Mometrix
TEST PREPARATION

OAE

Assessment of Professional Knowledge: Multi-Age (PK-12) (004)
Secrets Study Guide

DEAR FUTURE EXAM SUCCESS STORY

First of all, **THANK YOU** for purchasing Mometrix study materials!

Second, congratulations! You are one of the few determined test-takers who are committed to doing whatever it takes to excel on your exam. **You have come to the right place.** We developed these study materials with one goal in mind: to deliver you the information you need in a format that's concise and easy to use.

In addition to optimizing your guide for the content of the test, we've outlined our recommended steps for breaking down the preparation process into small, attainable goals so you can make sure you stay on track.

We've also analyzed the entire test-taking process, identifying the most common pitfalls and showing how you can overcome them and be ready for any curveball the test throws you.

Standardized testing is one of the biggest obstacles on your road to success, which only increases the importance of doing well in the high-pressure, high-stakes environment of test day. Your results on this test could have a significant impact on your future, and this guide provides the information and practical advice to help you achieve your full potential on test day.

Your success is our success

We would love to hear from you! If you would like to share the story of your exam success or if you have any questions or comments in regard to our products, please contact us at **800-673-8175** or **support@mometrix.com**.

Thanks again for your business and we wish you continued success!

Sincerely,
The Mometrix Test Preparation Team

Need more help? Check out our flashcards at:
http://MometrixFlashcards.com/OAE

TABLE OF CONTENTS

Introduction

Thank you for purchasing this resource! You have made the choice to prepare yourself for a test that could have a huge impact on your future, and this guide is designed to help you be fully ready for test day. Obviously, it's important to have a solid understanding of the test material, but you also need to be prepared for the unique environment and stressors of the test, so that you can perform to the best of your abilities.

For this purpose, the first section that appears in this guide is the **Secret Keys**. We've devoted countless hours to meticulously researching what works and what doesn't, and we've boiled down our findings to the five most impactful steps you can take to improve your performance on the test. We start at the beginning with study planning and move through the preparation process, all the way to the testing strategies that will help you get the most out of what you know when you're finally sitting in front of the test.

We recommend that you start preparing for your test as far in advance as possible. However, if you've bought this guide as a last-minute study resource and only have a few days before your test, we recommend that you skip over the first two Secret Keys since they address a long-term study plan.

If you struggle with **test anxiety**, we strongly encourage you to check out our recommendations for how you can overcome it. Test anxiety is a formidable foe, but it can be beaten, and we want to make sure you have the tools you need to defeat it.

1

Secret Key #1 – Plan Big, Study Small

There's a lot riding on your performance. If you want to ace this test, you're going to need to keep your skills sharp and the material fresh in your mind. You need a plan that lets you review everything you need to know while still fitting in your schedule. We'll break this strategy down into three categories.

Information Organization

Start with the information you already have: the official test outline. From this, you can make a complete list of all the concepts you need to cover before the test. Organize these concepts into groups that can be studied together, and create a list of any related vocabulary you need to learn so you can brush up on any difficult terms. You'll want to keep this vocabulary list handy once you actually start studying since you may need to add to it along the way.

Time Management

Once you have your set of study concepts, decide how to spread them out over the time you have left before the test. Break your study plan into small, clear goals so you have a manageable task for each day and know exactly what you're doing. Then just focus on one small step at a time. When you manage your time this way, you don't need to spend hours at a time studying. Studying a small block of content for a short period each day helps you retain information better and avoid stressing over how much you have left to do. You can relax knowing that you have a plan to cover everything in time. In order for this strategy to be effective though, you have to start studying early and stick to your schedule. Avoid the exhaustion and futility that comes from last-minute cramming!

Study Environment

The environment you study in has a big impact on your learning. Studying in a coffee shop, while probably more enjoyable, is not likely to be as fruitful as studying in a quiet room. It's important to keep distractions to a minimum. You're only planning to study for a short block of time, so make the most of it. Don't pause to check your phone or get up to find a snack. It's also important to **avoid multitasking**. Research has consistently shown that multitasking will make your studying dramatically less effective. Your study area should also be comfortable and well-lit so you don't have the distraction of straining your eyes or sitting on an uncomfortable chair.

 The time of day you study is also important. You want to be rested and alert. Don't wait until just before bedtime. Study when you'll be most likely to comprehend and remember. Even better, if you know what time of day your test will be, set that time aside for study. That way your brain will be used to working on that subject at that specific time and you'll have a better chance of recalling information.

Finally, it can be helpful to team up with others who are studying for the same test. Your actual studying should be done in as isolated an environment as possible, but the work of organizing the information and setting up the study plan can be divided up. In between study sessions, you can discuss with your teammates the concepts that you're all studying and quiz each other on the details. Just be sure that your teammates are as serious about the test as you are. If you find that your study time is being replaced with social time, you might need to find a new team.

Secret Key #2 – Make Your Studying Count

You're devoting a lot of time and effort to preparing for this test, so you want to be absolutely certain it will pay off. This means doing more than just reading the content and hoping you can remember it on test day. It's important to make every minute of study count. There are two main areas you can focus on to make your studying count.

Retention

It doesn't matter how much time you study if you can't remember the material. You need to make sure you are retaining the concepts. To check your retention of the information you're learning, try recalling it at later times with minimal prompting. Try carrying around flashcards and glance at one or two from time to time or ask a friend who's also studying for the test to quiz you.

To enhance your retention, look for ways to put the information into practice so that you can apply it rather than simply recalling it. If you're using the information in practical ways, it will be much easier to remember. Similarly, it helps to solidify a concept in your mind if you're not only reading it to yourself but also explaining it to someone else. Ask a friend to let you teach them about a concept you're a little shaky on (or speak aloud to an imaginary audience if necessary). As you try to summarize, define, give examples, and answer your friend's questions, you'll understand the concepts better and they will stay with you longer. Finally, step back for a big picture view and ask yourself how each piece of information fits with the whole subject. When you link the different concepts together and see them working together as a whole, it's easier to remember the individual components.

Finally, practice showing your work on any multi-step problems, even if you're just studying. Writing out each step you take to solve a problem will help solidify the process in your mind, and you'll be more likely to remember it during the test.

Modality

Modality simply refers to the means or method by which you study. Choosing a study modality that fits your own individual learning style is crucial. No two people learn best in exactly the same way, so it's important to know your strengths and use them to your advantage.

For example, if you learn best by visualization, focus on visualizing a concept in your mind and draw an image or a diagram. Try color-coding your notes, illustrating them, or creating symbols that will trigger your mind to recall a learned concept. If you learn best by hearing or discussing information, find a study partner who learns the same way or read aloud to yourself. Think about how to put the information in your own words. Imagine that you are giving a lecture on the topic and record yourself so you can listen to it later.

For any learning style, flashcards can be helpful. Organize the information so you can take advantage of spare moments to review. Underline key words or phrases. Use different colors for different categories. Mnemonic devices (such as creating a short list in which every item starts with the same letter) can also help with retention. Find what works best for you and use it to store the information in your mind most effectively and easily.

3

Secret Key #3 – Practice the Right Way

Your success on test day depends not only on how many hours you put into preparing, but also on whether you prepared the right way. It's good to check along the way to see if your studying is paying off. One of the most effective ways to do this is by taking practice tests to evaluate your progress. Practice tests are useful because they show exactly where you need to improve. Every time you take a practice test, pay special attention to these three groups of questions:

- The questions you got wrong
- The questions you had to guess on, even if you guessed right
- The questions you found difficult or slow to work through

This will show you exactly what your weak areas are, and where you need to devote more study time. Ask yourself why each of these questions gave you trouble. Was it because you didn't understand the material? Was it because you didn't remember the vocabulary? Do you need more repetitions on this type of question to build speed and confidence? Dig into those questions and figure out how you can strengthen your weak areas as you go back to review the material.

Additionally, many practice tests have a section explaining the answer choices. It can be tempting to read the explanation and think that you now have a good understanding of the concept. However, an explanation likely only covers part of the question's broader context. Even if the explanation makes perfect sense, **go back and investigate** every concept related to the question until you're positive you have a thorough understanding.

As you go along, keep in mind that the practice test is just that: practice. Memorizing these questions and answers will not be very helpful on the actual test because it is unlikely to have any of the same exact questions. If you only know the right answers to the sample questions, you won't be prepared for the real thing. **Study the concepts** until you understand them fully, and then you'll be able to answer any question that shows up on the test.

It's important to wait on the practice tests until you're ready. If you take a test on your first day of study, you may be overwhelmed by the amount of material covered and how much you need to learn. Work up to it gradually.

On test day, you'll need to be prepared for answering questions, managing your time, and using the test-taking strategies you've learned. It's a lot to balance, like a mental marathon that will have a big impact on your future. Like training for a marathon, you'll need to start slowly and work your way up. When test day arrives, you'll be ready.

Start with the strategies you've read in the first two Secret Keys—plan your course and study in the way that works best for you. If you have time, consider using multiple study resources to get different approaches to the same concepts. It can be helpful to see difficult concepts from more than one angle. Then find a good source for practice tests. Many times, the test website will suggest potential study resources or provide sample tests.

Practice Test Strategy

If you're able to find at least three practice tests, we recommend this strategy:

UNTIMED AND OPEN-BOOK PRACTICE

Take the first test with no time constraints and with your notes and study guide handy. Take your time and focus on applying the strategies you've learned.

TIMED AND OPEN-BOOK PRACTICE

Take the second practice test open-book as well, but set a timer and practice pacing yourself to finish in time.

TIMED AND CLOSED-BOOK PRACTICE

Take any other practice tests as if it were test day. Set a timer and put away your study materials. Sit at a table or desk in a quiet room, imagine yourself at the testing center, and answer questions as quickly and accurately as possible.

Keep repeating timed and closed-book tests on a regular basis until you run out of practice tests or it's time for the actual test. Your mind will be ready for the schedule and stress of test day, and you'll be able to focus on recalling the material you've learned.

Secret Key #4 – Pace Yourself

Once you're fully prepared for the material on the test, your biggest challenge on test day will be managing your time. Just knowing that the clock is ticking can make you panic even if you have plenty of time left. Work on pacing yourself so you can build confidence against the time constraints of the exam. Pacing is a difficult skill to master, especially in a high-pressure environment, so **practice is vital**.

Set time expectations for your pace based on how much time is available. For example, if a section has 60 questions and the time limit is 30 minutes, you know you have to average 30 seconds or less per question in order to answer them all. Although 30 seconds is the hard limit, set 25 seconds per question as your goal, so you reserve extra time to spend on harder questions. When you budget extra time for the harder questions, you no longer have any reason to stress when those questions take longer to answer.

Don't let this time expectation distract you from working through the test at a calm, steady pace, but keep it in mind so you don't spend too much time on any one question. Recognize that taking extra time on one question you don't understand may keep you from answering two that you do understand later in the test. If your time limit for a question is up and you're still not sure of the answer, mark it and move on, and come back to it later if the time and the test format allow. If the testing format doesn't allow you to return to earlier questions, just make an educated guess; then put it out of your mind and move on.

On the easier questions, be careful not to rush. It may seem wise to hurry through them so you have more time for the challenging ones, but it's not worth missing one if you know the concept and just didn't take the time to read the question fully. Work efficiently but make sure you understand the question and have looked at all of the answer choices, since more than one may seem right at first.

Even if you're paying attention to the time, you may find yourself a little behind at some point. You should speed up to get back on track, but do so wisely. Don't panic; just take a few seconds less on each question until you're caught up. Don't guess without thinking, but do look through the answer choices and eliminate any you know are wrong. If you can get down to two choices, it is often worthwhile to guess from those. Once you've chosen an answer, move on and don't dwell on any that you skipped or had to hurry through. If a question was taking too long, chances are it was one of the harder ones, so you weren't as likely to get it right anyway.

On the other hand, if you find yourself getting ahead of schedule, it may be beneficial to slow down a little. The more quickly you work, the more likely you are to make a careless mistake that will affect your score. You've budgeted time for each question, so don't be afraid to spend that time. Practice an efficient but careful pace to get the most out of the time you have.

Secret Key #5 – Have a Plan for Guessing

When you're taking the test, you may find yourself stuck on a question. Some of the answer choices seem better than others, but you don't see the one answer choice that is obviously correct. What do you do?

The scenario described above is very common, yet most test takers have not effectively prepared for it. Developing and practicing a plan for guessing may be one of the single most effective uses of your time as you get ready for the exam.

In developing your plan for guessing, there are three questions to address:

- When should you start the guessing process?
- How should you narrow down the choices?
- Which answer should you choose?

When to Start the Guessing Process

Unless your plan for guessing is to select C every time (which, despite its merits, is not what we recommend), you need to leave yourself enough time to apply your answer elimination strategies. Since you have a limited amount of time for each question, that means that if you're going to give yourself the best shot at guessing correctly, you have to decide quickly whether or not you will guess.

Of course, the best-case scenario is that you don't have to guess at all, so first, see if you can answer the question based on your knowledge of the subject and basic reasoning skills. Focus on the key words in the question and try to jog your memory of related topics. Give yourself a chance to bring the knowledge to mind, but once you realize that you don't have (or you can't access) the knowledge you need to answer the question, it's time to start the guessing process.

It's almost always better to start the guessing process too early than too late. It only takes a few seconds to remember something and answer the question from knowledge. Carefully eliminating wrong answer choices takes longer. Plus, going through the process of eliminating answer choices can actually help jog your memory.

Summary: Start the guessing process as soon as you decide that you can't answer the question based on your knowledge.

How to Narrow Down the Choices

The next chapter in this book (**Test-Taking Strategies**) includes a wide range of strategies for how to approach questions and how to look for answer choices to eliminate. You will definitely want to read those carefully, practice them, and figure out which ones work best for you. Here though, we're going to address a mindset rather than a particular strategy.

Your odds of guessing an answer correctly depend on how many options you are choosing from.

Number of options left	5	4	3	2	1
Odds of guessing correctly	20%	25%	33%	50%	100%

You can see from this chart just how valuable it is to be able to eliminate incorrect answers and make an educated guess, but there are two things that many test takers do that cause them to miss out on the benefits of guessing:

- Accidentally eliminating the correct answer
- Selecting an answer based on an impression

We'll look at the first one here, and the second one in the next section.

To avoid accidentally eliminating the correct answer, we recommend a thought exercise called **the $5 challenge**. In this challenge, you only eliminate an answer choice from contention if you are willing to bet $5 on it being wrong. Why $5? Five dollars is a small but not insignificant amount of money. It's an amount you could afford to lose but wouldn't want to throw away. And while losing

$5 once might not hurt too much, doing it twenty times will set you back $100. In the same way, each small decision you make—eliminating a choice here, guessing on a question there—won't by itself impact your score very much, but when you put them all together, they can make a big difference. By holding each answer choice elimination decision to a higher standard, you can reduce the risk of accidentally eliminating the correct answer.

The $5 challenge can also be applied in a positive sense: If you are willing to bet $5 that an answer choice *is* correct, go ahead and mark it as correct.

Summary: Only eliminate an answer choice if you are willing to bet $5 that it is wrong.

8

Which Answer to Choose

You're taking the test. You've run into a hard question and decided you'll have to guess. You've eliminated all the answer choices you're willing to bet $5 on. Now you have to pick an answer. Why do we even need to talk about this? Why can't you just pick whichever one you feel like when the time comes?

The answer to these questions is that if you don't come into the test with a plan, you'll rely on your impression to select an answer choice, and if you do that, you risk falling into a trap. The test writers know that everyone who takes their test will be guessing on some of the questions, so they intentionally write wrong answer choices to seem plausible. You still have to pick an answer though, and if the wrong answer choices are designed to look right, how can you ever be sure that you're not falling for their trap? The best solution we've found to this dilemma is to take the decision out of your hands entirely. Here is the process we recommend:

Once you've eliminated any choices that you are confident (willing to bet $5) are wrong, select the first remaining choice as your answer.

Whether you choose to select the first remaining choice, the second, or the last, the important thing is that you use some preselected standard. Using this approach guarantees that you will not be enticed into selecting an answer choice that looks right, because you are not basing your decision on how the answer choices look.

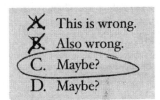

This is not meant to make you question your knowledge. Instead, it is to help you recognize the difference between your knowledge and your impressions. There's a huge difference between thinking an answer is right because of what you know, and thinking an answer is right because it looks or sounds like it should be right.

Summary: To ensure that your selection is appropriately random, make a predetermined selection from among all answer choices you have not eliminated.

9

Test-Taking Strategies

This section contains a list of test-taking strategies that you may find helpful as you work through the test. By taking what you know and applying logical thought, you can maximize your chances of answering any question correctly!

It is very important to realize that every question is different and every person is different: no single strategy will work on every question, and no single strategy will work for every person. That's why we've included all of them here, so you can try them out and determine which ones work best for different types of questions and which ones work best for you.

Question Strategies

⊘ READ CAREFULLY

Read the question and the answer choices carefully. Don't miss the question because you misread the terms. You have plenty of time to read each question thoroughly and make sure you understand what is being asked. Yet a happy medium must be attained, so don't waste too much time. You must read carefully and efficiently.

⊘ CONTEXTUAL CLUES

Look for contextual clues. If the question includes a word you are not familiar with, look at the immediate context for some indication of what the word might mean. Contextual clues can often give you all the information you need to decipher the meaning of an unfamiliar word. Even if you can't determine the meaning, you may be able to narrow down the possibilities enough to make a solid guess at the answer to the question.

⊘ PREFIXES

If you're having trouble with a word in the question or answer choices, try dissecting it. Take advantage of every clue that the word might include. Prefixes can be a huge help. Usually, they allow you to determine a basic meaning. *Pre-* means before, *post-* means after, *pro-* is positive, *de-* is negative. From prefixes, you can get an idea of the general meaning of the word and try to put it into context.

⊘ HEDGE WORDS

Watch out for critical hedge words, such as *likely, may, can, sometimes, often, almost, mostly, usually, generally, rarely*, and *sometimes*. Question writers insert these hedge phrases to cover every possibility. Often an answer choice will be wrong simply because it leaves no room for exception. Be on guard for answer choices that have definitive words such as *exactly* and *always*.

⊘ SWITCHBACK WORDS

Stay alert for *switchbacks*. These are the words and phrases frequently used to alert you to shifts in thought. The most common switchback words are *but, although*, and *however*. Others include *nevertheless, on the other hand, even though, while, in spite of, despite*, and *regardless of*. Switchback words are important to catch because they can change the direction of the question or an answer choice.

10

⊘ FACE VALUE

When in doubt, use common sense. Accept the situation in the problem at face value. Don't read too much into it. These problems will not require you to make wild assumptions. If you have to go beyond creativity and warp time or space in order to have an answer choice fit the question, then you should move on and consider the other answer choices. These are normal problems rooted in reality. The applicable relationship or explanation may not be readily apparent, but it is there for you to figure out. Use your common sense to interpret anything that isn't clear.

Answer Choice Strategies

⊘ ANSWER SELECTION

The most thorough way to pick an answer choice is to identify and eliminate wrong answers until only one is left, then confirm it is the correct answer. Sometimes an answer choice may immediately seem right, but be careful. The test writers will usually put more than one reasonable answer choice on each question, so take a second to read all of them and make sure that the other choices are not equally obvious. As long as you have time left, it is better to read every answer choice than to pick the first one that looks right without checking the others.

⊘ ANSWER CHOICE FAMILIES

An answer choice family consists of two (in rare cases, three) answer choices that are very similar in construction and cannot all be true at the same time. If you see two answer choices that are direct opposites or parallels, one of them is usually the correct answer. For instance, if one answer choice says that quantity x increases and another either says that quantity x decreases (opposite) or says that quantity y increases (parallel), then those answer choices would fall into the same family. An answer choice that doesn't match the construction of the answer choice family is more likely to be incorrect. Most questions will not have answer choice families, but when they do appear, you should be prepared to recognize them.

⊘ ELIMINATE ANSWERS

Eliminate answer choices as soon as you realize they are wrong, but make sure you consider all possibilities. If you are eliminating answer choices and realize that the last one you are left with is also wrong, don't panic. Start over and consider each choice again. There may be something you missed the first time that you will realize on the second pass.

⊘ AVOID FACT TRAPS

Don't be distracted by an answer choice that is factually true but doesn't answer the question. You are looking for the choice that answers the question. Stay focused on what the question is asking for so you don't accidentally pick an answer that is true but incorrect. Always go back to the question and make sure the answer choice you've selected actually answers the question and is not merely a true statement.

⊘ EXTREME STATEMENTS

In general, you should avoid answers that put forth extreme actions as standard practice or proclaim controversial ideas as established fact. An answer choice that states the "process should be used in certain situations, if…" is much more likely to be correct than one that states the "process should be discontinued completely." The first is a calm rational statement and doesn't even make a definitive, uncompromising stance, using a hedge word *if* to provide wiggle room, whereas the second choice is far more extreme.

⊘ Benchmark

As you read through the answer choices and you come across one that seems to answer the question well, mentally select that answer choice. This is not your final answer, but it's the one that will help you evaluate the other answer choices. The one that you selected is your benchmark or standard for judging each of the other answer choices. Every other answer choice must be compared to your benchmark. That choice is correct until proven otherwise by another answer choice beating it. If you find a better answer, then that one becomes your new benchmark. Once you've decided that no other choice answers the question as well as your benchmark, you have your final answer.

⊘ Predict the Answer

Before you even start looking at the answer choices, it is often best to try to predict the answer. When you come up with the answer on your own, it is easier to avoid distractions and traps because you will know exactly what to look for. The right answer choice is unlikely to be word-for-word what you came up with, but it should be a close match. Even if you are confident that you have the right answer, you should still take the time to read each option before moving on.

General Strategies

⊘ Tough Questions

If you are stumped on a problem or it appears too hard or too difficult, don't waste time. Move on! Remember though, if you can quickly check for obviously incorrect answer choices, your chances of guessing correctly are greatly improved. Before you completely give up, at least try to knock out a couple of possible answers. Eliminate what you can and then guess at the remaining answer choices before moving on.

⊘ Check Your Work

Since you will probably not know every term listed and the answer to every question, it is important that you get credit for the ones that you do know. Don't miss any questions through careless mistakes. If at all possible, try to take a second to look back over your answer selection and make sure you've selected the correct answer choice and haven't made a costly careless mistake (such as marking an answer choice that you didn't mean to mark). This quick double check should more than pay for itself in caught mistakes for the time it costs.

⊘ Pace Yourself

It's easy to be overwhelmed when you're looking at a page full of questions; your mind is confused and full of random thoughts, and the clock is ticking down faster than you would like. Calm down and maintain the pace that you have set for yourself. Especially as you get down to the last few minutes of the test, don't let the small numbers on the clock make you panic. As long as you are on track by monitoring your pace, you are guaranteed to have time for each question.

⊘ Don't Rush

It is very easy to make errors when you are in a hurry. Maintaining a fast pace in answering questions is pointless if it makes you miss questions that you would have gotten right otherwise. Test writers like to include distracting information and wrong answers that seem right. Taking a little extra time to avoid careless mistakes can make all the difference in your test score. Find a pace that allows you to be confident in the answers that you select.

⊘ Keep Moving

Panicking will not help you pass the test, so do your best to stay calm and keep moving. Taking deep breaths and going through the answer elimination steps you practiced can help to break through a stress barrier and keep your pace.

Final Notes

The combination of a solid foundation of content knowledge and the confidence that comes from practicing your plan for applying that knowledge is the key to maximizing your performance on test day. As your foundation of content knowledge is built up and strengthened, you'll find that the strategies included in this chapter become more and more effective in helping you quickly sift through the distractions and traps of the test to isolate the correct answer.

Now that you're preparing to move forward into the test content chapters of this book, be sure to keep your goal in mind. As you read, think about how you will be able to apply this information on the test. If you've already seen sample questions for the test and you have an idea of the question format and style, try to come up with questions of your own that you can answer based on what you're reading. This will give you valuable practice applying your knowledge in the same ways you can expect to on test day.

Good luck and good studying!

14

Student Development and Learning

Transform passive reading into active learning! After immersing yourself in this chapter, put your comprehension to the test by taking a quiz. The insights you gained will stay with you longer this way. Scan the QR code to go directly to the chapter quiz interface for this study guide. If you're using a computer, simply visit the bonus page at **mometrix.com/bonus948/oaeapkma** and click the Chapter Quizzes link.

Overview of Human Developmental Theories

ISSUES OF HUMAN DEVELOPMENT

Historically, there have been a number of arguments that theories of human development seek to address. These ideas generally lie on a spectrum, but are often essential concepts involved in developmental theories. For instance, the nature vs. nurture debate is a key concept involved in behaviorist camps of development, insisting that a substantial portion of a child's development may be attributed to his or her social environment.

- **Universality vs. context specificity**: Universality implies that all individuals will develop in the same way, no matter what culture they live in. Context specificity implies that development will be influenced by the culture in which the individual lives.
- **Assumptions about human nature** (3 doctrines: original sin, innate purity, and tabula rasa):
  - Original sin says that children are inherently bad and must be taught to be good.
  - Innate purity says that children are inherently good.
  - Tabula rasa says that children are born as "blank slates," without good or bad tendencies, and can be taught right vs. wrong.
- **Behavioral consistency**: Children either behave in the same manner no matter what the situation or setting, or they change their behavior depending on the setting and who is interacting with them.
- **Nature vs. nurture**: Nature is the genetic influences on development. Nurture is the environment and social influences on development.
- **Continuity vs. discontinuity**: Continuity states that development progresses at a steady rate and the effects of change are cumulative. Discontinuity states that development progresses in a stair-step fashion and the effects of early development have no bearing on later development.
- **Passivity vs. activity**: Passivity refers to development being influenced by outside forces. Activity refers to development influenced by the child himself and how he responds to external forces.
- **Critical vs. sensitive period**: The critical period is that window of time when the child will be able to acquire new skills and behaviors. The sensitive period refers to a flexible time period when a child will be receptive to learning new skills, even if it is later than the norm.

THEORETICAL SCHOOLS OF THOUGHT ON HUMAN DEVELOPMENT

- **Behaviorist Theory** – This philosophy discusses development in terms of conditioning. As children interact with their environments, they learn what behaviors result in rewards or punishments and develop patterns of behaviors as a result. This school of thought lies heavily within the nurture side of the nature/nurture debate, arguing that children's personalities and behaviors are a product of their environments.
- **Constructivist Theory** – This philosophy describes the process of learning as one in which individuals build or construct their understanding from their prior knowledge and experiences in an environment. In constructivist thought, individuals can synthesize their old information to generate new ideas. This school of thought is similar to behaviorism in that the social environment plays a large role in learning. Constructivism, however, places greater emphasis on the individual's active role in the learning process, such as the ability to generate ideas about something an individual has not experienced directly.
- **Ecological Systems Theory** – This philosophy focuses on the social environments in and throughout a person's life. Ecological systems theorists attempt to account for all of the complexities of various aspects of a person's life, starting with close relationships, such as family and friends, and zooming out into broader social contexts, including interactions with school, communities, and media. Alongside these various social levels, ecological systems discuss the roles of ethnicity, geography, and socioeconomic status in development across a person's lifespan.
- **Maturationist Theory** – This philosophy largely focuses on the natural disposition of a child to learn. Maturationists lean heavily into the nature side of the nature/nurture argument and say that humans are predisposed to learning and development. As a result, maturationists propose that early development should only be passively supported.
- **Psychoanalytic Theory** – Psychoanalytic theorists generally argue that beneath the conscious interaction with the world, individuals have underlying, subconscious thoughts that affect their active emotions and behaviors. These subconscious thoughts are built from previous experiences, including developmental milestones and also past traumas. These subconscious thoughts, along with the conscious, interplay with one another to form a person's desires, personality, attitudes, and habits.

FREUD'S PSYCHOSEXUAL DEVELOPMENTAL THEORY

Sigmund Freud was a neurologist who founded the psychoanalytic school of thought. He described the distinction between the conscious and unconscious mind and the effects of the unconscious mind on personality and behavior. He also developed a concept of stages of development, in which an individual encounters various conflicts or crises, called psychosexual stages of development. The way in which an individual handles these crises were thought to shape the individual's personality over the course of life. This general formula heavily influenced other psychoanalytic theories.

ERIKSON'S PSYCHOSOCIAL DEVELOPMENTAL THEORY

Eric Erikson's psychosocial development theory was an expansion and revision of Freud's psychosexual stages. Erikson describes eight stages in which an individual is presented with a crisis, such as an infant learning to trust or mistrust his or her parents to provide. The choice to trust or mistrust is not binary, but is on a spectrum. According to the theory, the individual's resolution of the crisis largely carries through the rest of his or her life. Handling each of the eight conflicts well theoretically leads to a healthy development of personality. The conflicts are spaced out throughout life, beginning at infancy and ending at death.

KOHLBERG'S STAGES OF MORAL DEVELOPMENT

Kohlberg's stages of moral development are heavily influenced by Erikson's stages. He describes three larger levels of moral development with substages. In the first level, the **preconventional level**, morality is fully externally controlled by authorities and is motivated by avoidance of punishment and pursuit of rewards. In the second level, the **conventional level**, the focus shifts to laws and social factors and the pursuit of being seen by others as good or nice. In the third and final level, the **postconventional** or **principled level**, the individual looks beyond laws and social obligations to more complex situational considerations. A person in this stage might consider that a law may not always be the best for individuals or society and a particular situation may warrant breaking the rule for the true good.

GEORGE HERBERT MEAD'S PLAY AND GAME STAGE DEVELOPMENT THEORY

George Herbert Mead was a sociologist and psychologist who described learning by stepping into **social roles**. According to his theory, children first interact with the world by imitating and playing by themselves, in which a child can experiment with concepts. Mead describes this development in terms of three stages characterized by increasing complexity of play. A child in the **preparatory stage** can **play** pretend and learn cooking concepts by pretending to cook. As a child develops socially, they learn to step in and out of increasingly abstract and complex **roles** and include more interaction. This is known as the **play stage**, including early interactive roles. For instance, children may play "cops and robbers," which are more symbolically significant roles as they are not natural roles for children to play in society. As social understanding develops, children enter the **game stage**, in which the child can understand their own role and the roles of others in a game. In this stage, children can participate in more complex activities with highly structured rules. An example of a complex game is baseball, in which each individual playing has a unique and complex role to play. These stages are thought to contribute to an individual's ability to understand complex social roles in adulthood.

IVAN PAVLOV

Ivan Pavlov was a predecessor to the behaviorist school and is credited with being the first to observe the process of classical conditioning, also known as Pavlovian conditioning. Pavlov observed that dogs would begin salivating at the sound of a bell because they were conditioned to expect food when they heard a bell ring. According to classical conditioning, by introducing a neutral stimulus (such as a bell) to a naturally significant stimulus (such as the sight of food), the neutral stimulus will begin to create a conditioned response on its own.

JOHN B. WATSON

Watson is credited as the founder of behaviorism and worked to expand the knowledge base of conditioning. He is famous for his experiments, including highly unethical experiments such as the "Little Albert" experiment in which he used classical conditioning to cause an infant to fear animals that he was unfamiliar with. Watson proposed that psychology should focus only on observable behaviors.

B.F. SKINNER

Skinner expanded on Watson's work in behaviorism. His primary contributions to behaviorism included studying the effect of **reinforcement** and **punishment** on particular behaviors. He noted that stimuli can be both additive or subtractive may be used to either increase or decrease behavior frequency and strengths.

LEV VYGOTSKY

Vygotsky's sociocultural theory describes development as a social process, in which individuals mediate knowledge through social interactions and can learn by interacting with and watching others. Vygotsky's ideas have been widely adopted in the field of education, most notably his theory of the "**zone of proximal development**." This theory describes three levels of an individual's ability to do tasks, including completely incapable of performing a task, capable with assistance, and independently capable. As an individual's experience grows, they should progress from less capable and independent to more capable and independent.

> **Review Video: Instructional Scaffolding**
> Visit mometrix.com/academy and enter code: 989759

BANDURA'S SOCIAL LEARNING THEORY

Albert Bandura's social learning theory argues against some of the behaviorist thoughts that a person has to experience stimulus and response to learn behaviors, and instead posits that an individual can learn from other peoples' social interactions. Bandura would say that most learning takes place from observing and predicting social behavior, and not through direct experience. This becomes a more efficient system for learning because people are able to learn information more synthetically.

BOWLBY'S ATTACHMENT THEORY

Bowlby's attachment theory describes the impact that early connections have on lifelong development. Working from an evolutionary framework, Bowlby described how infants are predisposed to be attached to their caregivers as this increases chance of survival. According to Bowlby's theory, infants are predisposed to stay close to known caregivers and use them as a frame of reference to help with learning what is socially acceptable and what is safe.

PIAGET'S COGNITIVE DEVELOPMENT THEORY

Piaget's theory of cognitive development describes how as individuals develop, their cognitive processes are able to become more complex and abstract. In the early stages, an infant may be able to recognize an item, such as a glass of water, on sight only. As that individual grows, they are able to think, compare, and eventually develop abstract thoughts about that concept. According to Piaget, this development takes place in all individuals in predictable stages.

MASLOW'S HIERARCHY OF NEEDS

Maslow defined human motivation in terms of needs and wants. His **hierarchy of needs** is classically portrayed as a pyramid sitting on its base divided into horizontal layers. He theorized that, as humans fulfill the needs of one layer, their motivation turns to the layer above. The layers consist of (from bottom to top):

- **Physiological**: The need for air, fluid, food, shelter, warmth, and sleep.
- **Safety**: A safe place to live, a steady job, a society with rules and laws, protection from harm, and insurance or savings for the future.
- **Love/Belonging**: A network consisting of a significant other, family, friends, co-workers, religion, and community.
- **Esteem or self-respect**: The knowledge that you are a person who is successful and worthy of esteem, attention, status, and admiration.

- **Self-actualization**: The acceptance of your life, choices, and situation in life and the empathetic acceptance of others, as well as the feeling of independence and the joy of being able to express yourself freely and competently.

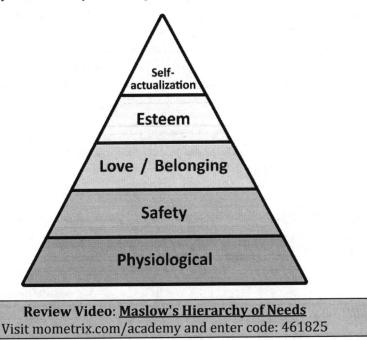

Review Video: Maslow's Hierarchy of Needs
Visit mometrix.com/academy and enter code: 461825

Cognitive Development

PIAGET'S THEORY OF COGNITIVE DEVELOPMENT

Jean Piaget's theory of cognitive development consists of four stages that a child moves through throughout life. The four stages are the **sensorimotor stage** (birth-2 years), **preoperational stage** (2-7 years), **concrete operational stage** (7-11 years), and **formal operational stage** (12 years and beyond). Piaget believed that the way children think changes as they pass through these stages. In the **sensorimotor stage**, infants exist in the present moment and investigate their world for the first time through their five senses, reflexes, and actions. Key skills infants acquire during this stage include object permanence and self-recognition. In the **preoperational stage**, children learn to express ideas symbolically, including through language and pretend play. Markers of this stage include engaging in animism, egocentrism, and the inability to understand conservation (the knowledge that the quantity of something does not change when its appearance does). In the **concrete operational stage**, children develop logical thought and begin understanding conservation. The **formal operational stage** brings the ability to think abstractly and hypothetically. Piaget believed that children learn through experimenting and building upon knowledge from experiences. He asserted that educators should be highly qualified and trained to create experiences that support development in each of these stages.

SKILLS TYPICALLY ACQUIRED AT EACH STAGE OF COGNITIVE DEVELOPMENT

- **Sensorimotor:** As children in the sensorimotor stage gain an increasing awareness of their bodies and the world around them, a wide range of skills are acquired as they mature from infancy to toddlerhood. Early skills at this stage include sucking, tasting, smiling, basic vocalizations, and **gross motor skills** such as kicking and grasping. These skills increase in complexity over time and come to include abilities such as throwing and dropping objects, crawling, walking, and using simple words or phrases to communicate. As children near the end of this stage, they are typically able to exhibit such skills as stacking, basic problem solving, planning methods to achieve a task, and attempting to engage in daily routines such as dressing themselves or brushing their hair.

[handwritten: birth – 2 yrs]

- **Preoperational:** This stage is marked by significant leaps in **cognition** and **gross motor skills**. Children in the preoperational stage are able to use increasingly complex language to communicate, and develop such skills as jumping, running, and climbing as they gain increasing control over their bodies. Preoperational children begin learning the basic categorization of alike objects, such as animals, flowers, or foods. This stage is also characterized by the development of pretend play and includes such skills as creating imaginary friends, role playing, and using toys or objects to symbolize something else, such as using a box as a pretend house.

[handwritten: 2 – 7 yrs]

- **Concrete Operational:** In this stage, children begin developing **logical reasoning** skills that allow them to perform increasingly complex tasks. Concrete operational children are able to distinguish subcategories, including types of animals, foods, or flowers, and can organize items in ascending or descending order based upon such characteristics as height, weight, or size. Children at this stage develop the understanding that altering the appearance of an object or substance does not change the amount of it. A classic example of this is the understanding that liquid transferred from one container to another retains its volume. This concept is known as **conservation**.

[handwritten: 7 – 11 yrs]

- **Formal Operational:** The formal operational stage is characterized by the development of **abstract** and **hypothetical** cognitive skills. Children at this stage are able to solve increasingly complex math equations, hypothesize and strategically devise a plan for engaging in science experiments, and develop creative solutions to problems. They are also able to theorize potential outcomes to hypothetical situations, as well as consider the nuances of differing values, beliefs, morals, and ethics.

[handwritten: 12 yrs +]

SUBSTAGES OF THE SENSORIMOTOR STAGE

Piaget's sensorimotor stage is divided into six substages. In each, infants develop new skills for representing and interacting with their world. In the first substage, infants interact **reflexively** and involuntarily to stimuli in the form of muscle jerking when startled, sucking, and gripping. Subsequent stages are circular, or repetitive, in nature, and are based on interactions with the self and, increasingly, the environment. **Primary circular reactions**, or intentionally repeated actions, comprise the second substage. Infants notice their actions and sounds and purposefully repeat them, but these actions do not extend past the infant's body. Interaction with the environment begins in the third substage as infants engage in **secondary circular reactions**. Here, infants learn that they can interact with and manipulate objects within their environment to create an effect, such as a sound from pressing a button. They then repeat the action and experience joy in this ability. In the fourth substage, secondary circular reactions become coordinated as infants begin planning movements and actions to create an effect. **Tertiary circular reactions** allow for exploration in the fifth substage, as infants start experimenting with cause and effect. In the sixth substage, infants begin engaging in **representational thought** and recall information from memory.

EXAMPLES OF PRIMARY, SECONDARY, AND TERTIARY CIRCULAR REACTIONS

The following are some common examples of primary, secondary, and tertiary circular reactions:

- **Primary:** Primary circular reactions are comprised of repeated **bodily** actions that the infant finds enjoyable. Such actions include thumb sucking, placing hands or feet in the mouth, kicking, and making basic vocalizations.
- **Secondary:** Secondary circular reactions refer to repeated enjoyable interactions between the infant and objects within their **environment** in order to elicit a specific response. Such actions include grasping objects, rattling toys, hitting buttons to hear specific sounds, banging two objects together, or reaching out to touch various items.
- **Tertiary:** Tertiary circular reactions are comprised of intentional and planned actions using objects within the environment to **achieve a particular outcome**. Examples include stacking blocks and knocking them down, taking toys out of a bin and putting them back, or engaging in a repeated behavior to gauge a caretaker's reaction each time.

DEFINING CHARACTERISTICS OF THE PREOPERATIONAL STAGE OF DEVELOPMENT

The preoperational stage of development refers to the stage before a child can exercise operational thought and is associated with several defining characteristics including **pretend play**, **animism**, and **egocentrism**. As children learn to think and express themselves symbolically, they engage in pretend play as a means of organizing, understanding, and representing the world around them as they experience it. During this stage, children do not understand the difference between inanimate and animate objects, and thus demonstrate animism, or the attribution of lifelike qualities to inanimate objects. Egocentrism refers to the child's inability to understand the distinction between themselves and others, and consequentially, the inability to understand the thoughts, perspectives, and feelings of others. During the preoperational stage, the brain is not developed enough to understand **conservation**, which is the understanding that the quantity of something does not change just because its appearance changes. Thus, children in this stage exhibit **centration**, or the focusing on only one aspect of something at a time at. Additionally, children struggle with **classification** during this stage, as they are not cognitively developed enough to understand that an object can be classified in multiple ways.

MILESTONES ACHIEVED DURING THE CONCRETE OPERATIONAL STAGE OF DEVELOPMENT

The concrete operational stage marks the beginning of a child's ability to think logically about the concrete world. In this stage, children develop many of the skills they lacked in the preoperational phase. For example, egocentrism fades as children in this stage begin to develop empathy and understand others' perspectives. Additionally, they develop an understanding of conservation, or the idea that the quantity of something does not change with its appearance. Children in this stage begin to learn to classify objects in more than one way and can categorize them based on a variety of characteristics. This allows them to practice **seriation**, or the arranging of objects based on quantitative measures.

DEVELOPMENT OF COGNITIVE ABILITIES IN THE FORMAL OPERATIONAL STAGE

In the formal operational stage, children can think beyond the concrete world and in terms of abstract thoughts and hypothetical situations. They develop the ability to consider various outcomes of events and can think more creatively about solutions to problems than in previous stages. This advanced cognitive ability contributes to the development of personal identity. In considering abstract and hypothetical ideas, children begin to formulate opinions and develop personal stances on intangible concepts, thus establishing individual character. The formal operational stage continues to develop through adulthood as individuals gain knowledge and experience.

LEV VYGOTSKY'S THEORY OF COGNITIVE DEVELOPMENT

Lev Vygotsky's theory on cognitive development is heavily rooted in a **sociocultural** perspective. He argued that the most important factors for a child's cognitive development reside in the cultural context in which the child grows up and social interactions that they have with adults, mentors, and more advanced peers. He believed that children learn best from the people around them, as their social interactions, even basic ones such as smiling, waving, or facial expressions, foster the beginning of more complex cognitive development. He is well-known for his concept of the **Zone of Proximal Development (ZPD)**, which is the idea that as children mature, there are tasks they can perform when they receive help from a more advanced individual. He believed that children could move through the ZPD and complete increasingly complicated tasks when receiving assistance from more cognitively advanced mentors. According to Vygotsky, children develop the most when passing through the ZPD. Vygotsky's contributions are heavily embedded in modern education, and often take the form of teacher-led instruction and scaffolding to assist learners as they move through the ZPD.

Zone of Proximal Development

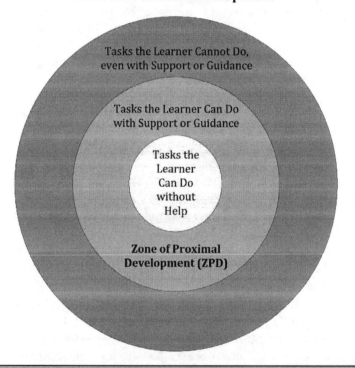

Review Video: Zone of Proximal Development (ZPD)
Visit mometrix.com/academy and enter code: 555594

Social and Emotional Development

ERIK ERIKSON'S EIGHT STAGES OF PSYCHOSOCIAL DEVELOPMENT

Erik Erikson defined eight predetermined stages of psychosocial development from birth to late adulthood in which an individual encounters a crisis that must be resolved to successfully transition to the next stage. The first is **trust vs. mistrust** (0-18 months), where the infant learns that the world around them is safe and they can trust caregivers to tend to their basic needs. The next stage is **autonomy vs. shame** (18 months-3 years), where children learn to control their actions and establish independence. In the **initiative vs. guilt stage** (3-5 years), children acquire a sense of purpose and initiative through social interactions. Next, children enter the **industry vs. inferiority stage** (6-11 years), where they develop mastery and pride in completing a task. The next stage is **identity vs. role confusion** (12-18 years), in which children explore and develop characteristics that will comprise their identity and determine their role in society. The sixth stage is **intimacy vs. isolation** (19-40 years), where one forms relationships by sharing the identity developed in the previous stage with others. **Generativity vs. stagnation** (40-65 years) occurs in middle adulthood and focuses on contributing to society's next generation through finding one's life purpose. The last stage is **ego integrity vs. despair** (65 to death), in which one reflects on the productivity and success of their life.

EXPECTED BEHAVIORS AT EACH STAGE OF PSYCHOSOCIAL DEVELOPMENT

Stage	Examples of expected behaviors
Trust vs. mistrust *0-18 mo*	In this stage, the infant's primary goal is ensuring the fulfillment of their **basic needs**. Infants will cry or make other vocalizations to indicate to caregivers when they want something, such as to be fed or picked up. Separation anxiety from parents is also typical during this stage.
Autonomy vs. shame *18mo - 3yrs*	Children in this stage begin attempting to perform daily tasks **independently**, such as making food, dressing themselves, bathing, or combing their hair. As children in this stage begin to realize they have a separate identity, they often begin attempting to assert themselves to parents and caregivers.
Initiative vs. guilt *3-5yrs*	Children at this stage often begin actively engaging and playing with other children. In play settings, these children will often assume **leadership roles** among a group of peers, create new games or activities, and devise their own rules for them. The initiative vs. guilt stage is also characterized by the development of feelings of sadness or guilt when making a mistake or hurting another's feelings.
Industry vs. inferiority *6-11yrs*	In this stage, children begin attempting to master concepts or skills with the intention of seeking **approval** and **acceptance** from others, particularly those older than themselves, in order to secure a feeling of competency. Children in this stage often become more involved in striving to succeed academically, extracurricular activities, and competitive sports.
Identity vs. role confusion *12-18yrs*	This stage is characterized by experimentation and uncertainty as young adolescents strive to establish an **independent identity**. Typical behaviors include interacting with new peer groups, trying new styles of dress, engaging in new activities, and considering new beliefs, values, and morals. As young adolescents in this stage are impressionable, they may potentially engage in risky or rebellious behavior as a result of peer pressure.
Intimacy vs. isolation *19-40yrs*	Individuals in this stage have typically established their identities and are ready to seek **long-term relationships**. This stage marks the development of a social network comprised of close friends and long-term romantic partners.
Generativity vs. stagnation *40-65yrs*	During this stage, individuals begin engaging in **productive** activities to benefit others and elicit personal fulfillment. Such activities include advancing in a career, parenting, or participating in community service projects.

Stage	Examples of expected behaviors
Integrity vs. despair 65yr – death	This stage occurs at the end of one's life and is characterized by **reflection** upon lifetime accomplishments and positive contributions to society. Doing so allows the individual to assess whether their life purpose was fulfilled and begin accepting death.

INCORPORATING LIFE SKILLS INTO CURRICULUM

In addition to academic achievement, the ultimate goal of education is to develop the whole child and provide a successful transition to independence and adulthood. Incorporating such valuable life skills as decision-making, goal setting, organization, self-direction, and workplace communication in early childhood through grade 12 curriculum is vital in ensuring students become productive contributors to society. Furthermore, the implementation of these life skills in early childhood is integral in allowing children to successfully progress in independence and maturity. The acquisition of such skills instills in students the self-motivation and ability to set goals, make decisions on how to effectively organize and manage time to complete them, and overcome obstacles. Additionally, teaching students to apply these skills promotes effective communication when working with others toward a goal. Through incorporating life skills into curriculum, teachers instill a growth mindset and foster self-empowered, confident lifelong learners with the necessary tools to navigate real-life situations and achieve success as they transition to adulthood. In the classroom, activities that promote leadership skills, cooperative learning, goal setting, self-monitoring, and social interaction foster an increasing sense of independence as children develop.

EFFECT OF EXTERNAL ENVIRONMENTAL FACTORS ON SOCIAL AND EMOTIONAL DEVELOPMENT

Social and emotional development is heavily influenced by a child's home environment. Children learn social and emotional skills such as self-regulation, self-awareness, coping, and relationship building through modeling from parents and caregivers. A positive and supportive home environment is integral for proper social and emotional development. External factors, including lack of affection and attention, parental divorce, and homelessness, pose profound negative impacts on this development. In terms of social development, such external factors could lead to attachment or abandonment issues, as well as distrust. Furthermore, children exposed to negative environmental factors could struggle forging relationships, cooperating, and following societal rules. Emotionally, negative impacts on development cause aggression, poor self-regulation, insecurity, anxiety, isolation, and depression. Since developmental domains are interconnected, the impacts that external factors have on social and emotional development ultimately damage cognitive and physical development. Underdeveloped social skills impair cognitive development because the inability to properly interact with peers impedes the ability to learn from them. Additionally, inadequate emotional skills can inhibit concentration and understanding in school, thus inhibiting cognitive development. Physically, struggling to interact with others leads to impaired development of gross and fine motor skills as well as large muscle development that would be achieved through play.

Physical Development

PHYSICAL CHANGES OCCURRING IN EARLY CHILDHOOD THROUGH ADOLESCENCE

As children pass through stages of development from early childhood through middle childhood and adolescence, they experience significant physical changes. Children in early childhood experience rapid growth in height and weight as they transition away from physical characteristics of infancy. In this stage, children begin to gain independence as they develop and improve upon gross and fine motor skills. By early childhood, children develop the ability to walk, run, hop, and as they mature through this stage, learn to throw, catch, and climb. They learn to hold and manipulate small objects such as zippers and buttons, and can grasp writing utensils to create shapes, letters, and drawings with increasing accuracy. Physical growth varies for individual children in middle childhood as some children begin experiencing prepubescent bodily changes. Children in middle childhood experience further improvements and refinements of gross and fine motor skills and coordination. Significant physical and appearance changes occur in adolescence as children enter puberty. These changes often occur quickly, resulting in a period of awkwardness and lack of coordination as adolescents adjust to this rapid development.

IMPACT OF EXTERNAL FACTORS ON PHYSICAL DEVELOPMENT

As children pass through physical development stages from early childhood to adolescence, it is important that environmental factors are supportive of proper growth and health. Physical development can be hindered by external factors, such as poor nutrition, lack of sleep, prenatal exposure to drugs, and abuse, as these can cause significant and long-lasting negative consequences. Exposure to such factors can lead to stunted physical growth, impaired brain development and function, poor bone and muscle development, and obesity. Furthermore, the negative impacts from such external factors ultimately impedes cognitive, social, and emotional development. Impaired brain development and function negatively affect cognitive development by impacting the ability to concentrate and grasp new concepts. In terms of emotional development, physical impairments due to external factors can cause a child to become depressed, withdrawn, aggressive, have low self-esteem, and unable to self-regulate. Improper physical growth and health impacts social development in that physical limitations could hinder a child's ability to properly interact with and play with others. Impacted brain development and function can limit a child's ability to understand social cues and norms.

Language Development

STAGES OF LANGUAGE DEVELOPMENT

The first stage of language development and acquisition, the **pre-linguistic stage**, occurs during an infant's first year of life. It is characterized by the development of gestures, making eye contact, and sounds like cooing and crying. The **holophrase** or **one-word sentence stage** develops in infants between 10 and 13 months of age. In this stage, young children use one-word sentences to communicate meaning in language. The **two-word sentence stage** typically develops by the time a child is 18 months old. Each two-word sentence usually contains a verb and a modifier, such as "big balloon" or "green grass." Children in this stage use their two-word sentences to communicate wants and needs. **Multiple-word sentences** form by the time a child is two to two and a half years old. In this stage, children begin forming sentences with subjects and predicates, such as "tree is tall" or "rope is long." Grammatical errors are present, but children in this stage begin demonstrating how to use words in appropriate context. Children ages two and a half to three years typically begin using more **complex grammatical structures**. They begin to include grammatical structures that were not present before, such as conjunctions and prepositions. By the age of five or six, children reach a stage of **adult-like language development**. They begin to use words in appropriate context and can move words around in sentences while maintaining appropriate sentence structure. Language development and acquisition has a wide range of what is considered normal development. Some children do not attempt to speak for up to two years and then may experience an explosion of language development at a later time. In these cases, children often emerge from their silent stage with equivalent language development to babies who were more

25

expressive early on. A child who does not speak after two years, however, may be exhibiting signs of a developmental delay.

ORAL LANGUAGE DEVELOPMENT

Oral language development begins well before students enter educational environments. It is learned first without formal instruction, with **environmental factors** being a heavy influence. Children tend to develop their own linguistic rules as a result of genetic disposition, their environments, and how their individual thinking processes develop. Oral language refers to both speaking and listening. Components of oral language development include phonology, syntax, semantics, morphology, and pragmatics. **Phonology** refers to the production and recognition of sounds. **Morphology** refers to how words are formed from smaller pieces, called morphemes. **Semantics** refers to meaning of words and phrases and has overlap with morphology and syntax, as morphemes and word order can both change the meaning of words. Semantic studies generally focus on learning and understanding vocabulary. **Syntax** refers to how words are morphemes are combined to make up meaningful phrases. In English, word order is the primary way that many components of grammar are communicated. Finally, **pragmatics** refers to the practical application of language based on various social situations. For instance, a college student is likely to use different vocabulary, complexity, and formality of language when speaking with a professor than when speaking with his or her peer group. Each of these five components of language are applied in oral language. Awareness and application of these components develops over time as students gain experience and education in language use. **Oral language development** can be nurtured by caregivers and teachers well before children enter educational environments. Caregivers and teachers can promote oral language development by providing environments full of language development opportunities. Additionally, teaching children how conversation works, encouraging interaction among children, and demonstrating good listening and speaking skills are good strategies for nurturing oral language development.

> **Review Video: <u>Components of Oral Language Development</u>**
> Visit mometrix.com/academy and enter code: 480589

HELPING STUDENTS DEVELOP ORAL LANGUAGE ABILITIES

Children pick up oral language skills in their home environments and build upon these skills as they grow. Early language development is influenced by a combination of genetic disposition, environment, and individual thinking processes. Children with **oral language acquisition difficulties** often experience difficulties in their **literacy skills**, so activities that promote good oral language skills also improve literacy skills. **Strategies** that help students develop oral language abilities include developing appropriate speaking and listening skills; providing instruction that emphasizes vocabulary development; providing students with opportunities to communicate wants, needs, ideas, and information; creating language learning environments; and promoting auditory memory. Developing appropriate speaking and listening skills includes teaching turn-taking, awareness of social norms, and basic rules for speaking and listening. Emphasizing **vocabulary development** is a strategy that familiarizes early learners with word meanings. Providing students with opportunities to **communicate** is beneficial for developing early social skills. Teachers can create **language learning environments** by promoting literacy in their classrooms with word walls, reading circles, or other strategies that introduce language skills to

26

students. Promoting **auditory memory** means teaching students to listen to, process, and recall information.

Review Video: <u>Types of Vocabulary Learning (Broad and Specific)</u>
Visit mometrix.com/academy and enter code: 258753

HELPING STUDENTS MONITOR ERRORS IN ORAL LANGUAGE

Oral language is the primary way people communicate and express their knowledge, ideas, and feelings. As oral language generally develops, their **speaking and listening skills** become more refined. This refinement of a person's language is called fluency, which can be broken down into the subdisciplines of language, reading, writing, speaking, and listening. **Speaking fluency** usually describes the components of rate, accuracy, and prosody. **Rate** describes how fast a person can speak and **prosody** describes the inflection and expressions that a person puts into their speech. **Accuracy** describes how often a person makes an error in language production. In early stages of language development, individuals generally do not have enough language knowledge to be able to monitor their own speech production for errors and require input from others to notice and correct their mistakes. As an individual becomes more proficient, they will be able to monitor their own language usage and make corrections to help improve their own fluency. In the classroom, the teacher needs to be an active component of language monitoring to help facilitate growth. Teachers can monitor **oral language errors** with progress-monitoring strategies. Teachers can also help students monitor their own **oral language development** as they progress through the reading curriculum. Students can monitor their oral language by listening to spoken words in their school and home environments, learning and practicing self-correction skills, and participating in reading comprehension and writing activities. Students can also monitor oral language errors by learning oral language rules for phonics, semantics, syntax, and pragmatics. These rules typically generalize to developing appropriate oral language skills.

EXPRESSIVE AND RECEPTIVE LANGUAGE

Expressive language refers to the aspects of language that an individual produces, generally referring to writing and speaking. **Receptive language** refers to the aspects of language that an individual encounters or receives, and generally refers to reading and listening. Both expressive and receptive language are needed for communication from one person to another.

	Expressive	**Receptive**
Written	Writing	Reading
Oral	Speaking	Listening

Expressive Language Skills

Expressive language skills include the ability to use vocabulary, sentences, gestures, and writing. People with good **expressive language skills** can label objects in their environments, put words in sentences, use appropriate grammar, demonstrate comprehension verbally by retelling stories, and more. This type of language is important because it allows people to express feelings, wants and needs, thoughts and ideas, and individual points of view. Strong expressive language skills include pragmatic knowledge, such as using gestures and facial expressions or using appropriate vocabulary for the listener or reader and soft skills, such as checks for comprehension, use of analogies, and grouping of ideas to help with clarity. Well-expressed language should be relatively easy for someone else to comprehend.

Receptive Language Skills

Receptive language refers to a person's ability to perceive and understand language. Good receptive language skills involve gathering information from the environment and processing it into meaning. People with good **receptive language skills** perceive gestures, sounds and words, and written information well. Receptive language is important for developing appropriate communication skills. Instruction that targets receptive language skills can include tasks that require sustained attention and focus, recognizing emotions and gestures, and listening and reading comprehension. Games that challenge the players to communicate carefully, such as charades or catchphrase, can be a great way to target receptive language skills. As one student tries to accurately express an idea with words or gestures, the rest of the class must exercise their receptive language skills. Lastly, focusing on **social skills and play skills instruction** encourages opportunities for children to interact with their peers or adults. This fosters receptive language skills and targets deficits in these skills.

Stages of Literacy Development

The development of literacy in young children is separated into five stages. Names and ranges of these stages sometimes vary slightly, but the stage milestones are similar. Stage 1 is the **Emergent Reader stage**. In this stage, children ages 6 months to 6 years demonstrate skills like pretend reading, recognizing letters of the alphabet, retelling stories, and printing their names. Stage 2 is the **Novice/Early Reader stage** (ages 6–7 years). Children begin to understand the relationships between letters and sounds and written and spoken words, and they read texts containing high-frequency words. Children in this stage should develop orthographic conventions and semantic knowledge. In Stage 3, the **Decoding Reader stage**, children ages 7–9 develop decoding skills in order to read simple stories. They also demonstrate increased fluency. Stage 4 (ages 8–15 years) is called the **Fluent, Comprehending/Transitional Reader stage**. In this stage, fourth to eighth graders read to learn new ideas and information. In Stage 5, the **Expert/Fluent Reader stage**, children ages 16 years and older read more complex information. They also read expository and narrative texts with multiple viewpoints.

> **Review Video: Stages of Reading Development**
> Visit mometrix.com/academy and enter code: 121184

Relationship between Language Development and Early Literacy Skills

Language development and early literacy skills are interconnected. **Language concepts** begin and develop shortly after birth with infant/parent interactions, cooing, and then babbling. These are the earliest attempts at language acquisition for infants. Young children begin interacting with written and spoken words before they enter their grade school years. Before they enter formal classrooms, children begin to make **connections** between speaking and listening and reading and writing. Children with strong speaking and listening skills demonstrate strong literacy skills in early grade school. The development of **phonological awareness** is connected to early literacy skills. Children with good phonological awareness recognize that words are made up of different speech sounds. For example, children with appropriate phonological awareness can break words (e.g., "bat" into separate speech sounds, "b-a-t"). Examples of phonological awareness include rhyming (when the ending parts of words have the same or similar sounds) and alliteration (when words all have the same beginning sound). Success with phonological awareness (oral language) activities depends on adequate development of speech and language skills.

PROMOTING LITERACY DURING THE EARLY STAGES OF LITERACY DEVELOPMENT

Teachers and parents can implement strategies at different stages of literacy development in order to build **good reading skills** in children with and without disabilities. During the **Emergent Reader stage**, teachers and parents can introduce children to the conventions of reading with picture books. They can model turning the pages, reading from left to right, and other reading conventions. Book reading at this stage helps children begin to identify letters, letter sounds, and simple words. Repetitive reading of familiar texts also helps children begin to make predictions about what they are reading. During the **Novice/Early Reader** and **Decoding Reader stages**, parents and teachers can help children form the building blocks of decoding and fluency skills by reading for meaning and emphasizing letter-sound relationships, visual cues, and language patterns. In these stages, increasing familiarity with sight words is essential. In the **Fluent, Comprehending/Transitional Reader stage**, children should be encouraged to read book series, as the shared characters, settings, and plots help develop their comprehension skills. At this stage, a good reading rate (fluency) is an indicator of comprehension skills. **Expert/Fluent readers** can independently read multiple texts and comprehend their meanings. Teachers and parents can begin exposing children to a variety of fiction and non-fiction texts before this stage in order to promote good fluency skills.

> **Review Video: Phonics (Encoding and Decoding)**
> Visit mometrix.com/academy and enter code: 821361
>
> **Review Video: Fluency**
> Visit mometrix.com/academy and enter code: 531179

Managing Developmental Transitions

DEVELOPMENTAL CHANGES EXPERIENCED IN EARLY ADOLESCENCE

Early adolescence is a time of considerable development in all domains. Physically, children enter puberty, and must learn to deal with its emotional, social, and academic impacts. Consequently, children at this stage are impressionable, and begin developing habits that influence success as they transition to adulthood. Thus, early adolescents have specific developmental needs, and an accommodating approach to instruction is required. As the goal of education is providing the necessary skills to successfully transition into adulthood and increasing independence, it must be recognized that the shift from elementary to high school is drastic, and high school curriculum is not developmentally appropriate for early adolescence. The shift from elementary to high school is stressful and may negatively impact a child's attitude toward acquiring necessary life skills for success. Thus, middle-level education is integral in providing a developmentally responsive curriculum that eases this transition yet allows for increasing personal and academic independence. Middle-level education considers the physical developmental changes of early adolescents and fosters cognitive, social, and emotional growth through engaging instruction that encourages self-direction and responsibility, and positive social relationships. Middle-level curriculum instills skills such as organization, time management, and goal setting that promote success in high school and ultimately, adulthood.

RISKS FACED BY STUDENTS WHEN EXPERIENCING CHALLENGES

As students in later childhood, adolescence, and young adulthood reconcile with rapid physical, cognitive, emotional, and social developments, they inevitably encounter challenges as they develop habits, beliefs, and relationships that will comprise their identity and future decisions. Such challenges as self-image, changing physical appearance, eating disorders, rebelliousness, identity formation, and educational and career decisions pose emotional, social, behavioral, and academic risks with long-term consequences if not addressed. Students may respond to challenges by engaging in risky behavior, or developing social and emotional issues such as depression, anxiety, or aggression. Such challenges may induce apathy toward academics and extracurricular activities and declining academic performance. These risks threaten the successful transition to adulthood and success throughout life in that they potentially hinder the educational and career choices that would lead to a successful future. Early intervention is imperative to provide supports for students facing challenges to try and prevent the consequences associated with them. Some supports include fostering and encouraging positive social relationships with peers and mentors, encouraging participation in extracurricular activities within the school and community, providing access to guidance counselors, and providing adequate health education to help students understand the challenges they are facing as they develop.

INDICATORS AND NEGATIVE IMPACTS OF RISKY BEHAVIORS IN STUDENTS

The likelihood that students will engage in risky behaviors, such as drug and alcohol use, gang involvement, or other dangerous activities, increases as they approach adolescence. Such behaviors pose serious negative consequences on development and learning. Cognitively, risky behaviors harm brain function and development, and lead to trouble sleeping, focusing, and learning. Socially, these students may have trouble maintaining positive relationships and are more likely to associate with others engaging in the same behaviors. Emotionally, these behaviors could cause depression, anxiety, and low self-esteem. Physically, negative impacts include injury, illness, or long-term health consequences. Furthermore, risky behaviors are detrimental to learning. Students participating in these behaviors have trouble focusing, grasping new concepts, and become apathetic toward academics. It is important to recognize indicators of risky behavior to intervene as early as possible and prevent long-term negative consequences. Indicators include being withdrawn, poor grades, poor appearance, hygiene, sleeping and eating habits, and lack of interest in academics or extracurricular activities. Schools and communities must do their best to prevent students from engaging in risky behaviors through encouraging positive social relationships, participation in extracurricular activities, providing access to guidance counselors, and providing access to proper health education.

ROLES OF PEERS, ACCEPTANCE, AND CONFORMITY DURING ADOLESCENT DEVELOPMENT

Adolescence is an insecure and impressionable time as students navigate rapid physical, emotional, social, and cognitive development. This stage introduces an increased sense of **independence** as adolescents begin developing the opinions, beliefs, values, and social relationships that will comprise their identity and establish the foundation for their future as they transition to adulthood. Social relationships are a vital part of identity formation during this stage, as adolescents engage with different peer groups, norms, and expectations, and seek acceptance in desired crowds. Adolescents will often conform their behavior to the social norms of a desired peer group for fear of rejection, and thus, the nature of the peer group has significant implications for teaching and learning. Involvement with unhealthy peer groups may lead to engaging in risky behaviors in seeking social acceptance, and a disinterest in learning and academic success. In contrast, association with healthy peer groups fosters the development of positive and supportive social relationships that encourage constructive behavior. Consequently, engaging in healthy peer groups increases the likelihood that the adolescent will be interested in academic involvement, achievement, and success.

Developmental Delays

DEVELOPMENTAL DIFFERENCES ENCOUNTERED AND STRATEGIES TO ADDRESS THEM

Cognitive, physical, social, and emotional milestones through which children pass as they mature are approximate, and development in any domain depends on the individual child as well as countless environmental factors that comprise each child's unique situation. Therefore, a teacher will encounter multiple variations in cognitive, physical, social, and emotional development in students that pose significant implications for instructional planning. Cognitively, a teacher will encounter several intelligences and learning styles. They will encounter students with various learning disabilities, gifted and talented students, or English Language Learners. Physically, students grow and develop at individual rates, and a teacher will encounter students with varying physical abilities or limitations. Social developmental differences vary as well and are heavily influenced by environmental factors. Variances in social cues, norms, relationship building, and communication are based on a child's culture and environment. Emotional development such as self-regulation and coping are impacted by environment also. Such an array of differences requires a teacher to be trained to recognize individual prior knowledge and learning needs to effectively teach to those differences. Strategies to achieve this include adjusting curriculum, activities, and assessments to match individual student needs, providing necessary scaffolds, and differentiating instruction to access learners of all abilities.

EFFECT OF DEVELOPMENTAL DELAYS ON LEARNING EXPERIENCES AND ASSESSMENTS

Developmental delays in any domain pose significant potential impacts on learning experiences and assessments through affecting comprehension and participation. A delay in cognitive development could impact information processing times, information retention, and the ability to understand complex ideas, thus hindering comprehension and ultimately impacting the willingness to participate. A student with a physical developmental delay may struggle with fine and gross motor skills that prevent effective participation in class activities that would improve comprehension of new instruction. Students with social developmental delays may have difficulty properly expressing a need for assistance, thus potentially discouraging participation and overall comprehension. Furthermore, students with social or emotional developmental delays may be withdrawn, depressed, anxious, or have behavioral issues that impede their self-motivation and ability to focus, thus affecting comprehension and willingness to participate. These potential impacts can have long-lasting consequences on students' overall learning experience, and early recognition is imperative for instilling the proper accommodations for each student.

ACCOMMODATIONS TO ASSIST STUDENTS WITH DEVELOPMENTAL DELAYS

In order to create an equitable and inclusive environment, the teacher must have an understanding of the developmental characteristics of each student. Furthermore, the teacher must be able to use this knowledge to make the proper accommodations to the curriculum, instruction, and assessments in such a way that addresses individual needs and abilities across the domains of development. Modifications should be specific to the student depending on their individual need and should provide the necessary support to allow for success in learning. Such accommodations may include scaffolding to break instruction into smaller, more manageable pieces, extended work time for assignments and assessments, shorter work periods with frequent breaks, reduced ratio of students to teacher, individualized instruction, and preferential seating based on the student's need for proximity. Additionally, students may require accommodations to address physical developmental delays, including scribes, text to speech for assignments, or enlarged fonts. Providing accommodations to address individual needs in the four areas of development allows for the teacher to effectively assess student progress and ultimately allows for success in learning.

RECOGNIZING SIGNS OF DEVELOPMENTAL DELAYS OR IMPAIRMENTS

Although each child develops at their own pace, there are often indicators that a student is not developing at a generally similar rate as their peers. Developmental delays or impairments can be cognitive, physical, emotional, or social. Some common indicators of developmental delays include but are not limited to lower-than-average assessment scores, difficulty concentrating and retaining new information, difficulty socializing or communicating with others, limited vocabulary compared to others in the same age group, clumsiness, and difficulty holding small objects. Delays can be difficult to detect, but a teacher can recognize signs through observation of the student and analyzing their progress across subject areas generally compared to their peers. Early recognition and detection are beneficial in allowing for early intervention to develop a treatment plan for the child that could improve their progress both inside and outside of the classroom.

Developmentally Appropriate Practices

DEVELOPMENTALLY APPROPRIATE PRACTICE

Developmentally Appropriate Practice **(DAP)** is an approach to teaching grounded in theories of child development. It is derived from the belief that children are naturally curious to learn, and when provided a stimulating environment, are encouraged to take initiative in their own learning. This approach allows for a great deal of choice in learning experiences. The teacher's role is to facilitate active learning by creating developmentally appropriate activities based on the awareness of similarities between children in various developmental stages and the knowledge that each child develops at their own rate. With this knowledge, the teacher can then adjust the curriculum, activities, and assessments to fit the needs of individual students based on an awareness of age, cultural, social, and individual expectations.

CREATING INSTRUCTION TAILORED TO COGNITIVE DEVELOPMENT

A developmentally responsive teacher understands that the needs of students change as they mature through the stages of cognitive development. Furthermore, an effective teacher uses this knowledge to plan instruction that coincides with each developmental level. The early childhood teacher understands the needs and abilities of preoperational children, and designs instruction that focuses on interacting with the world around them through hands-on activities and pretend play. Such activities foster exploration of the environment, roles, and connections. Developmentally responsive elementary school teachers are aware of the logical thinking patterns that occur during the concrete operational stage. Thus, they create instruction that allows children to interact with tangible materials to help them draw logical conclusions about their environment and understand abstract ideas. As children reach adolescence, a developmentally responsive teacher understands the increased ability to think abstractly, hypothetically, and reflectively in the formal operational stage. They use this knowledge to create instruction that encourages discussion, debate, creative problem solving, and opportunities to develop opinions, beliefs, and values.

COGNITIVE DEVELOPMENT
IMPORTANCE IN DESIGN OF APPROPRIATE LEARNING EXPERIENCES THAT FACILITATE GROWTH

The teacher must understand their students' cognitive developmental ability relative to their grade level in order to create effective, engaging learning experiences that facilitate growth. This understanding allows teachers to develop age-appropriate instruction, activities, and assessment that challenges students based on their skills and abilities but is attainable based on their cognitive developmental level. In knowing how students in a given grade level think and learn, the teacher can develop instruction that effectively facilitates learning and growth, such as creating opportunities for purposeful play with young children, opportunities for middle-school aged students to engage in logical problem solving, or activities that promote the development of abstract thinking and reasoning with adolescents. In addition, understanding students' cognitive abilities of each developmental level allow the teacher to better understand the nuances that exist within them, as students ultimately develop at their own pace and have individual learning needs.

IMPACT ON TEACHING AND LEARNING

Students' thinking and learning develops as they mature, as their thought processes and worldview changes. Consequently, teaching and learning must adapt to accommodate these changes and facilitate growth. In the early years of cognitive development, children learn through interacting with the surrounding environment using their physical senses and engage in independent play. To facilitate this, young children need learning experiences that stimulate their development through exploration. As children reach early elementary school, they begin to think symbolically and play with others. Purposeful play and interaction with learning materials becomes an important part of learning at this stage. Teachers should act as facilitators and provide multiple opportunities for children to engage in purposeful, self-directed play with interactive materials as they learn to categorize the world around them. By later childhood, children think concretely and logically, and thus, need hands-on learning experiences that provide opportunities for classification, experimentation, and problem-solving skills to facilitate their level of cognition and promote development. As children reach adolescence, they are increasingly able to think abstractly and consider hypothetical situations beyond what is concretely present. To enhance learning, teachers must provide opportunities for exploring different perspectives, values, and synthesizing information to engage in creative problem solving.

APPROPRIATE INSTRUCTIONAL ACTIVITIES

The following are some examples of appropriate instructional activities for early childhood, middle-level, and high school students:

- **Early childhood:** Activities that allow for exploration, play, and movement while teaching young children to function and cooperate in a group setting are most valuable in early childhood classrooms. **Movement activities** such as dancing, jumping rope, using outdoor play equipment, as well as structured and unstructured play, are beneficial in developing gross motor skills and teaching young children to properly interact with others. **Whole-group** activities such as circle time, class songs, and read-aloud sessions are also valuable in teaching young children appropriate communication skills within a group. **Thematic learning stations**, such as a science center, dramatic play area, library corner, block area, art center, and technology center, allow young children to explore their own interests on a variety of topics while developing creative and imaginative skills. **Sensory play** stations that include such items as a sand box or water table, are beneficial in further developing motor skills and allowing young children to explore and experiment with a variety of textures. Young children also require opportunities for quiet activities, such as naptime, self-selected reading, or meditation throughout the day in order to process information, reflect, and rest after active movement.

- **Middle-level**: Students at this age are best supported by the implementation of **hands-on** learning activities that develop **logical reasoning** and **collaboration** skills. Collaborative activities such as science experiments, mathematical word problems, the use of manipulatives, and projects that allow opportunities for building, creating, disassembling, and exploring, are beneficial in facilitating such a learning experience. Social and emotional learning activities are also important in developing middle school students' skills in these domains. Incorporating such activities as class meetings, community building activities, and self-reflection activities, are valuable methods for teaching social and emotional skills. In addition, cooperative learning opportunities should be implemented frequently across subject areas to further develop students' ability to work productively with others. Examples include literacy circles, creating teams for class review games, or group presentations.
- **High School:** Instructional activities for high school students should be designed to foster the development of **abstract** and **hypothetical** thinking abilities while preparing them to become productive members of society as they enter adulthood. Activities such as debates, class discussions, and mock trials are beneficial in providing high school students the opportunity to employ abstract reasoning, consider solutions to hypothetical situations, and develop empathy for opposing viewpoints. Assignments that require students to engage in the research process are valuable opportunities for developing higher-order thinking skills, as they encourage students to analyze, compare, and interpret information, as well as seek evidence to support their claims. In addition, incorporating activities that benefit the community, such as fundraisers or food and clothing drives, are beneficial in teaching high school students the importance of positively contributing to society.

EFFECTIVE AND DEVELOPMENTALLY APPROPRIATE LEARNING EXPERIENCES AND ASSESSMENTS

Effective developmentally appropriate instruction requires careful consideration when planning to ensure that students' individual needs across domains are supported to facilitate growth and a positive learning experience. The teacher must consider the developmental stage of their students based upon their age group, as well as students' individual differences. With this knowledge in mind, teachers must ensure that they provide an inclusive learning environment that fosters growth and development by creating challenging, yet attainable activities based on students' needs. Likewise, teachers must evaluate whether learning experiences and assessments are age, developmentally, and culturally appropriate while ensuring that they are tailored to students' unique learning differences. Learning experiences must provide opportunities for hands-on, cooperative, and self-directed learning, exploration, and participation to allow students to interact with their environment and build experiences. Additionally, lessons and activities should be flexible in nature to allow for inquiry and build upon students' prior experiences. Effective developmentally appropriate assessments are aimed at monitoring student progress and allow for flexibility based on students' learning differences. They should be intended to provide feedback to the teacher on how to better adapt instruction to meet students' individual needs and foster developmental growth.

FACILITATING DEVELOPMENT OF LIFE SKILLS AND ATTITUDES IN MIDDLE SCHOOL-AGE CHILDREN

Middle school-age children are at a pivotal development point in which they experience rapid and profound change. In this transition, they often demonstrate characteristics of younger and older children and are therefore at a critical stage for developing the beliefs, attitudes, and habits that will be the foundation for their future. Teachers must understand the implications of these changes and design instruction that addresses students' learning needs and facilitates the development of such important life skills as working and getting along with others, appreciating diversity, and committing to continued schooling. Cooperative learning and team building strategies instill the importance of working together positively to problem solve, building on one another's strengths, and valuing other's perspectives. These strategies also teach students to appreciate diversity through encouraging them to work with peers with different backgrounds and experiences. Additionally, teachers can teach students to embrace diversity through creating a culturally responsive classroom environment that models acceptance and incorporates elements of students' differences into instruction to demonstrate the value of diverse perspectives. Teachers promote positive attitudes toward academics that encourage a commitment to continued schooling by teaching organization, time management, and goal-setting skills that instill a growth mindset and provide a foundation for success.

IMPACT OF STUDENT CHARACTERISTICS ON TEACHING AND LEARNING

YOUNG CHILDREN

The developmental level of young children is characterized by defining attributes that impact teaching and learning, and for which several considerations must be made to design and implement effective instruction. As the attention span of young children is limited, the teacher must think about how to effectively act as a facilitator for learning more often than directly instructing students. **Direct instruction** must be delivered in small, manageable chunks to accommodate students' attention spans and ensure they retain and understand new concepts. Thus, the teacher must evaluate which elements of the curriculum require structured learning, while allowing for flexibility within instruction to accommodate student inquiry. Young children also need frequent **movement**, **physical activity**, and **social interaction**, as they learn and build experiences concretely through moving, playing, interacting with, and exploring their environment. To create a learning environment that accommodates these characteristics, the teacher must consider the physical arrangement of the classroom, and whether it adequately allows for movement. Additionally, teachers must incorporate **structured** and **unstructured activities** that foster and promote exploration, inquiry, play, cooperative learning, and hands-on interactions with the learning environment. With these considerations in mind, the teacher enhances students' learning experience by tailoring instruction to their developmental characteristics.

MIDDLE SCHOOL-AGED CHILDREN

As middle school-age children transition from childhood to adolescence, they experience vast changes across all developmental domains. Consequently, they exhibit characteristics that affect teaching and learning that require careful consideration when adapting instruction to their unique learning needs. While these students require increasing independence as they mature, they still need a structured, predictable environment to ease the transition into high school. The teacher must create a balance between fostering independence and growth while providing a schedule and routine. Opportunities for self-directed learning and student choice, as well as strategies for self-assessment and reflection foster autonomy and self-responsibility over learning while the teacher facilitates and monitors progress. Strategies to teach effective organizational and time management skills further promote independence and prepare students for success upon entering high school. As middle school-age students develop, the importance of peers becomes increasingly prevalent as they begin to search for their identity and shape their own values and beliefs. Teachers must ensure to provide opportunities for cooperative and small group learning to facilitate students' social development while considering the importance of promoting positive peer relationships at this impressionable developmental level.

ADOLESCENT CHILDREN

The developmental changes that occur in adolescence result in distinct characteristics as students in this age group transition into young adulthood. During this stage, students are discovering their identities, values, and beliefs and begin to explore long-term career and life choices. As they navigate their development and shape the person they will become, social relationships come to be increasingly important. Teachers must consider the impact of these characteristics when developing instruction to effectively address the unique needs of this age group and establish foundational attitudes, habits, and skills necessary for success in life. Effective instruction encourages adolescents to consider different perspectives, morals, and values to broaden their worldview and foster the development of their own beliefs. Lessons and activities should allow for exploration of personal interests, skills, and abilities as students shape their personalities and begin to consider long-term life goals. Moreover, the teacher should incorporate strategies that assist adolescents in goal setting to successfully foster a growth mindset and provide a foundation for success. Additionally, as socialization is highly influential at this stage, teachers must consider the importance of incorporating cooperative learning strategies and opportunities for socialization within instruction to encourage healthy peer relationships and foster positive identity development.

INTERCONNECTION OF DEVELOPMENTAL DOMAINS

Developmental domains are deeply interconnected. If one area of a child's development is negatively impacted, it is likely to pose negative consequences on other developmental areas. Proper physical development is key to developing cognitively, socially, and emotionally in that physical development allows children to acquire the necessary gross and fine motor skills to explore and experiment with the world around them, as well as interact with others. Physical development includes development of the brain, and factors such as poor nutrition, sleep, or prenatal exposure to drugs potentially hinder brain development. Consequentially, this may result in cognitive delays, and ultimately lead to social or emotional developmental delays through negatively impacting the child's ability to interact with others, build relationships, emotionally regulate, or communicate effectively.

FACTORS TO CONSIDER WHEN SELECTING MATERIALS FOR LEARNING AND PLAY

To plan meaningful, integrated, and active learning and play experiences, the teacher must have a deep understanding of both the developmental stage of the students and an understanding of students' individual needs. With this knowledge in mind, there are several factors that the teacher must consider when choosing materials that support active learning and play experiences, and ultimately, the development of the whole child. Materials should be adaptable in use to facilitate development in multiple areas. Versatility is also important in fostering imagination and creativity. The teacher must consider how the chosen materials will support understanding of concepts covered in instruction, as well as how they will support conceptual, perceptual, and language development. Furthermore, the teacher must ensure that materials are age-appropriate, stimulating, and encourage active participation both independently and cooperatively.

CHARACTERISTICS OF A DEVELOPMENTALLY RESPONSIVE CLASSROOM

A developmentally responsive classroom is one in which the teacher understands the cognitive, physical, social, and emotional developmental stages of students while recognizing nuances and individual developmental differences within these stages. The teacher understands that developmental domains are interconnected, and effectively responds to unique developmental differences by designing a learner-centered curriculum and classroom environment that caters to each students' abilities, needs, and developmental levels to develop the whole child. The developmentally responsive classroom is engaging, supportive, and provides challenging learning opportunities based on individual learner abilities. There are several factors the teacher must consider in the developmentally responsive classroom when planning an appropriate, engaging, and challenging learning experience. The teacher must have a deep understanding of which teaching strategies will most effectively appeal to students of varying developmental levels and be prepared to teach content in multiple ways. Furthermore, the teacher must consider how to plan and organize activities, lessons, breaks, and the overall classroom environment. This would include considering how to arrange the classroom, which activity areas to include, spacing, and classroom equipment. The developmentally responsive classroom should promote positivity and productivity through creating a supportive yet challenging learning atmosphere that welcomes and respects differences, thus encouraging students' curiosity and excitement for learning.

Factors that Impact Student Learning

HOME AND COMMUNITY FACTORS THAT IMPACT STUDENT LEARNING

Students are exposed to multiple social and cultural factors from their homes and communities that significantly impact learning, so it is imperative that the teacher is conscious of these factors to effectively adapt instruction and assessment to enhance students' learning. Students are often held to different academic and behavioral expectations by their parents, depending on their social and cultural background, that affect self-motivation, engagement, and academic performance. When adapting instruction and assessment, teachers must ensure that all students are held to high expectations while providing individual students with the necessary supports for success. Teachers must also consider the availability of community resources that offer support and enhance learning, as this differs among social and cultural groups. Students from low sociocultural backgrounds may lack quality resources such as libraries, tutoring, or after-school activities, so teachers must adapt to include time outside of instruction for completing assignments, additional support, and use of school resources. Community problems pose obstacles that hinder students' motivation, self-concept, and attitude toward learning. It is important that teachers establish a safe, welcoming, and engaging classroom while providing the necessary academic and behavioral supports to foster equity and promote a growth mindset.

SELF-DIRECTED LEARNING

In a **self-directed learning** environment, students are given a sense of agency that enhances self-motivation, feelings of ownership and responsibility for their own learning. By choosing what and how they learn based on their individual interests, learning styles, and preferences, students have the ability to explore and inquire freely, thus increasing their natural curiosity and motivation to do so. In choosing their own learning, students determine their own learning goals, thus creating a sense of ownership and self-responsibility. This sentiment is also increased when students can tailor their learning according to their own needs and challenge themselves based upon their skills and abilities. Furthermore, when students achieve self-decided goals, they develop a sense of ownership over their learning. In order to foster a self-guided environment in which students are fully engaged in their own learning, teachers must adopt a facilitator role in instruction and offer support when necessary. Instruction and assessment must allow multiple opportunities for student choice in how learning is determined and demonstrated. By providing opportunities for self-evaluation and reflection, teachers further facilitate self-motivation, ownership, and responsibility over students' own learning through encouraging them to make personal connections, reflect on accomplishments, and seek areas for self-improvement.

37

TEACHER ROLES IN STUDENT LEARNING

The teacher's role is multifaceted in nature, and teachers must often adopt multiple roles within a single lesson to effectively facilitate learning and accommodate individual students' needs. The role of the **lecturer**, **model**, and **facilitator** are applicable to different learning situations and have varying impacts on learning. As the lecturer, the teacher delivers direct instruction to students. This role is most appropriate when introducing a new concept, providing instructions for an upcoming activity, or reviewing material. In addition, teachers can effectively communicate new skills, ideas, and thought processes through modeling to students, as this is a highly influential method of instruction. When teachers serve as facilitators, they guide students in learning while offering support, scaffolding, and assistance when necessary. This role is effective in active and open-ended learning situations in which students are encouraged to explore, practice, and engage in creative problem solving. Through this method, teachers allow students to adopt a self-directed approach that encourages ownership over their own learning, thus creating an engaging, empowering learning experience.

IMPACT OF STUDENT ROLES ON LEARNING

Students adopt multiple roles in the learning process, and teachers must be cognizant of individual learning styles and specific learning situations to determine which role is most applicable and effective for enhancing learning. As **active learners**, students participate and interact throughout the learning process. In this role, students are encouraged to implement higher-order thinking skills through exploration, inquiry, and problem solving, thus creating an engaging learning environment that promotes the retainment of information. This role is particularly effective in learning situations in which students are practicing new skills, testing hypotheses, and exploring new concepts. The opportunity to actively participate in learning allows them to better internalize new information and formulate creative solutions to problems. Active learning also occurs in effectively designed collaborative learning situations. As **group participants**, students can build upon one another's skills, abilities, and experiences to solve problems, explore new information, and understand new perspectives to enhance the overall learning experience. When students are learning new skills, behaviors, or thought processes, they often adopt the role of the observer. Modeling is an influential instructional strategy, and in **observing** the teacher or another more experienced individual, students learn to utilize and implement new information in learning situations.

GARDNER'S THEORY OF MULTIPLE INTELLIGENCES

When determining instruction, activities, and assessment, teachers must consider and incorporate students' various approaches to learning. Every student learns differently and has unique needs, and thus, teachers must ensure that auditory, visual, kinesthetic, and tactile learning styles are addressed in all areas of curriculum to maximize students' learning potential. Through incorporating multiple modalities using Howard Gardner's **theory of multiple intelligences** as a framework, teachers can design content and activities that deliver instruction in a variety of ways simultaneously (visual-spatial, linguistic, musical, naturalistic, interpersonal, intrapersonal, logical-mathematical, bodily-kinesthetic). Through this approach, student understanding is reinforced, and each student is provided the opportunity to learn in the way that best suits their individual needs. By differentiating instruction with these modalities, teachers can incorporate several strategies simultaneously when teaching a concept, such as independent practice, cooperative learning, music, art, problem solving, and movement. Opportunities for student choice in learning further allows the integration of multiple modalities in instruction, as it lets students decide the method of learning that is best tailored to their individual learning style and needs.

Howard Gardner's Theory of Multiple Intelligences

Visual/Spatial	Prefers visual representations, able to visualize with the mind's eye, excels in activities that incorporate drawing, building, creative expression, and manipulatives.
Logical-Mathematical	Prefers activities that require order, analysis, and problem-solving using logical reasoning. Excels in solving math equations, conducting science experiments, puzzles, and analyzing data.
Verbal-Linguistic	Prefers learning through reading, writing, speaking, and listening. Often skilled in acquiring foreign languages. Excels in activities that incorporate discussion, debate, oral presentations, and written assignments.
Bodily-Kinesthetic	Prefers hands-on learning experiences that involve movement and physical interaction with the learning environment. Excels in activities that involve sports, dance, building, and hands-on projects.
Interpersonal	Prefers learning opportunities that involve communicating and collaborating with others. Excels in partner, small group, and whole-group learning activities.
Intrapersonal	Prefers to learn and work independently. Usually possesses a strong sense of self-awareness. Excels in activities that allow for independent, self-paced learning and self-reflection.
Musical	Learns best when music is incorporated into instruction. Prefers using songs, mnemonic devices and rhythms to learn concepts and retain information.
Naturalistic	Learns best when opportunities to connect with nature are incorporated into instruction. Prefers activities such as nature walks, identifying and classifying elements of nature, and working outside.

MULTIPLE LITERACIES

Multiple literacies are part of modern learning and business. To be successful, people must effectively process and share different types of information using **multiple media forms**. Therefore, teachers must devote instructional time to teaching students the skills they need to succeed in this technology-rich environment.

Teaching multiple literacies requires a mixture of explicit instruction, guided practice, and opportunities for application. For example, teachers need to teach students to find supporting details in digital texts. They may explicitly teach this skill during mini-lessons by modeling how they highlight key phrases. Teachers may then ask students to highlight key phrases in digital texts independently while they observe and provide feedback. Students may then be given multiple opportunities to apply this skill throughout the year to complete projects and assignments.

Teachers should also provide opportunities for students to interact with texts of all types and communicate using different media. They can offer choices in projects and assignments as long as instructional objectives are met. This method allows students to pursue their own interests and leads to increased engagement and ownership over learning.

CHARACTERISTICS OF AUDITORY LEARNERS

Auditory learners easily gather and process information through listening. For example, they may determine main ideas from lectures, assess subtle details from speakers' tones during conversations, and follow oral directions to complete multistep tasks. Auditory learners often enjoy speaking as well, and they may frequently participate in class discussions and conversations.

Teachers can implement many instructional strategies to support auditory learners. They can incorporate read-alouds, discussions, and lectures into classroom activities. They can provide audio versions of textbooks and storybooks. They can also record lectures so students can listen to them later to prepare for assignments and assessments. Teachers can allow students to interview others to gather information, and they can introduce songs, chants, and rhymes to assist with memorization. When designing projects and assessments, teachers can allow students to complete oral reports or presentations. Additionally, they can allow students to think through problems out loud and offer verbal feedback. Directions can also be given orally.

CHARACTERISTICS OF VISUAL LEARNERS

Visual learners easily gather and process information by observing. They may learn by seeing written words, photographs, models, or any other visual representations of information. For example, they may locate words signaling the main ideas of written texts, summarize events detailed in illustrations, or complete new tasks after seeing the steps modeled.

Teachers can implement many instructional strategies to support visual learners. They can encourage visual learners to take notes when reading new texts or learning new concepts. Notes can consist of words, pictures, or combinations of both. Teachers can also provide written directions to complete tasks, or they can visually model the steps. Additionally, teachers can use photos, realistic objects, diagrams, and other visual materials when introducing new concepts to learners. They can provide graphic organizers to help learners visualize the connections among concepts. When reading aloud, teachers can also share and discuss the illustrations. When teachers are designing projects and assessments, they can allow students to present their learning through multimedia presentations, models, or other visual means.

CHARACTERISTICS OF KINESTHETIC LEARNERS

Kinesthetic learners learn best by doing. They benefit from watching people model how to do things and being given opportunities to do things themselves. They also benefit from opportunities to be active within the classroom.

Teachers can implement many instructional strategies to support kinesthetic learners. They can consider active ways for students to learn and practice new concepts. For example, first grade students can trace sight words in chalk and hop along the letters, helping them memorize the spellings. Students of all ages can complete science experiments that allow them to mix, measure, and complete other scientific tasks. During math lessons on comparing and ordering numbers, students can form human number lines and discuss the processes they used.

Classroom arrangements and routines are also important for kinesthetic learners. Teachers can consider flexible seating arrangements and opportunities to move throughout the classroom to accommodate these students' needs.

CHARACTERISTICS OF TACTILE LEARNERS

Tactile learning is sometimes viewed as a synonym of kinesthetic learning, but there are some key differences. Kinesthetic learning refers to active learning by doing, and **tactile learning** refers to learning through **physical touch**. Tactile learners benefit from frequent opportunities to feel and manipulate items during instruction.

Teachers can implement many instructional strategies to support tactile learners. For example, early childhood students can trace letter cards made of different textures. Students can be given opportunities to spell words in rice, sand, or other textured materials. Manipulating letter tiles can also be used during word work activities. When completing science activities, students can feel objects and describe their textures. During math activities, students can use manipulatives to explore concepts and solve problems. When teachers are designing projects and assessments, they can also allow students to present their learning using models constructed from types of artistic materials.

USING INSTRUCTIONAL STRATEGIES THAT ADDRESS ALL LEARNING MODALITIES

Teachers should consider all learning modalities and accommodate auditory, visual, kinesthetic, and tactile learners within the classroom. This is important for several reasons, including the possibility that each student may display preferences for multiple modalities. Additionally, students can benefit from having information presented in multiple ways. For example, students may learn how to complete new tasks by watching their teachers model the steps. However, if given opportunities to practice the steps themselves, students may be better able to remember and apply them in the future.

Teachers need to consider the specifics of each concept they are teaching when determining which **modalities** to address during instruction. For example, it is difficult to teach letter formation using only oral directions. Students benefit from seeing the process teachers use to form each letter and from having opportunities to practice forming the letters independently. When teaching rhyming, auditory instruction is important. All modalities play a role in learning.

Classrooms are also made up of **diverse students** who prefer different modalities. To meet the needs of all learners, teachers can offer instructional choices and present information in multiple ways. For example, teachers can offer print and auditory versions of texts. Directions can be provided in written form and spoken verbally. Teachers can also offer project choices that allow students to present their learning in oral, written, or visual form.

Role of Play in Learning and Development

CHARACTERISTICS OF THE DEVELOPMENTAL PLAY STAGES

As children develop, so do their styles of play. Developmental play stages are divided into five primary phases: **solitary play** (Birth-2 years), **onlooker play** (2 years), **parallel play** (2-3 years), **associative play** (3-4 years) and **cooperative play** (4 years and beyond). During the **solitary play** stage, children play alone and are uninterested in playing with others, or what other children around them are doing. When they reach the **onlooker play** stage, children will watch other children play, but will not actively engage in playing with others. In **parallel play**, children do not play with one another, but will often play next to each other and will use similar materials. They may be curious about what other children are doing, and may copy them, but will not directly play with them. Children begin to intentionally play with others in the **associative play** stage, but the play is unorganized and still largely individual in its goals. In **cooperative play**, children begin to intentionally play and share materials in organized groups, and often have a common purpose or goal when playing.

PURPOSES AND BENEFITS OF PLAY IN EARLY CHILDHOOD EDUCATION

Purposeful play is an integral part of learning and development in the early childhood classroom. Its purpose is to aid and allow children to incorporate all aspects of development and thus provides cognitive, social, emotional, and physical benefits. Purposeful play deepens children's understanding of new concepts through allowing them to explore and experiment in the world around them using imagination and creativity. Integrating purposeful play into the early childhood classroom is further beneficial in that it allows children to construct and build on knowledge through experiences and helps develop divergent and convergent thinking. The socialization children get from play strengthens their language skills through speaking to one another, using new vocabulary, and listening to others. Purposeful play strengthens physical-motor development in that it calls for children to move their bodies in games, running, jumping, etc. Play is necessary for building important emotional and social skills that are necessary for being a successful member of society later in life.

Diverse Student Populations

UNDERSTANDING STUDENTS' DIVERSE BACKGROUNDS AND NEEDS
SELF-EDUCATION

Educating oneself on students' diverse backgrounds and needs enhances one's overall understanding of their students and creates a culturally sensitive, accepting classroom environment tailored to students' individual needs. There are several avenues through which teachers should educate themselves in an effort to build an accepting and respectful classroom climate. Communication is key for learning about diversities; thus, it is important for teachers to foster and maintain positive communications with students' families to deepen understanding of cultures, beliefs, lifestyles, and needs that exist within their classroom. This could include learning some language of students with different cultural backgrounds, attending family nights at school, or participating in social events within their students' communities to integrate themselves into the culture. Furthermore, teachers can learn more about their students' backgrounds and needs through gaining an understanding of student differences, incorporating these diversities into the curriculum, and encouraging students to participate in learning by sharing aspects of their lives with the class.

TEACHING, LEARNING, AND CLASSROOM CLIMATE BENEFITS

A deep understanding of students' diverse backgrounds and needs provides multiple benefits for teaching, learning, and overall classroom climate. Knowledge of students' diversities allows teachers to understand the individual needs and abilities of their students, and tailor instruction accordingly to maximize student development and achievement. Additionally, it allows teachers to know which authentic materials to incorporate in lessons and instructions to best create an engaging, relevant, and respectful learning experience that fosters student interest in learning and promotes success. Furthermore, by enhancing understanding of students' diverse backgrounds and needs, teachers consequently begin to model an attitude of inclusivity, acceptance, and respect for differences, which is then reflected by students and achieves a positive, welcoming classroom climate that promotes diversity.

IMPLICATIONS FOR TEACHING, LEARNING, AND ASSESSMENT IN DIVERSE CLASSROOMS

In any classroom, a teacher will encounter a wide range of variances among individual students that inevitably will influence teaching, learning, and assessment. Diversities in ethnicity, gender, language background, and learning exceptionality will likely exist simultaneously in a single classroom. Educators must be prepared to teach to these diversities while concurrently teaching students the value and importance of diversity. The curriculum and classroom environment must be adjusted to meet individual student needs and create an **inclusive**, **respectful**, and **equitable** environment that welcomes differences and allows for success in learning. This begins with the teacher developing an understanding of the unique diversities that exist within their students and using this knowledge to **differentiate** curriculum, materials, activities, and assessments in such a way that students of all needs, interests, backgrounds, and abilities feel encouraged and included. Furthermore, the teacher must understand how to instill appropriate supports to accommodate the diverse needs of students, as well as how to modify the classroom environment in such a way that is reflective of the diversity of the students.

CONSIDERATIONS FOR TEACHING IN DIVERSE CLASSROOMS
ETHNICALLY-DIVERSE CLASSROOMS

As society becomes increasingly diverse, teachers will certainly encounter classrooms with students of multiple ethnicities. Thus, to create an accepting and respectful classroom environment that allows for success in learning for all students, there are several factors to consider. Teachers must educate themselves on the various ethnicities within their classroom. This includes being mindful of **social norms, values, beliefs, traditions,** and **lifestyles** of different ethnic groups, and learning to communicate with students and families in a respectful, culturally sensitive manner. Additionally, the teacher must make a conscious effort to incorporate aspects of each ethnicity into the curriculum, activities, and classroom environment to create an inclusive atmosphere that teaches the acceptance, respect for, and celebration of differences. Teachers must be **culturally competent** and ensure that all materials are accurate, relevant, authentic, and portray the different ethnicities within the classroom in a respectful, unbiased manner. Furthermore, teachers must consider how their own ethnicity impacts their teaching style and interactions with students, how they may be perceived by other ethnic groups, and how to respond in a manner that fosters respect and inclusivity.

GENDER-DIVERSE CLASSROOMS

When approaching a gender-diverse classroom, teachers need to consider their perceptions, interactions with, and expectations of different genders, as well as how the classroom environment and materials portray gender differences. Teachers must work to eliminate possible stereotypical beliefs so all students feel respected, accepted, and encouraged to participate. Furthermore, teachers must consider how their behavior acts as a model for how students perceive gender roles and should act in a way that eliminates gender divisiveness. Teachers should use gender-neutral language when addressing students and ensure that all students receive equal attention. Teachers must maintain equal academic and behavioral expectations between genders and be sure to equally praise and discipline students so that neither gender feels superior or inferior to another. Regarding curriculum and classroom materials, teachers must ensure that the classroom environment encourages equal participation in, access to, and choice of all activities and procedures. Activities and materials should provide equal opportunities and foster collaboration between genders. Furthermore, teachers must ensure that curriculum materials avoid gender stereotypes, and highlight each gender equally in order to create an accepting and respectful learning environment that provides equal opportunities for students of all genders to develop their individual identities and abilities.

LINGUISTICALLY DIVERSE CLASSROOMS

In a **linguistically diverse** classroom, teachers must consider how to effectively demonstrate value for students' native languages while simultaneously supporting the development of necessary language skills to thrive in the school setting. By accepting and encouraging students to use their native languages, teachers can establish an inclusive learning environment that celebrates linguistic differences, and therefore, encourages students to want to build upon their language skills. Through this, teachers create an equitable learning environment that allows for academic success. To develop English language skills, the teacher must first consider each students' language ability and level of exposure to English prior to entering the classroom, as well as the level of language learning support each student has at home. Teachers can then implement effective instructional strategies and supports to modify curriculum in a way that addresses students' language needs. Teachers must also consider the implications of the classroom environment on language acquisition. By

43

creating an atmosphere that encourages language acquisition through **literacy-rich resources** and **cooperative learning**, teachers promote the use of language skills and ultimately provide opportunities for success for all students.

LINGUISTIC SUPPORTS AND INSTRUCTIONAL STRATEGIES PROMOTING ENGLISH LANGUAGE PROFICIENCY

Incorporating a variety of linguistic aids and instructional strategies is beneficial in supporting ELL students of varying levels of English language proficiency. **Visual representations** to accompany instruction, such as posters, charts, pictures, slide shows, videos, tables, or anchor charts, are valuable in providing clarification and reference while promoting vocabulary acquisition. When delivering instruction, **body language** such as hand gestures, eye contact, and movement to mimic verbal directions and explanations can provide clarification to enhance understanding. These students may also require **translation devices** for clarification, an interpreter to help with understanding instructions and new concepts, alternate assignments with simplified language, or **individualized instruction** from an ESL teacher. Frequently checking for understanding and providing clarification as necessary throughout instruction are necessary to ensuring ELL students understand learning materials, instructions, and assessments. In addition, creating a print and literacy-rich environment by including word walls for new vocabulary, reading materials that vary in complexity, labels, and opportunities for speaking, reading, and writing within instruction are valuable in promoting English language acquisition.

LEARNING DISABILITIES AND OTHER EXCEPTIONALITIES

In a classroom where learning disabilities and exceptionalities are present, teachers must consider accommodations for students of various learning needs while fostering an atmosphere of respect and acceptance. Teachers must understand the individual learning needs of each student and differentiate instruction accordingly to create an equitable and inclusive learning atmosphere. For **learning disabled** students, teachers must consider accommodations that allow for inclusion in all areas of curriculum and instruction. Such considerations may include extended work time, individualized instruction, and cooperative learning activities to ensure that learning disabled students are provided the necessary supports to achieve academic success. For students with other exceptionalities, such as **gifted and talented** students, teachers need to consider ways to provide challenging and stimulating opportunities for expansion and enrichment of curriculum. Furthermore, the teacher must be aware of their own interactions with students in order to demonstrate and encourage respect and acceptance among students. By providing supports for individual student success, teachers can effectively highlight students' strengths and therefore, teach students to accept and celebrate differences in learning abilities.

Educating Students about Diversity

GOALS OF TEACHING DIVERSITY IN THE CLASSROOM

Teaching diversity in the classroom aims to establish a welcoming and inclusive classroom environment that encourages academic achievement and whole-child development. Diversity education works to develop students' understanding, acceptance, and respect for others' perspectives while instilling the concept that people are ultimately more alike than different, and that diversities should be celebrated. Teaching the importance of differences creates a positive, inclusive classroom atmosphere in which all students feel respected, safe, and valued by their teacher and peers. Such an environment promotes academic achievement among students in that it encourages participation in learning and builds the self-esteem necessary for positive growth and development. Furthermore, teaching diversity has a significant role in **whole-child development** in that it instills the ability to understand and respect multiple frames of reference, thus increasing their ability to problem solve, cooperate with others, and develop a broader global perspective. Additionally, it allows for the development of cultural competency and ultimately creates accepting and respectful contributors to society.

RECOGNIZING AND ELIMINATING PERSONAL BIASES

Personal biases are often subtle and unconscious, yet it is essential that teachers work to recognize and eliminate them to create an accepting and respectful classroom environment. Personal biases may negatively impact teaching style, interactions with students, and ultimately, student learning and self-esteem. In eliminating personal bias, teachers ensure that they establish an inclusive classroom environment where each student is treated fairly. Furthermore, students' beliefs toward diversity are influenced by the attitudes and behaviors modeled by their teacher, and therefore, eradicating personal bias is vital in positively influencing students to accept and respect differences. To eliminate personal bias, teachers must **reflect** on their own culture's attitudes toward diversity, as well as how these attitudes influence their interactions toward other groups, and work to make positive changes. Teachers must **educate** themselves on the diversities among their students and work to deepen their understanding of different groups through **communicating** with families, **integrating** themselves into students' communities, and participating in **professional development** that focuses on **cultural competency** and the importance of teaching diversity. Through making positive changes against personal biases, teachers foster a classroom environment that promotes diversity and empowers all students to be successful.

IMPACT OF DIVERSE CULTURAL CLIMATE IN THE CLASSROOM

Creating a diverse cultural climate in the classroom results in an empowering and engaging learning environment that facilitates academic success. An atmosphere that respects and accepts differences fosters a sense of inclusivity and welcoming among teachers and students, which allows students to feel comfortable with differences, safe in their own identities, and consequently, comfortable to engage in learning. This fosters a positive attitude toward learning that promotes academic achievement. Additionally, when students accept one another's differences in a diverse cultural climate, they are better able to work together and adopt creative problem-solving solutions through others' perspectives, which results in success in learning. Furthermore, a successfully diverse cultural climate reflects the diversity of the students within it, which ultimately creates a more engaging and relevant academic environment that sparks motivation and curiosity toward learning. Learning environments that reflect students' diversity create a sense of unity and belonging in the classroom and positively contribute to success in learning through building students' self-esteem and self-concept to empower them in believing they can achieve academic success.

AUTHENTIC CLASSROOM MATERIALS

Authentic classroom materials are artifacts from various cultures, events, or periods of time. These items enhance the relevancy of instruction by promoting students' real-world connection to learning and may also be used to incorporate students' backgrounds and experiences into the classroom to increase engagement. Such materials include magazines, newspapers, advertisements, restaurant menus, and recipes. In addition, resources such as video clips, films, television shows, documentaries, news segments, and music serve as authentic media sources to incorporate into instruction. Original works or documents, including art pieces, literature, poetry, maps, or historical records, are also valuable authentic resources for providing students with a real-world learning experience.

LOCATING AND IMPLEMENTING

Authentic classroom materials and resources are integral in creating a classroom environment that fosters engaging, relevant, and positive learning experiences. Teachers must work to develop an understanding of the diversities among their students and use this knowledge to locate and implement authentic classroom materials into daily instruction. In doing so, teachers create a positive learning environment that accepts and respects differences through incorporating **relevant** and **familiar** materials that make students from all backgrounds feel valued and included in instruction. When students can see aspects of their culture reflected in authentic learning materials, they can make **personal connections** between what they are learning and their own lives, and learning becomes more valuable, engaging, and relevant, thereby promoting success in learning.

INCORPORATING DIVERSITY EDUCATION INTO THE CLASSROOM

Incorporating diversity into the classroom maximizes student opportunities for academic success through creating a welcoming, empowering, and inclusive atmosphere. Teachers can implement multiple strategies to incorporate **diversity education** into the curriculum both as its own unit and woven into content instruction once they develop an understanding of the diversities among their own students. Through **building relationships** with students, teachers can use their knowledge of students' lives to incorporate aspects of their backgrounds into the curriculum by creating specific **cultural lessons** on food, music, language, art, and history. Additionally, **cultural comparison** studies are an effective method of teaching students the value of diversity, as well as highlighting the fact that people from different backgrounds often have more similarities than differences. Teachers can further implement diversity education by encouraging students to participate in learning through having them share elements of their culture and background with the class through activities such as show and tell or hosting family nights. Furthermore, integrating **cooperative learning** activities into instruction allow and encourage students from different backgrounds to work together and gain an understanding of the perspectives and backgrounds of others.

INCORPORATING DIVERSITY IN THE CURRICULUM

Incorporating diversity into the curriculum is vital for teaching the value and importance of differences and for contributing to a respectful and accepting environment. Additionally, it is imperative that diversity education extend from the curriculum to the entire classroom environment to maximize student growth and opportunity to reach potential. When students learn in an atmosphere that celebrates diversity and identifies strengths in differences, they feel a sense of belonging and confidence that encourages them to engage in learning, thus maximizing the potential for academic success. Teachers can effectively integrate diversity into the classroom environment through making authentic cultural materials such as texts, music, and art readily accessible for students. Additionally, providing several opportunities for students to collaborate and socialize in a natural setting allows them to gain an understanding and respect for their peers' backgrounds. By encouraging students to share aspects of their own lives and backgrounds with the class through cultural activities, teachers facilitate a diverse climate that celebrates differences.

CULTURALLY RESPONSIVE TEACHING

Culturally responsive teaching is an instructional approach in which the teacher practices awareness, inclusivity, and sensitivity regarding the social and cultural diversities that are present within the classroom. With this awareness in mind, the culturally responsive teacher designs curriculum, instruction, activities, and assessments that are inclusive and reflective of students' social and cultural backgrounds and experiences. When planning instruction and learning experiences, the teacher can demonstrate awareness of social and cultural norms through consciously educating themselves on the beliefs, values, and norms of their students. This is achieved through connecting with students and building positive relationships to learn about their individual backgrounds and locate authentic learning materials that are reflective of their experiences. Through communicating with students' parents, family members, and members of the community, the teacher can practice and build awareness of the diverse social and cultural norms of their students to gain an understanding of how to design culturally responsive instruction. By educating themselves on the social and cultural norms of their students, the teacher can effectively ensure that students' diversities are reflected in all areas of instruction in a culturally sensitive manner to create an empowering learning environment that engages all students.

	Practices for Culturally Responsive Teaching
1	Create an inclusive classroom environment
2	Recognize personal biases and work to eliminate them
3	Self-educate on the community and students' social and cultural backgrounds
4	Use curriculum that reflects students' diversities using authentic materials
5	Frequently communicate with students' families
6	Build positive interpersonal relationships with students
7	Be involved in the community

Supporting Students with Varied Learning Needs

PLANNING AND ADAPTING LESSONS TO ADDRESS STUDENTS' NEEDS

VARIED BACKGROUNDS

Effectively planning lessons and adapting instruction to address students' varied backgrounds requires teachers to gain an understanding of individual students, and educate themselves on **customs, norms**, and **values** of the cultures in their classroom. This allows teachers to effectively plan **culturally responsive** lessons with **authentic materials** to make learning valuable, interesting, relevant, and allow students to feel included. Understanding students' backgrounds means teachers recognize variances in their knowledge and experiences on different topics and can effectively plan engaging and inclusive lessons that build upon it. Teachers must assess students' knowledge on material prior to creating lessons to effectively plan instruction that adapts to the needs of students' varied backgrounds and reflects students' experiences. Teachers must plan lesson materials such as texts, art, music, and language that accurately and sensitively reflect students' diverse backgrounds. Cooperative learning strategies should be incorporated to facilitate communication among students with varying backgrounds, as it helps them build knowledge from others' experiences, as well as teaches them to respect and value differences among their peers. Teachers must plan instruction that communicates high academic expectations for all students and adapt instruction as necessary by implementing supports to create equity and address the needs of varying backgrounds.

> **Review Video: <u>Adapting and Modifying Lessons or Activities</u>**
> Visit mometrix.com/academy and enter code: 834946

DIFFERENCES IN INDIVIDUAL STUDENTS' SKILLS

Teachers must use their knowledge of differences in students' skills to plan multifaceted, adaptable lessons that highlight students' strengths while providing instructional supports where needed based on individual skill level. To effectively plan, teachers must incorporate multiple strategies and mediums for instruction, activities, and assessments to allow students of all skill levels equitable and enriching access to content material. This includes allowing multiple opportunities for **student choice** in learning and demonstration of understanding through such strategies as choice boards, learning centers, project menus, and digital resources that allow students to approach content in multiple ways. In doing so, teachers effectively plan instruction that allows students to grasp new material and demonstrate learning in a way that best suits their skill level. Additionally, teachers must plan to incorporate **scaffolds** into their lessons and plan to adapt instruction as needed through continuous **formative assessments** to provide additional support for students of lower skill levels, while adding opportunities for enrichment and acceleration for gifted students. Supports can also be effectively planned into lessons through providing several opportunities for small-group activities in which students of various skill levels can work together, provide peer tutoring, and build upon one another's knowledge.

DIFFERENCES IN STUDENTS' INDIVIDUAL INTERESTS

In order to plan engaging instruction that fosters success in learning, teachers must plan lessons and adapt instruction to address differences in students' individual interests. To accomplish this, teachers first need to work to build relationships with students and develop an understanding of their unique interests to effectively tailor instruction that taps into these interests. Through **differentiated instruction** and the incorporation of **student-choice** opportunities for learning and assessment, teachers can effectively plan **student-centered** lessons that teach content in multiple ways that appeal to varying interests. Additionally, interest centers in the classroom foster engagement in learning, are easily adaptable, and can be planned into daily instruction. By frequently conducting **formative assessments**, teachers can gauge student interest in activities and adjust as necessary. This ultimately promotes self-direction, motivation, and curiosity in learning through providing students the opportunity to build content knowledge based on their individual interests.

DIFFERENCES IN STUDENTS' INDIVIDUAL LEARNING NEEDS

Differences in backgrounds, abilities, skills, and interests results in a wide spectrum of student learning needs that must be addressed when planning effective and adaptable instruction. Teachers must recognize the individual learning needs of students to plan lessons that are accommodating, equitable, and promote success in learning. Through **student-centered** and **differentiated** instruction, teachers can effectively provide multiple avenues for content instruction, learning, and assessment based on individual need. Planning for **student-choice** and **self-directed learning** allows teachers to successfully address all learning styles and needs. Additionally, teachers must incorporate scaffolds into their lessons to adapt instruction. This can be done through incorporating such supports as graphic organizers, outlines, charts, and visuals, as well as planning for small, mixed-ability group instruction based on learning needs to provide scaffolding. Teachers should plan to check frequently for understanding during instruction in order to adapt activities and adjust instruction to meet individual learning needs.

ELL STUDENTS

English language learners (ELLs) need support in both understanding content material and building their English proficiency levels. To effectively plan and adapt instruction to accommodate them and facilitate success in learning, it is important that teachers demonstrate respect for the student's native language while encouraging the acquisition of English language skills. Teachers should plan for some content instruction to be in the student's native language to begin to build knowledge. To effectively assist ELLs in building vocabulary on specific content areas, lessons should be planned around **themed units**. Additionally, planning multiple cooperative learning and peer-tutoring activities allows ELLs to practice and develop their English skills in a natural setting, as well provides support for understanding new instructional concepts. Teachers must plan to scaffold content material, texts, and writing assignments to align with students' proficiency levels through adding such supports as graphic organizers, labels, and charts. Incorporating **linguistic aids** such as verbal cues, gestures, pictures, and digital resources allow teachers to effectively adapt instruction as necessary to support understanding and develop English language skills.

STUDENTS WITH DISABILITIES

Students with disabilities may require **instructional or physical supports** in order to have an equitable learning experience that facilitates their academic success. Teachers must be cognizant of any student disabilities and work to effectively plan instruction in a subtle, sensitive, and inclusive manner. Students with learning disabilities may require the planning of supports such as preferential seating, extra time for work and assessments, graphic organizers, and shorter or chunked assignments. These students may need to be paired with others that can provide scaffolding and peer-tutoring or may require individualized instruction or small focused groups. Students with physical disabilities may require such supports as a modified classroom environment to address their physical needs, audiovisual supplements, enlarged font, or braille texts. Teachers must work to incorporate these supports into their lesson planning to ensure that all students are included and empowered to learn, while allowing for flexibility in their lesson plans to allow for necessary adaptations.

CULTURAL AND SOCIOECONOMIC DIFFERENCES
ADDRESSING DIFFERENCES IN AN INCLUSIVE AND EQUITABLE CLASSROOM ENVIRONMENT

In a **culturally responsive** classroom, the teacher recognizes and is sensitive to the importance of planning instruction that addresses cultural and socioeconomic differences among students for creating an **inclusive** and **equitable** learning environment. The teacher responds to differences in norms, values, interests, and lifestyles through designing relevant instruction that builds on students' experiences and facilitates personal connections that foster engagement in learning. This is important in conveying to students the value of their diverse experiences and highlighting their strengths in a manner that empowers them to achieve academic success while providing support where needed. It is important that the teacher incorporate supports in instructional planning to address academic, social, behavioral, and emotional needs of students from different cultural and socioeconomic backgrounds to provide all students an equitable opportunity for success in learning while maintaining high academic expectations.

POSSIBLE IMPACTS ON ACADEMIC ACHIEVEMENT

If not properly addressed, cultural and socioeconomic differences among students pose potentially negative impacts on academic achievement. It is vital that teachers recognize and accommodate these differences to instill the proper supports for engagement and success in learning. Students from different cultural or socioeconomic backgrounds may feel excluded from curriculum and instruction, which may result in lowered self-concept, self-esteem, and ultimately, disengagement toward learning. Thus, teachers must practice **culturally responsive teaching** to create instruction in which all students feel valued and included. These students may lack the support or resources for education at home due to various cultural and social challenges, and students from low socioeconomic backgrounds may face health, behavioral, or emotional challenges that impact their development and ability to learn. It is important that the teacher recognize these challenges and subtly address them in the classroom to establish an inclusive, equitable, and empowering environment that fosters engagement in learning. Some strategies for addressing these differences include providing community classroom materials, extra time for tutoring and assistance outside of classroom hours, individualized instruction, or opportunities to use the internet at school for students who lack access at home.

SIGNIFICANCE OF VARIED STUDENT LEARNING NEEDS AND PREFERENCES
IMPLICATIONS ON INSTRUCTION

Variances in students' learning needs and preferences implies that instruction must be **differentiated**, flexible, and allow for adaptations as necessary to accommodate students' individual needs, abilities, and interests. Furthermore, it means that teachers must work to build relationships with their students to develop an understanding of their different needs and preferences. This allows teachers to design instruction that emphasizes individual strengths while challenging students academically based on their abilities and providing instructional supports where necessary to ensure student success. To accomplish this, teachers must plan and deliver instructional material in multiple ways to address differences in learning needs and preferences, as well as allow for student choice in learning, processing, and demonstrating understanding of content.

POSSIBLE VARIANCES THAT MAY BE ENCOUNTERED

Teachers will inevitably encounter an array of learning needs and preferences among their students. As students have varying **learning styles**, including but not limited to visual, auditory, or kinesthetic, their methods for acquiring, processing, and retaining information will differ, as well as their **preferred modalities** for doing so. Some students may prefer written assignments in which they work independently, while others may prefer activities that involve active movement within a group. Similarly, some students require more individualized attention, while others may function better in a small group or whole-class setting. Students will also come to the classroom with differing **academic abilities**, and therefore, will require varying levels of assistance, support, and guidance to facilitate their success in learning. In addition, students may have specific learning, physical, social, or emotional **disabilities**, and as such, will need varying degrees of supports and accommodations to support their ability to learn effectively.

IMPORTANCE OF TAILORING CURRICULUM, INSTRUCTION, AND ASSESSMENTS

Through tailoring curriculum, instruction, and assessments according to student learning needs and preferences, teachers create a **student-centered** learning environment. This motivates and empowers students to take ownership of their learning and allows every student an equal opportunity to achieve academic success. By creating a flexible curriculum and presenting instruction through multiple methods, teachers ensure that the learning needs and preferences of all students are met by facilitating a dynamic and engaging learning environment in which students can learn in the way that best suits their needs. Furthermore, in adapting assessments based upon students' learning needs and preferences by allowing **student choice**, teachers maximize student understanding of content material, allowing them to demonstrate learning according to their interests and abilities.

Teaching English Language Learners

ENGLISH LANGUAGE LEARNERS
CHARACTERISTICS AND NEEDS OF LANGUAGE PROFICIENCY LEVELS

The term **English language learner** (ELL) refers to students acquiring English as a second language, and consists of beginner, intermediate, and advanced levels of English language proficiency. Each proficiency level is determined by specific characteristics and requires differing linguistic supports across listening, speaking, reading, and writing domains. **Beginning** ELLs have little or no ability to understand the English language across domains and rely heavily on linguistic aids such as visual representations, gestures, verbal cues, and environmental print. These students communicate through memorized high-frequency words or phrases and often require individualized instruction. **Intermediate** ELLs have acquired some foundational knowledge on the English language and can communicate with increasing complexity. They are generally able to understand, speak, read, and write in short, simple sentences and follow clear, routine directions. These students are able to seek clarification for misunderstandings but continue to require linguistic supports such as repetition, slowed speech, visual representations, and body language. **Advanced** ELL students are generally able to understand and utilize the English language with minimal error and often do not require extensive linguistic support outside of occasional repetition or clarification. Their proficiency is comparable to that of their native English-speaking peers.

ACQUIRING LISTENING AND SPEAKING SKILLS

The acquisition of **listening** and **speaking** skills are interrelated and often are the first two domains in which English language proficiency is developed. As the ELL hears and observes the teacher modeling proper speech and active listening, they begin acquiring listening skills. Additionally, listening to and observing classmates is integral for the development of listening and speaking skills. By watching and imitating their peers, ELLs build understanding of the nuances of the English language in different settings. When words and phrases heard are linked to a particular action or event, the ELL derives meaning and can utilize the newly acquired vocabulary, thus developing listening and speaking skills simultaneously. The development of listening and speaking skills is enhanced in a **language-rich environment** in which students are provided multiple opportunities to practice and develop their skills in a natural setting. Therefore, the teacher must include opportunities for ELLs to speak, actively listen, and work collaboratively. Incorporating materials such as songs, games, stories, and digital media further immerse the ELL in a language-rich environment and allow them to attach meaning to new vocabulary to build proficiency.

ACQUIRING READING AND WRITING SKILLS

The acquisition of listening and speaking skills in English provides the foundation for developing **reading** and **writing** skills. Reading and writing abilities develop in relation to one another, as when students begin acquiring reading skills, they learn to attach meaning to vocabulary and texts that enable them to express themselves in writing. The development of reading skills begins with understanding simple, high-frequency vocabulary and simple sentence structures as a foundation, building upon this knowledge with increasingly complex vocabulary and sentence structures. Similarly, writing ability increases in complexity from basic labels, lists, and copying and develops into expression though simple sentences on familiar topics, and ultimately, complex writing abilities that employ higher-order thinking on abstract concepts. Reading and writing skill development is enhanced through consistent practice in a **print** and **literacy-rich** environment. Students should be provided with multiple opportunities for reading and expressing themselves through writing throughout instruction. Reading materials with varying levels of complexity should be readily available for students, and literacy development must be incorporated into all subject areas to build vocabulary and comprehension.

> **Review Video: <u>Stages of Reading Development</u>**
> Visit mometrix.com/academy and enter code: 121184

PRINT AND LITERACY-RICH LEARNING ENVIRONMENT

A print and literacy-rich learning environment is beneficial for providing an **immersive** experience that promotes the development of students' reading, writing, speaking, and listening skills. Such an environment typically incorporates a variety of learning resources and strategies to encourage literacy. The walls are often decorated with a variety of print materials, such as posters, captions, word walls with high-frequency or thematic vocabulary words, signs, labels, bulletin boards, and anchor charts. Students are provided with authentic printed and digital literacy materials, such as newspapers, magazines, shopping advertisements, video clips, songs, and documentaries to increase relevancy and personal connections. A print and literacy-rich classroom also includes a class library that offers texts of varying genres, formats, and levels of complexity. Learning activities provide multiple opportunities to develop literacy skills in a natural setting, such as opportunities for collaborative learning, self-selected reading, and free-write sessions.

COMPONENTS OF LANGUAGE

All languages are comprised of syntax, semantics, morphology, phonology, and pragmatics.

- **Syntax** refers to the structure and arrangement of words within a sentence, which controls the functions of grammar.
- **Semantics** refers to how language conveys meaning.
- **Morphology** refers to how words are constructed of smaller parts, such as root words, prefixes, and suffixes.
- **Phonology** refers to how words are pronounced.
- **Pragmatics** refers to the practical, social applications of language and its use in the real world, including non-verbal communication.

These components heavily overlap with one another. For instance, morphology is heavily involved in constructing the meaning of a word, which largely falls under the category of semantics and without a logical ordering of the words in a sentence (syntax), the sentence could mean something completely different, or be altogether incoherent. Each of these systems needs to be well-established for communication in English or any other language. Some of these components, such as morphology, can be particularly targeted to support content-based instruction. For instance, a teacher might work on prefixes and root words that commonly occur in science, such as bio-, geo-, tele-, -logy, -scope, and -graphy.

ENGLISH LANGUAGE PROFICIENCY FOR LISTENING AND SPEAKING

DESCRIPTORS FOR ENGLISH LANGUAGE PROFICIENCY FOR EACH ABILITY LEVEL

Development of English language proficiency is marked by descriptors for each ability level in listening and speaking. **Beginner** ELLs are highly limited or unable to understand or speak English in any setting. They have difficulty understanding and using simple vocabulary even with the help of linguistic aids and rely on single words for basic communication. Grammatically, they are unable to construct full sentences. **Intermediate** ELLs understand and speak using high-frequency English vocabulary on familiar topics and settings. They speak and understand short sentences and demonstrate a basic understanding of English grammatical patterns for constructing simple sentences but need linguistic aids for unfamiliar vocabulary. Additionally, they make several errors when communicating, but can ask in English for clarification, and are usually understood by those familiar with working with ELLs. **Advanced** ELLs can speak and understand grade-appropriate English with linguistic supports. They understand and participate in longer conversations about familiar and unfamiliar topics, but may rely on linguistic aids, repetition, or clarification. These students still make some errors in communication but are often understood by people unfamiliar with working with ELLs. **Advanced high** ELLs require minimal linguistic support and can understand and speak English at a similar level to native English-speaking peers.

TEACHING STUDENTS AT DIFFERENT PROFICIENCY LEVELS

Teaching students with different proficiency levels for listening and speaking English implies that students will require varying degrees of linguistic support to develop their skills and provide them with an equitable learning environment. Specifically, students with lower proficiency levels in these areas will rely more on linguistic accommodations than students with more developed abilities. Teachers must be knowledgeable of the descriptors for each proficiency level to implement the proper supports and instructional strategies to address individual learning needs for developing listening and speaking skills in English. Instructional strategies should aim to promote the acquisition of skills through building background knowledge and providing context in multiple ways. This includes modeling proper speaking and listening skills, accompanying instruction with verbal cues, slower speech, repetition, gestures, and visual aids to improve student comprehension and build vocabulary. Additionally, incorporating several cooperative learning opportunities provides scaffolding and opportunities to practice and build upon listening and speaking abilities. Content instruction can be supported with the implementation of digital resources that promote the acquisition and development of listening and speaking skills and can be tailored to students' individual abilities.

> **Review Video: ESL/ESOL/Second Language Learning**
> Visit mometrix.com/academy and enter code: 795047

ENGLISH LANGUAGE PROFICIENCY FOR READING AND WRITING

DESCRIPTORS FOR ENGLISH LANGUAGE PROFICIENCY AT EACH ABILITY LEVEL

English language proficiency for ELLs is determined by descriptors for each ability level in reading and writing. **Beginning** ELLs possess little or no ability to read, understand, or write in English. Comprehension is restricted to single, familiar vocabulary words, and writing is limited to lists, labels, and vocabulary accompanied by pictures. These students rely heavily on linguistic supports for understanding, and their writing is unclear to those unfamiliar with working with ELLs. **Intermediate** ELLs can read, understand, and write short sentences and simple language structures on familiar material with the help of linguistic aids. They engage in writing assignments, but their writing contains errors and is unclear to those unfamiliar with working with ELLs. **Advanced** ELLs read, understand, and write using more expansive vocabulary and sentence structures with the help of linguistic accommodations. They may have difficulty with unfamiliar vocabulary but can read and write at a faster pace with increased accuracy. These students demonstrate more complex writing abilities, and their writing is usually understood by those unfamiliar with working with ELLs. **Advanced high** ELLs can read, understand, and write using grade-appropriate English with minimal linguistic support at a level similar to native English-speaking peers.

TEACHING STUDENTS AT DIFFERENT PROFICIENCY LEVELS

Teaching students with different proficiency levels for reading and writing English means linguistic accommodations in the classroom will need to be scaffolded to address the needs and abilities of individual students and promote the development of skills in these areas. Students with lower proficiency levels in reading and writing will require more linguistic aids than students with more developed abilities. Thus, the teacher must have a deep understanding both of individual student needs and of descriptors for proficiency at each level to effectively support students in their acquisition of reading and writing skills. Instructional strategies should foster the acquisition of these skills through providing several ways to allow students to build background knowledge and context to increase understanding. This includes creating a language-rich classroom environment that emphasizes the development of literacy skills in the form of environmental print, word walls and charts for new vocabulary and high-frequency words, labels, and visual aids. Reading materials on subject content should be available at each reading level. Additionally, the use of graphic organizers and outlines increases comprehension and writing ability through breaking information into smaller portions to provide scaffolding.

CREATING EQUITABLE LEARNING ENVIRONMENT FOR ELLS USING LINGUISTIC SUPPORTS

To create an equitable learning environment, ELL students must be provided with linguistic supports that are applicable across content areas in order to ensure they are provided with an equal opportunity for success in learning. Teachers can implement varying supports appropriate to students' levels of English language proficiency that are beneficial in facilitating both English language and content-specific learning. Such supports include incorporating verbal cues, gestures, and visual representations into instruction to provide context and build background knowledge. The use of environmental print, word walls, and labels are also effective in supporting English language skills while simultaneously providing context for facilitating learning in the content area. Teachers should model speaking and listening skills, and practice slow speech or repetition when necessary to ensure understanding. Scaffolding instruction and activities across content areas through such supports as graphic organizers, outlines, and cooperative learning opportunities serve to assist ELL students in building English language proficiency skills across content areas at a pace appropriate for their ability level. By implementing the proper supports, teachers can effectively foster English language learning in all subject areas while ensuring that students simultaneously learn content-specific material.

INSTRUCTIONAL STRATEGIES FOR ENGLISH LANGUAGE LEARNING IN ALL SUBJECT AREAS

Language acquisition occurs across content areas for ELL students, as each subject is comprised of different vocabulary, grammatical patterns, and methods of expressing ideas. Thus, it is important that teachers provide these students with learning strategies that are applicable in all subject areas in order to effectively support English language acquisition and content-specific learning. Through a metacognitive approach, teachers can facilitate ELL students in thinking about how they learn, reflecting on their strengths and weaknesses, and applying useful learning strategies from one content area to another to develop their English language skills in all subjects. This strategy enhances learning through teaching students how to apply learning strategies from one instructional context to another when developing language skills. By activating students' prior knowledge when introducing new material in a given subject area, teachers promote English language learning through providing context and encouraging students to consider what they may already know about a new concept. Such methods as pre-teaching, anticipatory guides, graphic organizers, and brainstorming allow ELL students to make connections that build their language abilities across content areas.

ADAPTING INSTRUCTION FOR VARYING LEVELS OF ENGLISH LANGUAGE PROFICIENCY

When encountering ELL students with varying English language skills, it is imperative to adapt instruction to accommodate these differences and ensure that all students receive appropriate linguistic support. Instruction must be communicated, sequenced, and scaffolded to support learners with different English proficiency abilities. The teacher must communicate instruction clearly while allowing time for repetition or slowed speech as necessary. In addition, teachers must supplement instruction with linguistic supports such as verbal cues, gestures, and visual representations as needed to provide assistance and context appropriate to individual ability levels. Instruction must also be sequenced logically and clearly communicate the expectations and steps of learning experiences. This is achieved by indicating an explicit beginning, middle, and end to activities through transition words and actions appropriate to students' levels of English proficiency. Teachers must scaffold instruction, activities, and assessments to meet individual students' language learning needs. Supports such as word walls, graphic organizers, charts, labels, and pairing students with others who can provide assistance are effective means of scaffolding learning to accommodate varying ability. By communicating, sequencing, and scaffolding instruction in a way that is tailored to ELL students' individual language needs, teachers effectively foster an equitable environment that promotes success in learning.

Promoting Higher-Order Thinking

STIMULATING REFLECTION, CRITICAL THINKING, AND INQUIRY AMONG YOUNG CHILDREN
OPPORTUNITIES FOR PLAY, MANIPULATING MATERIALS, AND TESTING IDEAS AND HYPOTHESES

In providing age-appropriate learning experiences, teachers effectively stimulate critical thinking, inquiry, and reflection. For young children, opportunities for play, manipulating learning materials, and testing ideas and hypotheses are integral components of development, as children at this stage learn through interacting with their environment. These learning experiences stimulate inquiry and critical thinking through providing children with the space to explore, imagine, create, and form new ideas by directly and concretely engaging with their surroundings. In forming and testing new ideas, critical thinking abilities are further developed, as young children are encouraged to utilize problem-solving skills to craft new solutions. These methods of learning also serve to stimulate reflection in that they foster the ability to understand, rationalize, and organize how the world around them functions. When young children have the opportunity to explore, inquire, and test new ideas, they are able to reflect on their learning through processing and integrating new information to build understanding and experience.

STRUCTURED, HANDS-ON PROBLEM-SOLVING ACTIVITIES, EXPLORATION, AND RISK-TAKING

Opportunities for structured, hands-on problem solving, exploration, and risk taking are integral components in enhancing the learning experience through stimulating inquiry, critical thinking, and reflection. Physically exploring and interacting with learning materials actively engages students in the learning process, thus fostering curiosity and inquiry, as students are more encouraged to take risks and test their ideas, as well as examine how materials work. When students are actively engaged through these learning methods, critical thinking is stimulated, as students must consider, analyze, and evaluate information to make informed choices for problem solving as they work to reach their desired outcome. Through hands-on learning experiences, student understanding is deepened in a way that fosters connections and stimulates reflection. These methods allow students to see and analyze the results of their own inquiry and problem solving, thus allowing them to evaluate and reflect upon their learning for further exploration and improvement.

PROMOTING POSITIVE CONTRIBUTIONS, COMMUNICATION, AND RESPECTFUL EXCHANGE OF IDEAS

Positive contributions, communication, and respectful exchanging of ideas facilitate a welcoming learning community that stimulates inquiry, critical thinking, and reflection. In such a learning environment, students feel a sense of security, inclusiveness, and trust that empowers them to engage in curiosity and inquiry through asking questions, exploring, and taking risks. When students can positively contribute to the learning experience through communicating their viewpoints with the trust that they will be respected, critical thinking is enhanced. Critical thinking encourages students to consider multiple viewpoints and challenges their own frames of reference. In addition, positive and respectful communication and exchanging of ideas stimulates inquiry and critical thinking through establishing a space in which students feel safe to share their experiences. This allows for students to constructively contribute to cooperative learning activities in which students can build critical thinking skills by feeling empowered to take risks, learning from others' perspectives, skills, and approaches to problem solving. When students feel comfortable discussing their learning in a respectful and positive environment, it allows for deeper reflection and understanding that enhances the learning experience.

ACTIVITIES THAT ENCOURAGE THE DEVELOPMENT OF HIGHER-ORDER THINKING SKILLS

The learning experience is enhanced and student understanding is strengthened when instruction focuses on the use and development of higher-order thinking skills. When instructional activities encourage students to **apply**, **analyze**, and **synthesize** information rather than simply knowing it, they develop the critical thinking and problem-solving skills necessary for academic and real-world success. By using **Bloom's taxonomy** when determining learning outcomes and creating instruction, teachers can effectively incorporate activities that foster students' refinement of higher-order thinking abilities. Activities that encourage exploration of diverse perspectives broaden students' worldview and teach them to consider different approaches to problem-solving by exposing them to new viewpoints. Cooperative learning experiences further allow students to explore others' approaches to problem solving, build upon one another's experiences, and synthesize different perspectives to create new solutions. Cooperative and other active learning experiences that allow for problem-solving, open-ended questioning, and inquiry promote the development of higher-order thinking skills through encouraging students to explore and analyze information, test hypotheses, make connections, and synthesize information to formulate their own conclusions. Activities that develop students' research skills promote higher order thinking through encouraging students to make inferences, consider and analyze other's perspectives, synthesize information to create new conclusions, and elaborate on their findings.

TEACHING AND MODELING ORGANIZATIONAL AND TIME-MANAGEMENT SKILLS
Helping Students Develop AND Build Upon Real-World Life Skills

Teaching and modeling time management and organizational skills to students is vital in instilling positive habits that serve as the foundation for academic success and the development of important life skills. As students progress through their academic careers and into the real world, these skills will allow them to succeed in setting and achieving measurable goals in an organized, timely fashion, as well as successfully managing increasing responsibilities, commitments, and schedules. Furthermore, mastering these skills fosters efficient learning through teaching students to effectively plan, organize, and maximize their time and prioritize the completion of tasks. **Modeling** these skills is necessary for students to observe how to effectively manage and organize their time to be successful. The development of these skills is integral in creating empowered, confident lifelong learners that are successful in real-world situations and in effectively preparing them for future academic achievement and success in the professional realm.

IMPORTANCE AND METHODS OF ADAPTING FOR DIFFERENT AGE GROUPS

Organizational and time management skills are developed over time, and thus, it is integral to introduce these concepts to students in their early school years at an age-appropriate level. In teaching, modeling, and monitoring these skills, teachers provide a strong foundation which students can develop with increasing independence throughout their academic careers. By adapting organizational and time management techniques to address different age groups' needs, teachers ensure that students internalize, implement, and develop these habits. For younger children, these skills can be taught and modeled through creating specific places for classroom materials, keeping like items together, and establishing smooth transitions between activities based on a schedule. Teachers can then monitor to ensure that students successfully follow these procedures. As students mature, their academic and extracurricular schedules become increasingly complex, and therefore, it is important that teachers continue to build organizational and time management skills while adapting to students' age levels through allowing increasing independence. Through teaching, modeling, and monitoring organizational tools such as a daily agenda and teaching effective strategies for systematically locating and organizing information, students develop and learn to independently implement tools that will allow for success as they transition through their academic careers and into adulthood.

TEACHING AND MODELING STUDY SKILLS FOR ACADEMIC AND PROFESSIONAL SUCCESS

Establishing strong study skills from an early age is integral for acquiring the tools necessary for academic and professional success. By teaching, modeling, and monitoring age-appropriate study techniques in the early school years, teachers provide students with foundational skills to develop and build upon as they progress through their academic careers and into the real world. Teachers can begin instilling effective study habits by teaching and modeling the use of graphic organizers and outlines to organize and process information with increasing levels of difficulty and independence based on age level. As students mature and academics become progressively challenging, effectively teaching, modeling, and monitoring note taking, summarizing, and test taking strategies with increasing levels of independence teaches students to organize and prepare new information. When study skills are taught and modeled at an age-appropriate level through adapting the amount of monitoring to address the needs of different age groups, teachers equip students with the tools necessary and the ability to develop these skills for lifelong learning and success.

IMPORTANCE OF APPROPRIATELY STRUCTURED RESEARCH PROJECTS

The research process instills valuable organizational, time management, and study skills that contribute to academic preparedness and success. When teachers effectively structure and monitor the research process, they teach students strategies that can be implemented for success in real-world situations. Teachers should begin by instructing students on the steps in research. This includes identifying a problem, issue, or argument for research, how to gather pertinent information related to the topic, and strategies for organizing, prioritizing, processing, and synthesizing supporting evidence. These steps teach students important organizational skills that will allow them to successfully think critically and problem solve in real-world situations. Throughout the project, teachers should establish checkpoints to monitor student progress and foster independence through encouraging the use of time management tools. In doing so, teachers foster the development of important real-world life skills by instilling in students the ability to effectively and efficiently structure and prioritize their time for the completion of tasks, thus preparing them for future success.

The Research Process

IMPACT OF TEACHER ATTITUDES AND BEHAVIORS ON STUDENT ACHIEVEMENT AND SELF-CONCEPT

Teachers' behavior significantly impacts the learning experience, as their actions are highly influential to students. Often unconsciously, teachers exhibit attitudes and behaviors that impact students' self-concept, self-esteem, and consequently, academic achievement. If a teacher indicates negative sentiments toward students, it hinders their self-perception and belief in their abilities, thus negatively impacting their academic performance. To minimize negative factors, promote students' growth mindset, and enhance learning, teachers must engage positively with all students in communication, instruction, and assessment. They must be cognizant of their own bias toward students and eliminate all negative notions to ensure that exchanges with students are equally positive. Teachers must display positive modeling and be conscientious of interactions both with individual students and the class as a whole. Additionally, teachers must ensure that they hold equally high academic and behavioral expectations for students, and make certain that each student receives equal attention, praise, and discipline. Teachers must be aware of how they group students and do so in a way that does not insinuate bias, negative connotation, or difference in expectations. Instruction and assessments must also be free of bias and include necessary supports for individual student needs to provide equal opportunities for success in learning.

Equity in Education

EQUALITY VS. EQUITY

Equality refers to providing everyone with the same resources when working toward a goal, regardless of the unique needs or situation of the individual. **Equity** means considering an individual's needs and circumstances to provide the proper supports that allow them a fair opportunity to achieve a common goal. In the classroom, creating an equitable environment requires the consideration of students' individual learning styles, needs, and personal situations, and using this knowledge to instill necessary supports to help each student achieve the same objectives relative to their peers. Equity in the classroom is especially important for closing the achievement gap, particularly in low socioeconomic areas, because many of these students come from disadvantaged situations and need additional help to gain a fair opportunity for academic success.

> **Review Video: Equality vs Equity**
> Visit mometrix.com/academy and enter code: 685648

SUPPORTS UTILIZED TO PROVIDE AN EQUITABLE LEARNING ENVIRONMENT

The nature of academic, physical, and behavioral supports depends largely on the needs of the individual student. However, some common supports are effective in addressing an array of needs to facilitate an equitable learning environment. Students with **learning disabilities** may benefit from such academic supports as preferential seating near the front of the room and minimized distractions to enhance focus. Modified test questions or alternate assignments, graphic organizers, scaffolded texts, extra copies of class notes, and individualized instruction as necessary are also valuable in enhancing focus, preventing overwhelm, and ensuring learning activities are aligned with students' capabilities. Students with **physical disabilities** may require wheelchair access, a sign language interpreter or scribe, braille text, enlarged fonts, or the use of technology devices to aid in reading and writing. Common **behavioral supports** in the classroom include opportunities for frequent breaks or movement as needed, a daily check-in with a caseworker or other dedicated staff member, or a behavior chart to allow students to self-monitor.

ESTABLISHING HIGH ACADEMIC EXPECTATIONS

In any classroom, establishing high academic standards is imperative for motivating and empowering students to succeed. By communicating high expectations clearly and frequently, the teacher demonstrates belief that each student can overcome obstacles and excel academically, thus inspiring student engagement, curiosity for learning, and an overall positive and productive learning environment. To create an environment of high academic standards, the teachers' expectations must be apparent in instruction. The teacher must provide lessons and activities that are rigorous but not so challenging that students are unable to complete them without assistance, as this would disempower and disengage students from learning. The teacher must set achievable learning goals based on knowledge of student abilities and encourage self-reflection. Additionally, the teacher must utilize knowledge of students' individual needs to instill necessary supports to help students in achieving tasks and create an equitable environment for learning. This will ultimately empower students to overcome obstacles and motivate them for academic success.

Chapter Quiz

Ready to see how well you retained what you just read? Scan the QR code to go directly to the chapter quiz interface for this study guide. If you're using a computer, simply visit the bonus page at **mometrix.com/bonus948/oaeapkma** and click the Chapter Quizzes link.

Assessment, Instruction, and the Learning Environment

Transform passive reading into active learning! After immersing yourself in this chapter, put your comprehension to the test by taking a quiz. The insights you gained will stay with you longer this way. Scan the QR code to go directly to the chapter quiz interface for this study guide. If you're using a computer, simply visit the bonus page at **mometrix.com/bonus948/oaeapkma** and click the Chapter Quizzes link.

Learning Environments in Early Childhood

GUIDELINES FOR INDOOR AND OUTDOOR SPACE USE

Indoor and outdoor early childhood learning environments should be safe, clean, and attractive. They should include at least 35 square feet indoors and 75 square feet outdoors of usable play space per child. Staff must have access to prepare spaces before children's arrival. Gyms or other larger indoor spaces can substitute if outdoor spaces are smaller. The youngest children should be given separate outdoor times/places. Outdoor scheduling should ensure enough room and prevent altercations/competition among different age groups. Teachers can assess if enough space exists by observing children's interactions and engagement in activities. Children's products and other visuals should be displayed at child's-eye level. Spaces should be arranged to allow individual, small-group, and large-group activity. Space organization should create clear pathways enabling children to move easily among activities without overly disturbing others, and should promote positive social interactions and behaviors; activities in each area should not distract children in other areas.

ARRANGEMENT OF LEARNING ENVIRONMENTS
ARRANGING INDOOR LEARNING ENVIRONMENTS ACCORDING TO CURRICULAR ACTIVITIES

EC experts indicate that rooms should be organized to enable various activities, but not necessarily to limit activities to certain areas. For example, mathematical and scientific preschool activities may occur in multiple parts of a classroom, though the room should still be laid out to facilitate their occurrence. Sufficient space for infants to crawl and toddlers to toddle is necessary, as are both hard and carpeted floors. Bolted-down/heavy, sturdy furniture is needed for infants and toddlers to use for pulling up, balancing, and cruising. Art and cooking activities should be positioned near sinks/water sources for cleanup. Designating separate areas for activities like block-building, book-reading, musical activities, and dramatic play facilitates engaging in each of these. To allow ongoing project work and other age-appropriate activities, school-aged children should have separate areas. Materials should be appropriate for each age group and varied. Books, recordings, art supplies, and equipment and materials for sensory stimulation, manipulation, construction, active play, and dramatic play, all arranged for easy, independent child access and rotated for variety, are needed.

ARRANGING LEARNING ENVIRONMENTS TO CHILDREN'S PERSONAL, PRIVACY, AND SENSORY NEEDS

In any early childhood learning environment, the indoor space should include easily identifiable places where children and adults can store their personal belongings. Since early childhood involves children in groups for long time periods, they should be given indoor and outdoor areas allowing solitude and privacy while still easily permitting adult supervision. Playhouses and

60

tunnels can be used outdoors, while small interior rooms and partitions can be used indoors. Environments should include softness in various forms like grass outdoors; carpet, pillows, and soft chairs indoors; adult laps to sit in and be cuddled; and soft play materials like clay, Play-Doh, finger paints, water, and sand. While noise is predictable, even desirable in early childhood environments, undue noise causing fatigue and stress should be controlled by noise-absorbing elements like rugs, carpets, drapes, acoustic ceilings, and other building materials. Outdoor play areas supplied by a school or community should be separated from roadways and other hazards by fencing and/or natural barriers. Awnings can substitute for shade, and inclines/ramps for hills, when these are not naturally available. Surfaces and equipment should be varied.

Student Motivation

INTERNAL AND EXTERNAL MOTIVATION

Internal motivation is the desire to perform an activity for personal enjoyment, reward, and satisfaction. In the classroom, students with strong internal motivation engage in learning because they enjoy it and are interested in the topic of instruction. The overall learning atmosphere contributes to internal motivation. A positive, welcoming, and interesting environment excites students and promotes genuine curiosity for learning. In addition, attitudes and behaviors modeled by the teacher influence the classroom atmosphere, and ultimately, student motivation. When the teacher is enthusiastic about learning, they positively affect students' internal motivation to participate in instruction. In employing multiple instructional strategies, the teacher effectively elicits internal motivation by providing an engaging environment that addresses students' needs and interests. **External motivation** is the desire to complete a task for a tangible reward, such as extra credit, prizes, or special privileges, or to avoid something unwanted, such as bad grades or punishment. Students' individual backgrounds heavily influence external motivation. Additionally, the value placed on education at home and parental expectations contribute to students' engagement as motivational factors. The frequency of external rewards ultimately determines the effectiveness of external motivation. While external motivation can promote a desired outcome, when used too frequently, it can diminish students' internal motivation for learning.

INSTRUCTIONAL STRATEGIES FOR ACTIVATING STUDENTS' INTERNAL MOTIVATION

When the teacher employs multiple instructional strategies, they create an engaging environment that activates students' **internal motivation** for success in learning. Community building strategies establish an engaging, respectful, and welcoming environment that fosters positive attitudes toward learning that activate students' internal motivation. Modeling is an effective technique for engaging students in learning, as when the teacher demonstrates an enthusiasm toward education, they positively influence students' excitement and desire for learning. Incorporating growth-mindset strategies serves to develop students' self-esteem and self-concept, which empowers them and enhances their personal desire to actively engage in learning and achieve success. In addition, when the teacher is cognizant of students' needs, interests, backgrounds, and preferences, they can employ a variety of strategies to individualize instruction and enhance relevancy, thus establishing a clear purpose for learning that activates internal motivation. Providing multiple active and self-directed learning opportunities that promote inquiry and curiosity further motivate and engage students in learning. Such opportunities create a personalized learning experience that promotes autonomy and ownership over learning, thus encouraging active participation. When students have an internal drive to participate in their own learning, they are ultimately more engaged, productive, and successful throughout the learning process.

INSTRUCTIONAL STRATEGIES FOR ACTIVATING STUDENTS' EXTERNAL MOTIVATION

External motivational strategies are effective for promoting engagement in achieving **short-term** desired outcomes or behaviors, particularly when internal motivation is already present. Implementing tangible rewards such as extra credit, class prizes, or special privileges when students accomplish a specific task enhances students' desire to engage and succeed in learning. In addition, incorporating competition amongst students by gamifying instruction or creating class contests is another strategy for providing external motivation that excites students for success in learning. By establishing clear academic and behavioral expectations, the teacher can effectively activate students' external motivation for academic success, as when students understand classroom operations and what is expected of them, they are more willing to engage in learning. This includes establishing a clear classroom management plan with explicit procedures, expectations, and consequences, as well as utilizing and maintaining an effective grading system. It is important to note that although external motivation techniques can be immediately successful in promoting engagement and learning, the teacher must be selective in implementing them, as when used too frequently, they may diminish students' internal motivation and the overall effectiveness of instruction.

SELF-MOTIVATION

SIGNIFICANCE IN THE LEARNING PROCESS AND INFLUENTIAL FACTORS

Student **self-motivation** is necessary for a productive learning experience. The student must be personally motivated to actively engage in learning. Students' internal drive for academic success affects their willingness to achieve learning goals, participate in instructional activities, and perform well on assignments. When students are self-motivated, they are more likely to put forth strong effort toward understanding and considering complex ideas on a deeper level to enhance comprehension and retainment. Students' **self-esteem** and **self-concept** influence their motivation toward learning, as students that feel poorly about themselves are less likely to actively engage in learning, whereas students with a high sense of self-worth feel confident and empowered to succeed. Students' self-concept is influenced by the interactions and methodology of the teacher, as the teacher's attitudes and behaviors can either empower and excite students for learning or hinder their self-confidence, and therefore, motivation to participate. In addition, **parental expectations** and the value placed on education at home can determine students' attitudes toward learning and whether they are self-motivated to achieve academically. **Peer relationships** are highly influential on students' self-motivation as well, as the regard a students' peers place on learning affects their own attitudes toward academic success.

STRATEGIES TO ENHANCE SELF-MOTIVATION

The teacher's role in enhancing students' **self-motivation** is integral to a productive and successful learning environment. An effective teacher implements a variety of teaching strategies throughout instruction to activate students' self-motivation by addressing their individual learning needs and providing variation in instruction to enhance engagement. By learning the unique needs, interests, and preferences of students, the teacher can locate and implement **authentic materials** that make learning relevant and enable students to make personal connections, thus promoting self-motivation in that a clear purpose for learning is established. **Modeling** enthusiasm for learning and ensuring all interactions in the classroom are positive fosters positive attitudes toward learning and establishes a welcoming, engaging environment that enhances excitement and motivation for success. In addition, incorporating **growth-mindset** strategies such as goal setting and teaching students to overcome obstacles empowers students to become confident learners, thus developing students' self-esteem, and ultimately, self-motivation to engage in learning. Furthermore, when students feel they have control over their learning, they are more motivated, engaged, and successful in learning. By incorporating several opportunities for autonomy through student-choice and self-directed learning opportunities, the teacher effectively enhances self-motivation that promotes success in learning.

IMPACT OF ENCOURAGING STUDENTS' SELF-MOTIVATION

When students' **self-motivation** is encouraged in the academic setting, they develop vital life skills necessary for real-world situations that serve as a foundation for lifelong success. Self-motivated students are more inclined to take initiative in setting goals and taking active steps to achieve them for a sense of personal accomplishment and satisfaction, rather than a tangible reward. In addition, when self-motivation is promoted, students develop the ability to commit to a goal, navigate obstacles, and reflect on their performance to seek areas for improvement, thus enabling them to be successful in a real-world, professional setting. When self-motivation is established early, students develop the desire to continuously pursue goals, challenge themselves, and learn through improvement, thus becoming lifelong learners with the necessary real-world skills for success.

Learning Goals and Objectives

DETERMINING INSTRUCTIONAL GOALS AND OBJECTIVES

ROLE OF ASSESSMENT IN MEETING INDIVIDUAL STUDENT LEARNING NEEDS

Assessing students' prerequisite skills and knowledge is integral in gaining the understanding necessary to effectively determine instructional goals and objectives. This understanding provides the teacher with information about students' background knowledge, diverse experiences, and individual needs. With this information in mind, the teacher can establish goals and objectives based on state standards that are tailored to meet students' individual learning needs, and ensure that learning targets are relevant, challenging, and attainable. In assessing background knowledge, the teacher can develop high quality instruction that builds on students' prior experiences, thus fostering engagement in learning by allowing students to make personal connections in their learning. Additionally, assessing prerequisite skills and knowledge allows the teacher to identify gaps in learning, misunderstandings, or specific learning needs. This information allows the teacher to adjust and adapt instructional goals and objectives that align with students' abilities, learning styles, and knowledge, thus maximizing student learning potential by establishing student-centered instruction.

ASSESSMENT STRATEGIES

Several assessment strategies can be utilized when determining student prerequisite knowledge and skills. Assessments may be either formal or informal and serve to provide valuable information to the teacher for effectively determining an instructional plan that is tailored to students' individual needs. Before introducing new content, the teacher can administer a formal diagnostic test that contains the new material to assess prior knowledge and skill level and can analyze the results to adjust goals and objectives as necessary. Additionally, knowledge and abilities can be evaluated by analyzing prior test scores or project portfolios to gauge student understanding of previously taught material. This allows the teacher to identify gaps in knowledge or make necessary clarifications to information. Some informal methods of assessment include conducting individual or whole-class formative assessments such as concept maps, polls, or observations to gain understanding of students' background knowledge on new material prior to teaching it. Teachers can also have students self-assess their prerequisite knowledge on new instruction through administering a test or questionnaire about content material. Often, when assessing prerequisite knowledge and skills, it is important that the teacher keep assessments anonymous to ensure they receive accurate and unbiased data on student understanding and ability.

ROLE OF STANDARDS IN DETERMINING INSTRUCTIONAL GOALS AND OBJECTIVES

State standards for achievement provide a guideline and reference point for specific benchmarks of student academic progress based on grade level. Additionally, they serve to ensure that teachers and students are held to the same expectations for teaching and learning, thus focusing instructional goals and objectives. Teachers must have a solid understanding of state standards, as they are responsible for referring to them as an outline for planning instruction, lessons, learning outcomes, and assessments and ensuring that students achieve these learning targets. State standards provide a structure for teachers to effectively plan and adjust instructional goals and objectives based on individual student learning needs and ensure that all students have the necessary support to reach these academic standards. State standards are also the reference point for establishing the pace of instruction, monitoring student progress, and determining if learning goals have been met before progressing through the curriculum.

APPROPRIATE LEARNING GOALS AND OBJECTIVES

Setting appropriate learning goals and objectives is an integral component of quality, effective instruction that communicates high expectations, is developmentally appropriate, and is tailored to students' individual learning needs. Specific learning targets allow the teacher to effectively determine the path of instruction based on students' skills and abilities in a manner that is challenging and attainable while supporting students in achieving state academic standards. Through focusing the method of instruction on specific targets, teachers can better determine which lesson materials, activities, and assessments will best support students' learning needs to achieve success in learning. Additionally, appropriate learning goals and objectives are necessary for student academic success because they communicate clear expectations and the purpose of learning. When students understand why they are learning a given concept and what they are expected to achieve, they are encouraged to be engaged and focused in learning. Clear learning goals and objectives are also important for monitoring student progress, as they allow teachers to concretely measure student achievement and provide specific, meaningful feedback that allows for student growth.

ELEMENTS OF APPROPRIATE LEARNING GOALS AND OBJECTIVES

When determining learning outcomes, the teacher must consider the elements of appropriate learning goals and objectives. Effective **learning goals** communicate long-term learning targets, such as at the end of a unit or chapter, whereas **objectives** should dictate what students are expected to learn at the end of a daily lesson or activity. Proper learning goals and objectives are derived from state academic standards and simultaneously reflect individual student learning needs. They are age and grade-level appropriate, challenging, and aimed toward higher order thinking while still attainable to students according to their developmental level and learning differences. Appropriate learning goals and objectives clearly and succinctly communicate measurable expectations and define a clear purpose for instruction to make learning relevant. Additionally, they consider students' current skills and abilities in order to set targets that build upon background knowledge and allow students to make personal connections in their learning.

DETERMINING EFFECTIVENESS OF LEARNING GOALS AND OBJECTIVES

Learning goals and objectives provide a necessary foundation for successful students. Proper learning targets clearly and succinctly communicate expectations, engagement, and achievement. The effectiveness of goals and objectives can be determined by their level of clarity, relevance, and significance desired outcomes to students, thus allowing for focused instruction and learning. Goals and objectives are most successful when they are relevant to both curriculum material and students' individual experiences, as this fosters engagement through allowing students to forge personal connections and apply new concepts to their own experiences. Moreover, appropriate goals and objectives convey significance to overall learning. When students understand why what they are learning is important, they are more likely to be engaged and focused on instruction, and ultimately, achieve success in learning.

FRAMING LEARNING GOALS AND OBJECTIVES TO PROMOTE STUDENT UNDERSTANDING

The language of learning objectives and goals must be **age-appropriate, clear**, and **succinct** for students to comprehend them. Learning goals must represent broader learning outcomes, whereas learning objectives outline the steps for doing so. This includes utilizing verbs that align with the level of understanding that teachers intend for their students to achieve. For example, when introducing a concept, learning objectives may include such verbs as *identify*, *match* or *define*. As students develop mastery, the language of objectives should incorporate **higher-order thinking** verbs, such as *analyze*, *interpret*, or *predict*. Learning objectives and goals should also be measurable in order to communicate to students exactly what they are expected to achieve by the end of the lesson or unit. For example, a learning objective written as, "students will be able to discuss the economic impact of World War II," provides students with a specific and tangible goal to work toward. Academic goals and objectives should include the **purpose** for learning, such as to prepare for an assessment, or complete part of a project, and should be connected to state or district standards.

> **Review Video: Learning Objectives**
> Visit mometrix.com/academy and enter code: 528458

DETERMINING IF LEARNING GOALS AND OBJECTIVES ARE RESPONSIVE TO STUDENT NEEDS

In order for instruction and learning to be successful, goals and objectives must be responsive to student developmental levels and individual needs. Teachers must determine the responsiveness of learning targets by their age-appropriateness, consideration of students' skills and abilities, and reflection of their needs, interests, cultures, and backgrounds. Age-appropriate goals and objectives promote student achievement by providing realistic, yet rigorous expectations based on developmental level that facilitate academic success. Expectations must also match students' individual skill levels and abilities to design instruction and activities that are challenging, but not overwhelming, to ensure that students feel empowered in their learning. Responsive learning goals and objectives also consider students' individual needs and interests, thus allowing for instruction that is relevant and engaging. Additionally, learning targets should be sensitive to and incorporate elements of students' cultures and backgrounds. This fosters engagement and success in learning through allowing students to make personal connections between instruction and their own experiences.

EVALUATING APPROPRIATENESS OF LEARNING GOALS AND OBJECTIVES

When evaluating the appropriateness of learning goals and objectives, the teacher should first consider their relevance and specificity to the academic standard from which they are deriving learning targets, as well as how well they facilitate the design of effective instruction. Learning goals should express the desired outcomes of long-term learning, whereas objectives should measure daily achievement as students work toward the learning goal and the specified state standard. The teacher should evaluate whether the goals and objectives precisely communicate what the students are expected to achieve to effectively design instruction that supports students in achieving learning targets. Furthermore, they must ensure that learning targets are tailored to students' individual learning needs to design challenging and realistic instruction. Additionally, the teacher should consider the purpose of the learning goals and objectives to determine whether they communicate clear intentions for learning to students. The teacher must then decide which activities, instructional strategies, materials, and resources are most effective for supporting the achievement of learning targets and how they will design assessments to determine student achievement.

ROLE OF CAMPUS AND DISTRICT GOALS IN STUDENT ACADEMIC READINESS

Aligning instructional learning goals and objectives with campus and district goals is imperative for student academic readiness. These standards indicate benchmarks of achievement that students are expected to reach at a given grade level and act as a framework for the design of goals and objectives that help facilitate this achievement. This allows for the focusing of instruction and learning, as well as providing a measurable framework for assessing student progress. Additionally, it ensures that all students are held to the same academic expectations and that all students are given the same opportunities for learning. Creating learning targets based upon campus and district goals ensures that students are successfully able to advance to the next grade level with the same academic preparedness relative to their peers.

DESIGNING GOALS AND OBJECTIVES TO ADDRESS DIFFERENT SKILLS AND ABILITY LEVELS

While learning targets must be aligned with state academic standards, they simultaneously must be tailored to address students' unique skills and abilities. By differentiating instructional goals and objectives, teachers ensure that the instructional strategies, activities, and materials that they implement are effectively varied to meet students' individual learning needs. Additionally, they ensure that instructional expectations challenge students based on their skill and ability while supporting all students in meeting academic benchmarks. The language of objectives and goals should be layered to include varying levels of rigor to accommodate students' differing abilities as they work toward achieving intended learning outcomes. Learning targets should include scaffolding in order to ensure students have necessary supports and allow opportunities for expansion or enrichment as necessary. They should include differentiation in skills students are expected to attain based on their background knowledge and ability, as well as variances in approaches to completing tasks and demonstrating understanding. In differentiating objectives and goals, teachers ensure that all students are challenged and supported as they work to achieve grade level academic standards.

Instructional Planning

DESIGNING AND SEQUENCING LESSON PLANS AND UNITS TO ALIGN WITH INSTRUCTIONAL GOALS

The effective sequencing of units and lesson plans is key to developing coherent, comprehensible instruction that aligns with instructional goals and fosters success in learning. The teacher must first determine the instructional goals that students will be expected to achieve based on state academic standards as a framework, as well as students' individual needs, knowledge, and abilities. The teacher must then logically arrange specific units of instruction aimed toward achieving the determined instructional goals. Each unit should build upon knowledge from the prior unit. Within each unit, the teacher must determine what students must achieve as they work toward instructional goals and determine objectives that facilitate success based on individual need and ability. Once objectives are defined, teachers must design lesson plans in a logical sequence that will facilitate students in reaching these objectives and increasingly build upon knowledge as students work toward achieving the learning goal. When planning lessons, teachers must decide which activities, procedures, and materials are necessary for successfully completing lesson objectives while ensuring that individual learning needs are met. The teacher must also decide what will be assessed at the end of each lesson and unit to determine student success in achieving instructional goals.

CREATING DEVELOPMENTALLY APPROPRIATE LEARNING EXPERIENCES AND ASSESSMENTS

Multiple factors must be considered when designing developmentally appropriate learning experiences and assessments that effectively facilitate student growth and achievement. Teachers must consider the general cognitive, physical, social, and emotional developmental levels of students, as well as individual differences in background, skill, knowledge, and learning needs. With this understanding, teachers must then evaluate whether learning experiences are simultaneously appropriate to students' developmental levels and individual needs. This includes ensuring that learning activities and teaching strategies are varied in approach, tailored to students' interests and incorporate student choice in learning. Learning experiences must build upon students' background knowledge and experiences and provide challenging, yet attainable learning opportunities based on individual skills and abilities. Additionally, the teacher must consider whether learning experiences promote student participation and engagement as well as cooperative learning to ensure development across domains. Just as with learning experiences, the developmental appropriateness of assessments must also be evaluated. The teacher must consider whether assessments allow for choice in how students demonstrate their learning so as to address individual learning needs. Furthermore, it is important that teachers consider the purpose of each assessment regarding the feedback they are seeking and how it can help determine further instruction.

ROLE OF LEARNING THEORY IN INSTRUCTIONAL PROCESS AND STUDENT LEARNING

Multiple learning theories exist to explain how people acquire knowledge, abilities, and skills. Each theory proposes its own approach for best practices in teaching and learning, and therefore, each is most effective and applicable based on the context of learning and individual student needs. Thus, learning theory has a significant role as the framework for the instructional process and facilitating student learning. The teacher must understand the principles of various learning philosophies as well as their students' unique learning needs to effectively design and implement instruction from the perspective of the most applicable theory. Learning theories serve as a context from which, upon identifying desired learning outcomes, teachers can make informed decisions about designing instruction, activities, and assessments that are most effective based on their students' learning styles, skills, and abilities. In developing an understanding of students' learning needs, teachers can determine which learning theory is appropriate in order to design the most effective instruction possible. This facilitates student learning in that it allows for the implementation of student-centered methodologies tailored to students' learning needs and preferences and enhances instruction through allowing the teacher to implement methods from the theory most relevant to students' needs.

The following are examples of some common learning theories that can be used as a framework in the instructional process:

- **Constructivism (Jean Piaget):** This theory proposes that students learn by interacting with the learning environment and connecting new information to their background knowledge to build understanding. This active process allows students to personalize their learning and construct their own perceptions of the world through the lens of their previous experiences.
- **Humanism (Carl Rogers):** This theory proposes that everyone seeks the fulfillment of a hierarchy of basic needs. This begins with physiological needs, such as food and water, and extends to the need for safety, love and belonging, esteem, and ultimately, self-actualization. In the classroom, teachers can create a learning environment that strives to meet these needs by establishing a safe, accepting learning environment, celebrating students' differences, and praising academic and personal achievement.

- **Connectivism (George Siemens, Stephen Downes):** This theory proposes that learning occurs by making a series of connections across pieces of information, ideas, concepts, and perspectives. Connectivism is rooted in the notion that learning occurs externally, and technology resources facilitate connections, as learners have access to several outlets for acquiring and processing new information.
- **Experiential Learning (David Kolb):** This theory proposes that students learn and retain information best through physical exploration and interaction with the learning environment. In the classroom, teachers can facilitate this student-led approach by providing students with varying relevant experiences and opportunities for hands-on learning, such as projects or learning centers.
- **Multiple Intelligences (Howard Gardner):** Gardner's theory proposes there are several versions of intelligence, and as such, the process of learning differs among individuals. Some learners may have a stronger intelligence in one domain, but perhaps have difficulty in another, and therefore, learn best when instruction is presented through the lens of their dominant intelligence. Intelligences are categorized as logical-mathematical, verbal-linguistic, visual-spatial, bodily-kinesthetic, interpersonal, intrapersonal, musical, and naturalistic.

CONNECTING NEW INFORMATION AND IDEAS TO PRIOR KNOWLEDGE

When students connect new information to prior knowledge, learning becomes relevant and engaging. Effective instruction encourages students to connect learning to background knowledge and experiences, which increases retainment, deepens understanding, and enhances the effectiveness of the overall learning experience. Fostering personal connections to learning is achieved through incorporating an array of strategies and technologies into instruction. Activities including KWL charts, anticipatory guides, graphic organizers, and brainstorming encourage students to consider what they know before learning new concepts, thus allowing them to build upon their prior knowledge and ability to make connections that strengthen learning. Cooperative learning strategies promote sharing and building prior knowledge with other students, thus increasing students' connections to new information. Numerous technologies exist to enhance the learning experience by fostering connections between prior knowledge and new information. Teachers can incorporate a wide range of apps and games across subject areas that build upon prior knowledge by providing activities with increasing levels of difficulty. Online polls, surveys, and word association websites allow students to demonstrate prior understanding of a topic to begin making connections. Self-reflection and closure opportunities at the end of instruction further strengthen learning by encouraging students to connect new material to prior knowledge and experiences.

MAKING LEARNING MEANINGFUL AND RELEVANT

Effective instruction occurs when learning is meaningful and relevant. When the purpose of learning is clear, students are engaged, motivated, and retain new information. Instruction must be student-centered, foster personal connections, and be applicable to real-life situations to create meaningful and relevant instruction. Teachers achieve this through an array of methods and technologies that are tailored to students' learning needs. Through forging positive relationships with students, teachers learn their unique interests, preferences, and experiences. Activities such as interest inventories, surveys, and community building develop a positive rapport between teachers and students. This allows teachers to make learning meaningful by creating learner-centered instruction that facilitates personal connections and builds upon prior knowledge. Field trips and community outreach programs are effective in enhancing relevancy through demonstrating the real-world applications of instruction. Additionally, technologies including virtual field trips and tours, videos, and documentaries, assist in increasing students' understanding the purpose of learning by illustrating the real-world applications of instruction. Self-assessments make learning meaningful and relevant through encouraging student ownership and responsibility over learning as students seek areas for improvement. Moreover, closure activities serve to demonstrate overall purpose for learning through encouraging students to connect learning to the lesson's objective and their prior knowledge.

INTRADISCIPLINARY AND INTERDISCIPLINARY INSTRUCTION

Intradisciplinary and interdisciplinary instruction are both valuable strategies for teaching and learning. In **intradisciplinary** instruction, several elements of a single broad subject area are incorporated into the lesson. For example, in a science lesson, the teacher could incorporate elements of chemistry, biology, and physics into instruction. This method of instruction is beneficial in deepening students' understanding of the nuances of a particular subject area through demonstrating the various components that comprise the overarching discipline. **Interdisciplinary** instruction refers to the simultaneous integration of ideas, knowledge, and skills from several subject areas when approaching an idea, problem, or theme, and applying principles of one subject area to another. For example, in an interdisciplinary unit on food, the teacher could incorporate elements of math by teaching students to measure ingredients, language arts by teaching them to read or write a recipe, science through examining chemical reactions of the cooking process, and social studies through having students explore the impact of food agriculture on economy and society. Interdisciplinary instruction is beneficial in deepening students' understanding across subject areas and developing real-world critical thinking skills by encouraging them to make connections between disciplines and teaching them to consider an idea or problem from multiple perspectives.

EXAMPLES OF INTRADISCIPLINARY INSTRUCTION

- **Language Arts:** A single language arts lesson can incorporate components of reading, writing, grammar, and listening skills. For example, a lesson on a particular poem can include a close reading of the poet's use of grammar, symbolism, imagery, and other literary techniques, as well as an audio recording of the poet reading aloud. At the end of the unit, students can be assigned to use what they learned to compose their own original poems.
- **Social Studies:** Social studies units can incorporate elements of history, anthropology, archaeology, sociology, psychology, or any other field that involves the study of humans, civilizations, cultures, and historical events. For example, a unit on the Aztec people may include an examination of their religious beliefs, customs, architecture, and agricultural practices.
- **Science:** Intradisciplinary units in science can include several branches within the field, such as chemistry, biology, physics, earth science, botany, or geology. For example, a unit on volcanoes may incorporate lessons on plate tectonics, the Earth's layers, chemicals released during a volcanic eruption, islands formed from cooled volcanic rock, as well as plants that grow best near volcanoes.
- **Mathematics:** An intradisciplinary math lesson may simultaneously include several branches within the field, such as arithmetic, algebra, or geometry. For example, in a geometry lesson on the Pythagorean theorem, students must utilize algebraic equations and arithmetic to determine the length of the sides of a right triangle.

EXAMPLES OF INTERDISCIPLINARY INSTRUCTION

- **Language Arts:** A unit based in language arts may also incorporate several other disciplines, such as social studies, art, or music. For example, a unit on William Shakespeare's *Romeo and Juliet* may include a reading of the play and an analysis of the use of literary techniques within it, as well as a study of William Shakespeare's life and the society in which he lived to incorporate social studies. Students can also act out the play to incorporate the arts and participate in a rhythmic study on iambic pentameter to incorporate music.
- **Social Studies:** Units based in social studies can include lessons focused on multiple disciplines, including language arts, music, science, and math. For example, an interdisciplinary unit on Ancient Egypt may include a historical study of the culture, religion, architecture, and practices of the Ancient Egyptians while integrating other subject areas, such as a study of hieroglyphics to incorporate language arts and creating Egyptian masks to incorporate art. Students can also study the scientific advancements of the Ancient Egyptians, as well as incorporate math to study how the ancient pyramids were constructed.
- **Science:** Scientific units can also incorporate elements of art, math, social studies, and language arts in order to become interdisciplinary. For example, a unit on Punnett squares focuses on biology and genetics but can also include several other subject areas. Math can be incorporated by integrating lessons on probability, students can be assigned to research their genetics, create a family tree, and write a report on their findings to incorporate language arts and social studies. Art can also be incorporated by having students create portraits of the potential outcomes from Punnett squares.
- **Mathematics:** Interdisciplinary units in mathematics can also include lessons focused on such disciplines as art, social studies, science, and music. For example, a geometry unit on measuring triangles may also incorporate songs to memorize equations, lessons on the pyramids of Ancient Egypt to incorporate social studies, as well as an art project in which students use only triangles to create an original piece.

INCORPORATING COOPERATIVE LEARNING ALLOWING CONSIDERATION FROM MULTIPLE VIEWPOINTS

In any classroom, teachers will encounter a wide range of diversities among students' backgrounds, cultures, interests, skills, and abilities. Thus, providing students with several opportunities for cooperative learning gives them access to others' perspectives and is highly valuable in teaching students to consider ideas from multiple viewpoints. As each student has different experiences and background knowledge, collaborative learning allows them to share their views on ideas with others. Additionally, in working together, students have the opportunity to work with others from different backgrounds that they may have otherwise never encountered and gain exposure to approaching ideas from multiple viewpoints. Cooperative learning opportunities allow students to understand and appreciate others' perspectives and teaches them that there are multiple approaches to problem solving and ideas.

LEARNING EXPERIENCES THAT DEVELOP REAL-WORLD LIFE SKILLS

The ultimate goal of education is to develop the whole child and ensure that students develop into productive, contributing members of society once they leave the classroom. Therefore, it is imperative to provide learning experiences that will develop life skills that are applicable and beneficial in the real world. In an increasingly fast-paced global society, students must be prepared to enter the professional and societal world as confident, independent, responsible, and adaptive individuals. They must have the leadership skills necessary to compete in the professional arena.

Students must be able to work cooperatively with others, respect and value multiple perspectives, and be effective problem solvers and critical thinkers in order to be successful outside of the classroom. Teachers must also aim to help students develop the skills necessary to become lifelong learners to ensure continuous growth and development as they enter society. Therefore, learning experiences that promote the development of real-world life skills in addition to academic skills are necessary in adequately preparing students for success.

CROSS-CURRICULAR INSTRUCTION FOR EXPLORING CONTENT FROM VARIED PERSPECTIVES

Cross-curricular instruction allows teachers to demonstrate that elements from one subject area can be applied to ideas or problem solving in another. Thus, this instructional strategy is highly valuable in developing students' abilities to explore content from varied perspectives. As this method incorporates several disciplines in approaching a topic, it deepens students' understanding that there are several perspectives that one can take when solving a problem, and that elements of one subject area are relevant in another. In addition, cross-curricular instruction prepares students for the real world through developing critical thinking skills and allowing them to make connections between disciplines, thus allowing them to understand how to successfully approach ideas from varied perspectives.

BENEFITS OF MULTICULTURAL LEARNING EXPERIENCES

Multicultural learning experiences demonstrate to students the array of diversities that exist both inside and outside of the classroom. Just as each culture has its own values, norms, and traditions, each has its own perspectives and approaches to ideas and problem solving. Incorporating multicultural experiences in the classroom exposes students to cultures and groups that they may have otherwise never encountered and teaches them to respect and value perspectives outside of their own. As students learn other cultures' beliefs, customs, and attitudes, they develop the understanding that each culture solves problems and considers ideas from multiple viewpoints and that each approach is valuable. As students learn other perspectives, they can apply this knowledge, and ultimately build problem solving and critical thinking skills that will be beneficial in developing successful lifelong learning habits.

INCORPORATING MULTIPLE DISCIPLINES INTO A THEMATIC UNIT

In **cross-curricular**, or **interdisciplinary** instruction, multiple disciplines are incorporated into a thematic unit in order to deepen students' understanding through fostering connections and demonstrating multiple perspectives and methods of problem solving. Effective interdisciplinary instruction requires careful planning to ensure that all activities are relevant to the overall lesson theme and effectively support students in achieving desired learning outcomes. The teacher must first select a thematic unit based on state academic standards and then determine desired learning outcomes. Then, the teacher must design lessons and activities for students to reach learning goals and objectives. When integrating multiple disciplines into a thematic unit, the teacher must seek out materials, resources, and activities from various subject areas that are applicable to the main topic and reinforce lesson objectives. The teacher can then integrate these elements into lesson planning to create multifaceted instruction. Additionally, the teacher can create activities that approach the overarching lesson theme from the perspective of different subject areas. The activities and materials should be coordinated and relate to one another in order to deepen students' understanding of the overall concept.

EFFECTIVELY ALLOCATING TIME WHEN CREATING LESSONS AND UNITS

Effective time management is vital for successful teaching and learning. To ensure that all academic standards are covered within a school year, teachers must consider how to best allocate specific amounts of time for units and lessons that allow for review, enrichment, and reteaching. A unit plan for the school year is an effective strategy in allowing the teacher to visualize and plan the amount of content that must be covered. A unit plan can also be utilized on a smaller scale, as a framework for designing and allotting time for instructional goals, objectives, and lessons within each unit. By setting learning goals and daily objectives within individual units, the teacher can determine the amount of time available for completing each unit, thus ensuring more effective lesson planning by allowing the teacher to develop a daily schedule with dedicated time for teaching and learning. When planning lessons, the teacher must consider how much instructional time is necessary to cover each topic and the time students will need to complete lesson activities. Additionally, teachers must ensure that they allow time at the end of each lesson for reteaching if students have misconceptions, as extra time can be utilized for enrichment if reteaching is unnecessary.

OPPORTUNITIES FOR REFLECTION

Opportunities for reflection within lesson plans are beneficial in enhancing learning experiences through strengthening student understanding and influencing further instruction. When students are given the opportunity to reflect, they are able to connect their learning back to the original objective and better understand the overall purpose for learning, thus fostering engagement. Reflection deepens students' understanding by allowing them to connect new concepts to their own personal experiences, which ultimately helps in comprehension and retainment through making learning relevant. Reflecting on performance empowers students to become self-motivated lifelong learners by allowing them to analyze what they understood and did well, as well as encouraging them to identify areas for improvement. Teachers can utilize students' reflections to influence and drive further instruction. Students' reflections also allow teachers to identify areas in which students excelled, areas for improvement, and can aid them in tailoring future lesson plans to adapt to students' needs and interests.

OPPORTUNITIES FOR SELF-ASSESSMENT

Self-assessments within lessons are a valuable formative assessment strategy that enriches student learning and provides insight to the teacher. Providing students with the opportunity to monitor their progress and assess their learning supports them in developing a wide range of skills that are beneficial both inside and outside of the classroom. Self-assessments empower students in their learning by creating a sense of ownership and responsibility over their own learning, thus fostering self-motivation and engagement. They also serve to foster a sense of independence and objectivity within students to effectively review their own work and identify areas of improvement, which is a vital skill needed to becoming a lifelong learner. When students evaluate their own performance, the teacher is able to effectively assess student understanding, thus allowing them to identify areas of weakness or misconception for reteaching.

OPPORTUNITIES FOR CLOSURE ACTIVITIES

Closure activities at the end of each lesson or topic are beneficial for both students and teachers. These short activities allow teachers to formatively assess student understanding of content covered within a lesson and identify areas of misconception for reteaching. Additionally, closure activities are valuable in measuring whether the intended lesson objective was achieved before moving to the next topic. For students, closures at the end of a lesson provide structure and organization to learning, as well as emphasize the purpose for instruction by allowing them to connect what they learned back to the original objective. Moreover, in having students restate what they have learned in a closure activity, learning is strengthened by giving students the opportunity to internalize new information. In demonstrating their understanding, they can better make personal connections between their own learning, background knowledge, and experiences.

Instructional Techniques

IMPLEMENTING MULTIPLE INSTRUCTIONAL TECHNIQUES TO MAXIMIZE STUDENT LEARNING

Incorporating multiple instructional techniques into the classroom maximizes student learning by enhancing intellectual involvement and overall engagement. When instructional material is presented through a variety of means, it facilitates an **active learning** environment in which students' interest is captured and they are motivated to participate in learning. Varying teaching strategies stimulates engagement and fosters achievement by encouraging students to actively participate in their own learning and implement critical thinking skills to consider information more deeply. Students' understanding is strengthened when content is presented in different ways through various instructional techniques by providing them with multiple frames of reference for making connections and internalizing new concepts. In addition, utilizing multiple instructional techniques allows the teacher to effectively **differentiate instruction** to access multiple learning styles and address individual student needs to ensure understanding and enhance the overall learning process.

INSTRUCTIONAL STRATEGIES TO DIFFERENTIATE INSTRUCTION

Implementing a variety of strategies for differentiation helps to ensure that instruction appeals to students' varying learning styles and needs. By incorporating **multiple modalities** into direct instruction, such as visual representations, written directions, video or audio clips, songs, graphs, or mnemonic devices, teachers can differentiate the presentation of new concepts and information. Using strategies to differentiate instructional activities is also beneficial in diversifying the learning experience. By providing opportunities for **independent, collaborative**, and **hands-on** learning, teachers can ensure that learning is accessible and engaging to all students. In addition, learning activities should allow for a degree of flexibility in order to appeal to students' varying needs and preferences. Activities such as task cards, educational technology resources, and learning stations provide this **flexibility** and allow for a student-directed experience in which they can choose to learn in the way that best suits their needs. Similarly, assigning open-ended projects as summative assessments allows for a degree of **student-choice**, thus differentiating the method in which students demonstrate their understanding.

VARYING THE TEACHER AND STUDENT ROLES IN THE INSTRUCTIONAL PROCESS

Varying the roles of the teacher and students as an instructional technique is beneficial in creating an engaging, dynamic classroom environment that maximizes learning. When different roles are implemented, instruction is diversified, thus stimulating student interest and engagement. In addition, certain teacher and student roles are most applicable and effective in specific learning situations. When teachers acknowledge this and understand when to adopt and assign particular roles, they can effectively deliver instruction in a way that deepens student understanding and fosters success in learning. In presenting new content, directions, or modeling new skills for example, the roles of **lecturer** and student **observer** are effective. In hands-on learning situations, students can take on the role of **active participant** while the teacher acts as a **facilitator** to create a student-centered and engaging learning environment in which students are given ownership over their own learning. Such variation enhances intellectual involvement by promoting critical thinking and problem-solving skills through self-directed learning. Skillfully assigning different roles throughout the learning process also allows the teacher to effectively address students' individual learning needs and preferences to promote engagement and enhance the learning experience.

FOSTERING INTELLECTUAL INVOLVEMENT AND ENGAGEMENT

Effective instruction includes a variety of strategies for fostering intellectual involvement and engagement to promote academic success. Presenting instruction using various approaches provides multiple avenues for learning new content, thus ensuring and strengthening student understanding to facilitate achievement. In addition, diversifying instructional strategies creates variety in the classroom that effectively stimulates students' interest and motivation to engage in learning. Such strategies as **cooperative learning**, **discussion**, and **self-directed opportunities** encourage active student participation that enhances intellectual involvement by allowing students to build on background knowledge, deepen understanding by exploring others' perspectives, and take ownership over their own learning. This ultimately increases student engagement and motivation for success in learning. Similarly, incorporating **inquiry**, **problem-solving**, and **project-based** strategies promote curiosity in learning, creativity, and the development of critical thinking skills that stimulate intellectual participation and engagement to create a productive learning environment. Implementing **digital resources** and media throughout instruction is integral in enhancing academic success by making learning relevant, interesting, and differentiated to accommodate various learning needs. At the end of a lesson or activity, allowing students the opportunity to reflect is a valuable strategy in increasing intellectual involvement, retainment, and academic success by facilitating personal connections with learning to build understanding.

ACTIVELY ENGAGING STUDENTS BY INCORPORATING DISCUSSION INTO INSTRUCTION

Classroom discussion is a valuable instructional technique in engaging students throughout the learning process. When the teacher skillfully poses higher-level questions in discussions, they establish an active learning environment in which students are encouraged and motivated to participate, thus enhancing overall engagement. Effective discussions prompt students to become **intellectually invested** in instruction by promoting the use of **critical** and **higher-order thinking** skills to consider information more deeply and devise creative solutions to problems. In addition, discussions stimulate engagement by providing students the opportunity to express their own thoughts and reasoning regarding a given topic to establish a sense of ownership over their learning. Furthermore, discussions foster a collaborative learning environment that actively engages students by prompting them to understand others' perspectives, consider alternative approaches, and build on one another's experiences to make deeper connections to learning.

PROMOTING STUDENT INQUIRY

The promotion of inquiry is a valuable instructional technique in enhancing student engagement and intellectual involvement. In an **inquiry-based** learning environment, students are encouraged to explore instructional material and devise their own conclusions or solutions to problems. This increases the effectiveness of the learning process by providing students with a sense of agency over their own learning. In addition, implementing this strategy fosters curiosity, self-motivation, and active participation, as it allows for hands-on, **student-led** learning that increases overall engagement. Incorporating inquiry into the classroom stimulates critical and higher-order thinking skills as students construct their own understanding by interacting with learning materials, analyzing their findings, and synthesizing their learning to create new conclusions, results, and responses. To effectively incorporate inquiry int the learning process, the teacher must provide several opportunities for self-directed and project-based learning, as well as student choice, to stimulate curiosity. Questions must be open-ended, and students must be encouraged to hypothesize, predict, and experiment in their learning. The teacher must be flexible in instruction to allow space and opportunity for exploration and allow time for reflection and extended learning opportunities to facilitate further inquiry.

INCORPORATING PROBLEM-SOLVING INTO INSTRUCTION

Providing opportunities for creative problem solving within instruction effectively creates an engaging and successful learning experience. Students become more **intellectually involved** when encouraged to actively participate in learning and utilize **critical thinking skills** to test hypotheses, analyze results, and devise creative solutions to problems. This hands-on, **student-directed** approach promotes success in learning by allowing students to interact with learning materials as they seek answers to complex ideas and problems in an engaging environment. Problem-solving enables students to make deeper connections to their learning to enhance understanding, as this strategy prompts them to employ and develop background knowledge. In addition, problem-solving activities allow for collaborative learning in which students can actively engage with peers to build on one another's knowledge and experience, thus enhancing successful learning.

RELATIONSHIP BETWEEN INTELLECTUAL INVOLVEMENT, ACTIVE STUDENT ENGAGEMENT, AND SUCCESS IN LEARNING

A productive learning environment is comprised of intellectually involved students that are actively engaged in successful learning. A strong correlation exists between **intellectual involvement**, **active student engagement**, and **success in learning**, and each component is necessary for effective instruction. Effective instruction consists of challenging students based on their abilities and teaching them to think deeply about new ideas and concepts. This ultimately encourages students' intellectual involvement, as it prompts them to utilize their critical thinking skills to build on their background knowledge, consider alternative perspectives, and synthesize their learning to devise creative solutions. When students are intellectually involved in instruction, they become more personally invested and engaged, as learning becomes relevant, interesting, and challenging. Engaged students are active participants in their learning, thus enhancing their overall productivity and academic success.

EFFECTIVELY STRUCTURING LESSONS

When developing instruction, it is imperative that the teacher is knowledgeable on how to effectively structure lessons to maximize student engagement and success. Each lesson must include a clear **objective** and explicitly state the process for achieving it. To initiate engagement, effective lessons begin with an **opening**, or "warm-up," activity to introduce a new topic, diagnose student understanding, and activate prior knowledge. Instruction of new material must be delivered through a variety of teaching strategies that are consciously tailored to students' individual learning needs to enhance participation and ensure comprehension. Direct instruction should be followed by **active learning** activities with clear directions and procedures to allow students to practice new concepts and skills. Throughout a successful lesson, the teacher checks frequently for understanding and comprehension by conducting a variety of **formative assessments** and adjusts instruction as necessary. Including **closure** activities is essential to successful learning, as it gives students the opportunity to reflect, process information, make connections, and demonstrate comprehension. In structuring lessons effectively according to students' learning needs, the teacher establishes a focused and engaging learning environment that promotes academic success.

Example of a Daily Lesson Plan Structure

Academic Standard → Learning Goals → Learning Objectives → Warm-Up/Opening Activity → Directed Instruction/Guided Learning → Active Learning Activities → Closure Activity/Reflection

FLEXIBLE INSTRUCTIONAL GROUPINGS

Flexible instructional groupings provide the teacher and students with a versatile, engaging environment for successful learning. Skillfully grouping students allows for productive, cooperative learning opportunities in which individual strengths are enhanced and necessary support is provided, thus enhancing motivation and engagement. When working in groups, students' understanding of instruction is strengthened, as they are able to learn and build upon one another's background knowledge, perspectives, and abilities. Instructional groups can include students of the **same** or **varied abilities** depending on the learning objective and task to increase productivity and provide scaffolding as necessary for support. This strategy is effective in enabling the teacher to **differentiate** instruction and adjust groups as needed to accommodate varying learning styles, abilities, and interests to maximize engagement and success in learning.

EFFECTIVE PACING OF LESSONS AND IMPORTANCE OF FLEXIBILITY TO STUDENTS' NEEDS

Effective pacing is imperative to focused and engaging instruction. The teacher must be conscientious of the pace of their instruction and ensure that it is reflective of their student's learning needs and sustains their attention. Instruction that is delivered too quickly results in confusion and discouragement, whereas if instruction is too slow, students will lose interest and become disengaged. A well-paced lesson states clear learning goals and objectives while clearly outlining the means to achieve them to elicit student motivation. The teacher must consider the most **efficient** and **engaging** instructional strategies for presenting new material to establish a steady pace and maintain it by incorporating smooth **transitions** from one activity to the next. It is important that the teacher is conscious of the rate of instruction throughout all stages of learning while maintaining **flexibility** in pacing in order to be responsive to their students. As individual students have different learning needs and processing times, they may require a faster or slower rate of instruction to understand new concepts and remain engaged in learning. Frequent checks for understanding and reflection activities are essential strategies in determining if the pace of instruction must be adjusted to accommodate students' needs.

CONNECTING CONTENT TO STUDENTS' PRIOR KNOWLEDGE AND EXPERIENCES

When the teacher implements effective instructional strategies for connecting content to students' prior knowledge and experiences, it enhances the relevancy of learning and fosters deeper connections that strengthen understanding. To achieve this, the teacher must educate themselves on students' backgrounds, experiences, communities, and interests to determine what is important and interesting to them. With this knowledge in mind, the teacher can successfully locate and implement **authentic materials** into instruction to enhance relevancy. Additionally, encouraging students to bring materials to class that reflect their backgrounds and including these materials in instruction makes learning relevant by allowing students to make **personal connections** to content. Instructional strategies such as brainstorming, KWL charts, prereading, and anticipation guides allow the teacher to determine what students know prior to learning a new concept, thus enabling them to connect content to students' background knowledge in a relevant way. Incorporating digital resources further enhances relevancy in learning in that the teacher can locate videos or audio clips that relate to instruction and reflect students' background experiences and interests. Using digital resources to introduce a new concept is a valuable strategy in developing students' **schema** on a topic to build prior knowledge and make learning meaningful by fostering connections.

MAKING LEARNING RELEVANT AND MEANINGFUL

For learning to be relevant and meaningful, it is essential that the teacher present content in a way that connects with students' **prior knowledge** and experiences. When students are able to apply new ideas and information to what they already know through effective instructional techniques, it facilitates strong **personal connections** that make learning relevant and meaningful. In addition, personal connections and **relevancy** are strengthened when the teacher consciously incorporates materials to reflect students' individual backgrounds and experiences in instruction. Linking content to students' background experiences enables them to relate instruction to real-world situations, thus establishing a sense of purpose for learning by making it applicable to their lives.

Intentionally connecting content with students' prior knowledge and experiences enhances the effectiveness of the instructional process and fosters positive attitudes toward learning.

ENHANCING STUDENT ENGAGEMENT AND SUCCESS IN LEARNING

Engaging instruction employs a variety of instructional strategies and materials to create a relevant, meaningful, and successful learning experience. Effective content establishes a clear and applicable purpose for instruction that increases student participation in the learning process. Presenting relevant and meaningful content enhances understanding and engagement by enabling students to create real-world, **personal connections** to learning based upon their own backgrounds and experiences. In addition, when instruction is tailored to reflect students' unique interests and preferences, content becomes more appealing and students' willingness to learn is enhanced. When students can perceive content through their own frames of reference with instructional materials that reflect their unique differences, they are able to effectively internalize and relate information to their lives, thus increasing engagement. Engaged learning ultimately facilitates academic success in that when students are motivated to learn, they demonstrate positive attitudes toward learning and are more likely to actively participate.

Adapting Instruction to Individual Needs

EVALUATING ACTIVITIES AND MATERIALS TO MEET INDIVIDUAL CHARACTERISTICS AND LEARNING NEEDS

The careful selection of instructional activities and materials is integral to accommodating students' varying characteristics and needs to foster success in learning. When evaluating the appropriateness of activities and materials, several considerations must be made. The teacher must consider whether activities and materials align with state and district **academic standards**, as well as their quality and effectiveness in supporting students' unique differences as they achieve learning goals and objectives. All materials and activities must be **developmentally appropriate** across domains, yet adaptable to individual students' learning needs. In addition, they must be challenging, yet feasible for student achievement relative to students' grade level and abilities to promote engagement and the development of critical and **higher-order thinking** skills. The teacher must evaluate activities and materials for versatility to allow for student choice and differentiation in order to address varying characteristics and needs. The teacher must also ensure that activities and materials are accurate, **culturally sensitive**, and reflective of students' diversities to foster an inclusive learning environment that promotes engagement.

INSTRUCTIONAL RESOURCES AND TECHNOLOGIES

The implementation of varied instructional resources and technologies is highly valuable in supporting student engagement and achievement. Effective use of resources and technologies requires the teacher to evaluate their appropriateness in addressing students' individual characteristics and learning needs for academic success. The teacher must be attuned to students' unique differences in order to seek high quality technologies and resources that address their students' needs to support and enhance the achievement of learning goals and objectives. Technologies and resources must be **accurate, comprehensible**, and easily **accessible** to students, as well as **relevant** to the curriculum and the development of particular skills. The teacher must also consider the grade-level and **developmental appropriateness** of technologies and resources, as well as their adaptability to allow for differentiation. Effective technologies and resources are interactive, engaging, and multifaceted to allow for varying levels of complexity based on students' abilities. This allows the teacher to provide appropriate challenges while diversifying instruction to appeal to varied characteristics and learning needs, thus fostering an engaging environment that supports success in learning for all students.

ADAPTING ACTIVITIES AND MATERIALS TO MEET INDIVIDUAL CHARACTERISTICS AND NEEDS

In effective instruction, activities and materials are adapted to accommodate students' individual characteristics and needs. The teacher must be attuned to students' unique differences and understand how to adjust activities and materials accordingly to facilitate academic success and growth. To achieve this, the teacher must incorporate a **variety** of activities and materials that appeal to all styles of learners. Activities and materials should provide **student choice** for engagement in learning and demonstration of understanding. By differentiating instruction, the teacher can effectively scaffold activities and materials to provide supports as necessary, as well as include extensions or alternate activities for enrichment. **Chunking** instruction, allowing extra time as necessary, and accompanying activities and materials with aids such as graphic organizers, visual representations, and anticipation guides further differentiates learning to accommodate students' learning characteristics and needs. Conducting **formative assessments** provides the teacher with valuable feedback regarding student understanding and engagement, thus allowing them to modify and adjust the complexity of activities and materials as necessary to adapt to varied characteristics and learning differences.

INSTRUCTIONAL RESOURCES AND TECHNOLOGIES

When the teacher understands students' individual characteristics and needs, they can adapt instructional resources and technologies accordingly to maximize learning. To do so effectively, the teacher must incorporate a diverse array of **multifaceted** resources and technologies that support and enhance learning through a variety of methods. This ensures that varying learning needs are met, as students of all learning styles are provided with several avenues for building and strengthening understanding. Additionally, the teacher can adapt resources and technologies to accommodate individual students by **varying the complexity** to provide challenges, support, and opportunities for enrichment based on ability level. Supplementing technologies and resources with **scaffolds**, such as extra time, visual representations, or opportunities for collaborative learning, further enables the teacher to adapt to individual learning needs. When effectively implemented and adapted to students' characteristics and needs, instructional technologies and resources serve as valuable tools for differentiating curriculum to enhance the learning experience.

Flexible and Responsive Instructional Practices

EVALUATION OF INSTRUCTION

Evaluating the appropriateness of instructional materials, activities, resources, and technologies is integral to establishing a successful learning environment. Doing so provides students with high-quality and inclusive instruction by ensuring **clarity**, **accuracy**, **relevancy**, and **reflection** of student diversities. By determining whether these components of instruction meet varying characteristics and learning needs, the teacher can deliver **student-centered** instruction, that is challenging based on individual ability, to promote development and academic success. This process also allows the teacher to effectively **differentiate** instruction to provide necessary personalized support for success in achieving learning targets, as well as create engaging learning opportunities tailored to students' unique differences and interests. Effectively determining the appropriateness of activities, materials, resources, and technologies in meeting students' learning needs ultimately maximizes academic achievement and fosters positive attitudes toward learning that establish a foundation for future success.

CONTINUOUS MONITORING OF INSTRUCTIONAL EFFECTIVENESS

Successful instruction must be flexible and adaptable to meet students' dynamic learning needs. To achieve this, teachers must continuously monitor the effectiveness of their instruction to determine if their teaching strategies, activities, and communication are effective. Frequent evaluation of instructional effectiveness is necessary to ensure that students understand **foundational concepts** before moving on to more advanced concepts. **Adaptations** to instruction, communication, or assessment may be necessary to ensure students are able to comprehend and retain concepts before moving on to more advanced topics. **Remediation** of missed concepts is often much more challenging and less successful than checking for comprehension within context and providing more detailed instruction. This ultimately fosters long-term achievement, as the teacher can identify and address student needs as they arise and prevent compounding issues. Continuous monitoring enables the teacher to ensure that learning opportunities are engaging, relevant, and challenging based on students' ability levels, as it provides immediate feedback on the effectiveness of instruction, which allows the teacher to make necessary changes. This ultimately enhances instruction by establishing a student-centered learning environment that is tailored to individual needs, interests, and abilities.

PRE-INSTRUCTIONAL, PERI-INSTRUCTIONAL, AND POST-INSTRUCTIONAL STRATEGIES

Instructional effectiveness must be monitored on a whole-class and individual level throughout all stages of teaching. Prior to instruction, administering **pre-tests** provides the teacher with insight regarding whole-class and individual understanding. This enables them to select effective and appropriate instructional strategies that can be differentiated to meet individual needs. Pre-tests allow the teacher to identify and clarify misunderstandings before instruction to ensure effectiveness. During instruction, **observation** of students' participation in instruction during independent and group activities enables the teacher to evaluate overall and individual understanding and engagement. Frequent checks for understanding and **formative assessments** throughout instruction provide feedback on whole-group and individual learning, as the teacher can assess understanding and participation to adapt teaching strategies or individualize instruction. Leading student discussions allows the teacher to identify areas of misunderstanding among the class or individuals that may need reteaching through a different approach. Closure and reflection activities after instruction are valuable in monitoring effectiveness, as they indicate both whole-class and individual comprehension and retainment of new concepts. Likewise, incorporating **summative assessments** and analyzing the results provides the teacher with information regarding the overall effectiveness of their teaching process, as well as students' individual strengths and weaknesses to consider for future instruction.

APPLYING FEEDBACK TO MAKE NECESSARY CHANGES TO INSTRUCTION

Continuous monitoring of instruction indicates the instruction's effectiveness on a **whole-class** and **individual** level, as it provides the teacher with immediate insight on student understanding, progress, and areas for improvement. Monitoring instructional effectiveness enables the teacher to evaluate students' **pace** in achieving learning goals and adjust the rate of instruction as necessary. Additionally, it allows the teacher to identify whole-class and individual **misconceptions** that require correction to ensure students do not fall behind schedule in meeting academic benchmarks. If monitoring reveals misunderstanding among the whole class, the teacher must alter their overall instructional approach and teaching strategies to clarify and regain understanding. Individual misconceptions indicate the need to differentiate instruction, adjust groupings, and provide supports and remediation as necessary to ensure the student progresses at the same rate as the rest of the class. By identifying student strengths and weaknesses through consistent monitoring of instructional effectiveness, the teacher can effectively make instructional decisions that are attuned to whole-class and individual student needs to maximize learning.

FLEXIBILITY IN INSTRUCTION
SITUATIONS REQUIRING FLEXIBILITY

The classroom environment is dynamic in nature. Teachers will inevitably encounter situations throughout instruction and assessment in which **flexibility** is integral to successful teaching and learning. As students have varying learning styles, needs, and interests, teachers may find that their instructional approaches are ineffective in maintaining engagement and may need to adjust strategies, activities, or assessments to better meet learning needs. Students may have difficulty grasping new material, which could result in a lack of engagement in instructional activities and, potentially, disruptive behavior. Teachers must consistently be attuned to students' level of comprehension and allow flexibility with their lesson plans to modify strategies, activities, or pacing as necessary to facilitate engagement and understanding before advancing in instruction. Students may also progress more quickly than others through instructional activities or assessments. **Scaffolding** activities to include opportunities for extension and enrichment allows for flexibility within instruction to ensure that all students are adequately challenged and engaged in learning. Throughout instruction and assessments, teachers may find valuable, unexpected learning opportunities. By remaining open and flexible to these instances, teachers can enhance the learning process by incorporating them into instruction to strengthen student understanding.

ENHANCING THE OVERALL LEARNING EXPERIENCE

Flexibility is an integral component of effective instruction, as it enables the teacher to adequately address and accommodate students' individual needs and interests for maximized success in learning. When the teacher considers their lesson plan as a **framework** while allowing for flexibility, they demonstrate an awareness of their students' individual differences and the potential for deviation from original instruction. This enables them to more effectively modify instructional and assessment strategies, activities, and approaches to create a **responsive**, **student-centered** environment that enhances the overall learning experience and promotes achievement. When instructional activities and assessments are adaptable to accommodate students' needs and interests, learning becomes more personalized and relevant, thus strengthening understanding and increasing motivation to engage in active learning. A flexible approach to instruction and assessment also provides students with the ability to explore content of interest on a deeper level and potentially encounter unanticipated learning opportunities that foster personal connections and enhance learning. In addition, this approach allows for **versatility** in assessment, as flexibility enables the teacher to modify assessments by providing necessary support to meet students' individual needs and supports students' choice in demonstrating learning.

POOR STUDENT COMPREHENSION

Throughout instruction and assessments, students may have difficulty **comprehending** new or difficult material, despite being engaged in instruction. This may lead to confusion that can cause students to become discouraged and disengaged in learning, as well as have continued and compounded difficulty in grasping increasingly complex concepts. Difficulties with comprehension hinders academic success, as students that struggle face challenges in building the foundation of understanding necessary for advancing through curriculum. To ensure student comprehension throughout all stages of learning, the teacher must be aware of students' individual learning styles and needs and be able to respond flexibly to obstacles they may encounter. **Formative assessments** during instruction enable the teacher to evaluate the level of student comprehension and identify areas of need for flexible **adjustment** or additional support. This includes modifying **pacing** and allowing additional time for student processing to ensure understanding. In addition, the original lesson plan may require **chunking** into smaller, more manageable parts to allow students to internalize new concepts before moving on. The teacher may also need to respond flexibly to students' needs during instruction by **differentiating** teaching strategies, activities, groupings, or assessments to ensure that material is accessible and comprehensible to all students for enhanced success.

UNANTICIPATED LEARNING OPPORTUNITIES

Unanticipated learning opportunities, when embraced by the teacher, are often highly valuable in establishing a classroom environment that promotes student engagement, motivation, and success. These instances often divert from the original lesson plan, but when utilized effectively, serve to strengthen student understanding and foster **personal connections** for an enhanced learning experience. Facilitating such opportunities allows students to investigate topics of interest and relevancy to them on a deeper level, thus increasing active engagement and promoting **self-directed** learning. This ultimately supports students in forming connections and recognizing the real-world applications of their learning, which increases the likelihood that they will internalize and **retain** new information. Responding flexibly to unanticipated learning opportunities includes acknowledging students' questions and comments, as well as demonstrating an awareness of their individual differences and learning needs. This enables the teacher to maximize the effectiveness of these opportunities by facilitating student-led instruction that is attuned to their learning styles, interests, and preferences for enhanced engagement and achievement.

CONDUCTING ONGOING ASSESSMENTS AND MAKING ADJUSTMENTS

Conducting **ongoing assessments** throughout instruction provides the teacher with continuous feedback regarding student comprehension, engagement, and performance. When practiced consistently, the teacher is more attuned and responsive to students' individual learning needs. This enables them to effectively modify instructional strategies, activities, and assessments accordingly for a **student-centered** learning environment that provides the support necessary for enhanced engagement, comprehension, and achievement. It allows the teacher to identify and address areas of **misconception** and student need to ensure understanding prior to progressing through the curriculum. Feedback from ongoing evaluation of student performance indicates to the teacher areas of instruction in which adjustment is necessary to effectively support students in achieving learning goals. The teacher may need to adjust their pacing to ensure comprehension and engagement, as well as differentiate instruction based on feedback regarding individual progress to ensure all students are adequately challenged and supported based on their ability levels. Student groupings may need to be adjusted to scaffold instruction and facilitate increased comprehension. When the teacher effectively applies feedback from ongoing assessments of student engagement and performance, they can tailor instruction to accommodate their individual needs and interests to enhance success in learning.

PROGRESSING AHEAD OF SCHEDULE

Throughout instruction, the teacher will encounter instances in which individual students or the whole class progresses **faster than anticipated**. When this arises, the teacher must be prepared to respond flexibly to ensure that all students are engaged, on task, and challenged based on their ability level. Lesson plans should be **scaffolded** to include opportunities for enrichment and extended learning for students that finish before others. This includes incorporating such material as increasingly complex texts, practice activities, and project opportunities. The teacher can also establish a designated area in the classroom in which individuals or small groups that finish early can participate in **extended learning** or **review** activities that reinforce learning objectives. Such activities allow students to explore instructional topics on a deeper level for strengthened understanding and ensure they are engaging productively in meaningful activities that are relevant to instruction. When the whole class progresses faster than expected, the teacher can respond flexibly by incorporating **total participation** activities to reinforce instructional material. Such activities as review games, class discussions, and digital resources for extra practice ensure that the class remains engaged in instruction when they finish a lesson early.

Schedules, Routines, and Activities for Young Children

IDEAL SCHEDULE FOR YOUNG CHILDREN

An ideal schedule for young children reflects their developmental characteristics and capabilities to maximize their learning. A **predictable** routine is necessary for young children to feel secure in their learning environment, and therefore, each day should follow a similar schedule while allowing room for **flexibility** if an activity takes longer than expected. Each day should begin with a clear routine, such as unpacking, a "warm-up" activity, and a class meeting to allow students to share thoughts, ask questions, and allow the teacher to discuss what will occur that day. This establishes a positive tone for the day while focusing the attention on learning. Similarly, the end of the day should have a specific routine, such as cleaning up materials and packing up for dismissal. Young children learn best by physically interacting with and exploring their environment. As such, each day should include large blocks of time for **active movement** throughout the day in the form of play, projects, and learning centers. Periods of **rest** must follow such activities, as this enables young children to process and internalize what they learned. **Direct instruction** should occur before active movement periods and last approximately 15-20 minutes to sustain engagement and attention on learning.

Example Daily Schedule for the Early Childhood Education Classroom	
8:00-8:30	Welcome, unpack, morning work
8:30-8:45	Circle time, review class calendar
8:45-9:30	Literacy/Language Arts
9:30-10:15	Learning Stations
10:15-11:00	Math
11:00-11:30	Music/Dance/Movement
11:30-12:15	Lunch
12:15-1:00	Recess/Unstructured play
1:00-1:20	Rest/Quiet time
1:20-2:00	Science
2:00-2:45	Creative Arts
2:45-3:15	Daily reflection, pack up, dismissal

Some examples of restful and active movement activities for young children are discussed below:

- **Restful:** Incorporating restful activities into the early childhood classroom are beneficial in helping young children process and retain new concepts and providing them the opportunity to unwind after active movement activities. Examples of such activities include nap time, class meditation, self-reflection activities, independent art projects, or self-selected reading time. Teachers can also read aloud to students or play an audiobook during these periods.

- **Active:** Providing young children with multiple opportunities for active movement throughout the day is beneficial in promoting the development of gross motor skills, connections to learning, and the ability to function in a group setting. Active movement opportunities should include whole-class, small group, and independent activities. Examples include class dances, songs, or games, nature walks, or total participation activities such as gallery walks or four corners. Physical education activities, such as jump rope, tag, sports, or using playground equipment are also beneficial. Young children should also be provided with ample time for both structured and unstructured play throughout the day.

BALANCING RESTFUL AND ACTIVE MOVEMENT ACTIVITIES

A schedule that balances **rest** and **active movement** is necessary for positive cognitive, physical, emotional, and social development in young children. Connecting learning to active movement strengthens students' understanding of new concepts, as it allows them to physically explore and interact with their environment, experiment with new ideas, and gain new experiences for healthy **cognitive development**. In addition, incorporating active movement encourages the use of **gross motor skills** and provides students with the space to physically express themselves in an appropriate setting, thus promoting physical and emotional development. Active movement also encourages the development of positive **interpersonal skills** as young children interact and explore with one another. Restful periods are equally as important to young children's development. Incorporating rest after a period of active movement further strengthens young children's connection to learning by providing them the opportunity to reflect, process, and internalize new information.

PROVIDING LARGE BLOCKS OF TIME FOR PLAY, PROJECTS, AND LEARNING CENTERS

Providing young children with ample time for play, projects, and learning centers throughout the school day is integral to fostering their development across domains. Young children learn most effectively through active movement as they physically interact with their environment, and incorporating large blocks of time for such activities allows them to do so. Significant time dedicated to active play, projects, and learning centers on a variety of topics allows young children to explore and experiment with the world around them, test new ideas, draw conclusions, and acquire new knowledge. This supports healthy **physical** and **cognitive development**, as it provides young children the opportunity to engage in learning across subject areas while connecting it to active movement for strengthened understanding. In addition, allowing large blocks of time for these activities is necessary for **social** and **emotional development**, as it provides young children the space to interact with one another and develop important skills such as cooperation, sharing, conflict resolution, and emotional self-regulation. Dedicating large blocks of time to play, projects, and learning centers establishes a student-led, hands-on learning environment that is reflective of the developmental characteristics and needs of young children.

DEVELOPMENTAL CHARACTERISTICS OF YOUNG CHILDREN IN RELATION TO INTERACTIONS WITH OTHERS

Designing group activities that align with young children's ability to collaborate while supporting social development requires a realistic understanding of their capacity to do so. This entails understanding the **developmental characteristics** of young children at varying stages, including how the nature of their interactions with others evolves. Young children learn by exploring and interacting with their environment, so they need ample opportunities for play and active movement to do so. However, the teacher must recognize that the way young children play and collaborate develops over time. Young children typically exhibit little interest in actively playing with others until approximately age four. Until then, they progress through stages of solitary play, observing their peers, playing independently alongside others, and eventually, loosely interacting, perhaps with the same toys, while still primarily engaging in independent play. During these stages, it is important that the teacher foster **collaboration** by providing multiple opportunities for play as well as learning materials that encourage **cooperation** and **sharing**. The teacher must, however, maintain the understanding that these children have yet to develop the capacity to intentionally work with others. Once this ability is developed, the teacher can integrate coordinated group activities that encourage collaboration toward a common goal.

CONSIDERATIONS WHEN DESIGNING GROUP ACTIVITIES FOR YOUNG CHILDREN

For young children, thoughtfully designed group activities are integral in promoting development across domains. These opportunities facilitate social and emotional development by encouraging collaboration and positive communication, as well as physical and cognitive growth as children play, explore, and interact with others in the learning environment. It is therefore important that the teacher carefully consider the particulars of group activities when planning to ensure maximized learning and development. The teacher must consider the **developmental characteristics** of their students' age group, including their capacity to collaborate with others. This enables the teacher to plan group activities that align with students' abilities while promoting collaboration and development. All **learning materials** must be carefully selected to encourage collaboration, sharing, and the development of positive social skills at a developmentally appropriate level. The teacher must also consider **desired learning outcomes** and the nature of the learning taking place to determine whether group activities should be structured or unstructured. Unstructured play is valuable in allowing students to develop their social and emotional skills in a natural setting, whereas structured, teacher-led group activities allow for more focused learning. Desired outcomes also determine the size of groups for the activity to best promote collaboration and learning.

GROUP ACTIVITIES THAT REFLECT AND DEVELOP YOUNG CHILDREN'S ABILITY TO COLLABORATE

Young children benefit from a variety of **whole-class** and **small-group** activities designed to reflect and develop their collaborative skills. When the teacher incorporates group activities to encourage cooperation, sharing, and positive interactions, young children gain important social and emotional skills necessary for development across domains. Whole-group activities such as **circle time** provide young children with the opportunity to interact with others, express ideas, and ask questions in a developmentally appropriate setting. This activity develops important collaborative skills, such as taking turns, active listening, and respectful communication. Other **whole-group activities**, such as reading aloud, group songs, dances, games, or class nature walks, are effective in teaching young children how to productively contribute to and function in a group setting. **Small-group activities** can be incorporated throughout all aspects of structured and unstructured learning to develop young children's collaborative skills. Learning centers, such as a science area, pretend play area, or building block center, provide materials that encourage collaboration while allowing students to interact with others according to their abilities in a student-led setting. Problem-solving activities, such as puzzles, games, age-appropriate science experiments, or scavenger hunts, are effective in teaching young children how to work together toward a common goal.

ORGANIZING AND MANAGING GROUP ACTIVITIES TO PROMOTE COLLABORATIVE SKILLS AND INDIVIDUAL ACCOUNTABILITY

Well-planned group activities are beneficial in developing students' collaborative skills and sense of individual accountability. Such group activities are well-organized, effectively managed, and intentionally structured with a **clear goal** or problem that must be solved while allowing room for creativity to enhance the collaborative process. When designing these activities, the teacher must incorporate enough **significant components** to ensure all students within the group can productively contribute. If the assignment is too simple, students can easily complete it on their own, whereas a multifaceted activity instills a sense of interdependence within the group that fosters the development of collaborative skills. To promote individual accountability, **meaningful roles** and responsibilities should be assigned to each group member because when students feel others are relying on their contributions to complete a task, they develop a sense of ownership that motivates active participation. To further develop collaborative skills and individual accountability, students should be graded both as a **whole-group** and **individually**. This encourages group cooperation while ensuring that students' individual contributions are recognized. Including **self-assessments** at the end of group activities is beneficial in allowing students to reflect on the quality of their contributions to the group and ways they could improve their collaborative skills.

Thoughtful consideration of how to best organize and manage collaborative activities helps establish an environment that supports students in learning to work together productively and assume responsible roles within a group. When planning group activities, the teacher must consider the **desired learning outcomes** and the **nature of the task** to determine whether there are enough significant components that would benefit from collaboration. **Group size** must also be considered to most effectively foster collaboration and individual accountability when assuming responsible roles. Groups with too few students may be inadequate for addressing all the components of a complex task, whereas grouping too many students together limits productive collaboration and makes it difficult for each member to assume a significant, responsible role. The teacher must be selective regarding which students are grouped together to best facilitate productive collaboration. This includes determining which students will work well together, as well as grouping students that may need support with others that can provide scaffolding. It is also important to consider how **responsibilities** will be divided to ensure each member is given a significant role that allows them to contribute productively to the group, as well how their contributions will be monitored and **assessed**.

Communicating Effectively with Students

CLEAR AND ACCURATE COMMUNICATION
SIGNIFICANCE
Successful teaching and learning is reliant on clear, accurate communication throughout all stages of the learning process. To create a positive and productive learning environment, it is vital that the teacher practice effective speaking, listening, reading, and writing skills to ensure focused instruction in which students understand expectations and desired learning outcomes. When communication is clear and accurate, learning becomes relevant and engaging, as students understand the purpose of instruction and are more successfully able to complete tasks and achieve learning targets. This ultimately enhances the overall learning experience in that it allows teachers to efficiently progress through the curriculum and challenge students with increasingly complex material as they master desired learning outcomes. In addition, effective communication is multifaceted and increases student comprehension and deepens their understanding of subject matter. When the teacher skillfully communicates instruction through a variety of methods, students of varying learning styles are better able to internalize new information according to their individual needs. By enhancing teaching and learning through clear and accurate communication, the teacher establishes positive attitudes toward learning among students that serve as a foundation for future academic success.

APPROPRIATE LANGUAGE FOR VARYING AGE GROUPS

Students' cognitive abilities develop as they mature, and therefore, the ability to focus, comprehend and process information differs among age groups. For successful teaching and learning, the teacher must be aware of these variances to clearly and accurately communicate in an age-appropriate manner that facilitates student understanding. The use of age-appropriate language throughout the teaching and learning process is vital in supporting students' attention and ability to focus, as well as challenging them according to their developmental levels to ensure prolonged engagement in instruction. Furthermore, age-appropriate language is necessary in promoting student understanding through making information accessible and relevant. When designing and communicating instruction, the teacher must consider students' cognitive and linguistic abilities, as well as their attention span relative to their age group to ensure a comprehensible, rigorous, and engaging learning environment. The teacher must also be sure to support verbal communication with eye contact, body language, and visuals appropriate to the specific age group to reinforce and deepen understanding.

TAILORING COMMUNICATION TO STUDENTS' INTERESTS

Communicating instruction to reflect students' interests enhances the teaching and learning process by fostering an engaging, student-centered environment. Instruction that appeals to students by incorporating their interests strengthens comprehension and understanding through increasing relevancy by allowing for personal connections to learning. To accomplish this, the teacher must get to know individual students and work to build positive relationships to gain an understanding of their unique interests and preferences. With this understanding in mind, the teacher can provide learning experiences that reflect individual interests through examples, relevant activities, and encouraging active participation to allow students to express their own interests and connections when learning. In addition, the teacher must seek student feedback and evaluate their reactions when delivering instruction to determine whether it is reflective of their interests and adjust accordingly. When instruction is communicated according to students' interests and preferences, the teacher creates an inclusive and personalized learning experience that fosters positive attitudes toward learning and enhances academic achievement.

USING LANGUAGE APPROPRIATE TO STUDENTS' BACKGROUNDS

Understanding students' backgrounds and adjusting language accordingly is imperative for ensuring clear, accurate, and respectful communication that promotes success in learning. When communicating in the classroom, using language appropriate to students' individual backgrounds is essential in ensuring culturally **relevant**, **sensitive**, and **responsive** instruction. In addition, when teachers understand what is important to students based upon their background experiences, beliefs, and values, they can more effectively and accurately communicate instruction, as they can tailor their language in a manner that is responsive to students' needs and avoids misunderstanding. Such **culturally competent** communication promotes academic success by fostering an inclusive environment in which all students feel respected and are therefore motivated to learn. Moreover, using language that is appropriate to students' backgrounds enhances the teaching and learning process by making instruction engaging and relevant to students, as it enables personal connections to deepen understanding. When the language of instruction is easily accessible to students and reflective of their experiences, they can apply their learning to their own personal contexts. This ultimately fosters positive attitudes toward learning among students that promote academic success.

INSTRUCTIONAL STRATEGIES FOR ENSURING CLEAR AND ACCURATE COMMUNICATION

In effective instruction, the teacher frequently implements strategies to ensure and evaluate the clarity and accuracy of communication and adjusts accordingly to meet students' individual needs.

In order to provide instruction that is easily accessible to students, the teacher must incorporate a variety of **verbal** and **nonverbal** communication techniques to strengthen understanding. Verbal information must be accompanied by nonverbal means of communication, such as proper eye contact, body language, gestures, visuals, and written information. Additionally, the teacher can determine whether they are communicating clearly and accurately by asking students to repeat instructions and key information. Frequently monitoring student progress by conducting formative assessments throughout the learning process allows the teacher to determine student comprehension and adjust communication techniques as necessary to enhance clarity and accuracy. Moreover, allowing students opportunities to provide feedback on the learning process through discussions and reflection activities is an effective strategy in providing insight on the clarity and accuracy of communication. By implementing cooperative learning and small group activities, the teacher can further ensure clarity and accuracy of communication by allowing for more focused instruction that is tailored to students' individual learning needs.

ENSURING STUDENT UNDERSTANDING
EFFECTIVELY COMMUNICATING DIRECTIONS, EXPLANATIONS, AND PROCEDURES

Successful learning requires the effective communication of directions, explanations, and procedures to ensure student understanding. When this information is clearly communicated, student confusion and misconception is avoided, allowing for smoother and more focused instruction. Effective and skillful communication eliminates distractions from instruction, thus allowing students to engage in learning confidently and successfully because they clearly understand the objectives, expectations, and methods for completing tasks. In addition, allocating specific time to provide specific directions, explanations, and procedures enhances student understanding by establishing consistency, order, and effective classroom management that enables students to focus on learning. This creates a safe, predictable, and ultimately, more engaging classroom environment that facilitates student understanding and success in learning.

STRATEGIES FOR ADJUSTING COMMUNICATION

In all stages of the teaching and learning process, the teacher must be flexible in instruction and implement strategies for adjusting communication to ensure student understanding. The teacher may have to adapt communication by adjusting their tone, pace, vocabulary, or method of communicating to meet students' individual learning needs. The teacher must get to know their students to understand their unique needs as well as what is interesting and relevant to them to tailor their communication accordingly. By building positive relationships and learning students' communication styles, the teacher can effectively deliver instruction that is easily understandable to students. Modeling good active listening skills, conducting formative assessments throughout instruction, and eliciting student feedback allows the teacher to evaluate student understanding and adjust their communication style as necessary. In addition, incorporating technology into instruction is a valuable strategy for adapting communication to meet students' needs and ensure understanding. By accompanying instruction with digital resources, the teacher can deliver information, directions, and explanations through a variety of methods to make communication accessible and comprehensible to students of varying learning styles.

PROVIDING EXAMPLES WHEN COMMUNICATING DIRECTIONS, EXPLANATIONS, AND PROCEDURES

When the teacher skillfully provides examples to support directions, explanations, and procedures, instruction is more effective because students' overall understanding is enhanced. In selecting appropriate, relevant examples, the teacher makes learning concrete and establishes a frame of reference for students to visualize the real-world application of the given information. Effective examples allow students to make personal connections to their learning by relating information to their own experiences, thus enhancing their understanding by making learning more engaging and meaningful. Additionally, as modeling is an influential instructional strategy, incorporating practical examples enhances student understanding by providing them with a model to reference, compare, and replicate. The use of effective examples in communicating directions, explanations, and procedures ultimately increases retainment of information, thus fostering success when students engage in learning.

TYPES OF EXAMPLES

Accompanying directions, explanations, and procedures with a variety of examples is beneficial in strengthening student's connections for enhanced understanding. **Visual representations**, such as images, illustrations, diagrams, graphs, or charts, serve as valuable examples for student reference, as reminders, as well as to supplement instruction. Modeling is a highly effective instructional strategy, and **demonstrating** to students how to perform directions, routines, and procedures ensures that students are clear regarding what is expected of them. When communicating criteria for assignments, showing examples of **past student work** provides students with clarity regarding how they will be graded, as well as the characteristics of quality work. In addition, using real-life **scenarios** or **personal experiences** as examples is beneficial in making new information relevant, applicable, and as a result, easier for students to comprehend.

SIMPLIFYING COMPLEX IDEAS

To strengthen student understanding of content material, complex ideas often must be simplified. The teacher must take care with their communication and be aware of effective implementation of teaching strategies to provide comprehensible instruction. The language of instruction must be clear, succinct, free of distractions, and age-appropriate to ensure that new content is easily accessible to students. Complex ideas should be **chunked** into smaller parts when teaching to allow for focused instruction that avoids misconceptions and builds a solid foundation of understanding. This also enhances student understanding by allowing the teacher the opportunity to formatively assess comprehension throughout the learning process and adjust instructional strategies as necessary to simplify difficult content material. Accompanying instruction with visual aids such as graphic organizers, anchor charts, or infographics make complex topics easier to internalize by emphasizing key information. Likewise, incorporating media and other digital resources enhances student understanding by diversifying the instructional approach to make learning more accessible and reinforcing complex ideas.

EFFECTIVE COMMUNICATION TOOLS

In a productive learning environment, the teacher implements a variety of communication tools to ensure that students have a clear understanding of directions, explanations, and procedures. **Visual aids** throughout the classroom in the form of posters, anchor charts, and class bulletin boards serve to reinforce and remind students of pertinent information and expectations. Effective **transitions** communicate to students the process for moving from one activity or subject to the next. Allowing students opportunities for **reflection** provides the teacher with feedback on the clarity of directions, explanations, and procedures and enables them to adjust communication as necessary to enhance understanding. In addition, several digital communication tools are available to increase communication and understanding, including interactive apps that enable teachers to formatively assess clarity and apps to remind students and families of important information to reinforce understanding. Establishing communication with families by creating a classroom newsletter or website and requiring students to keep a daily agenda book are examples of valuable tools for ensuring understanding, as these allow students to be reminded of events, assignments, and expectations at home.

VERBAL AND NONVERBAL MEANS OF COMMUNICATION

Directions, explanations, and procedures often must be communicated throughout instruction to enhance student understanding. In communicating this information through a variety of **verbal** and **nonverbal** methods, the teacher ensures that students are aware of every part of the instructional process, thus allowing for a focused and productive learning experience. When introducing a new lesson or activity, using effective speaking and listening skills, repeating explanations as necessary, and varying tone, pacing, and inflection to verbally communicate pertinent information and processes effectively establishes understanding. Verbally conducting formative assessments during instruction further supports student understanding by providing the teacher with feedback to adjust communication as needed for clarity. In addition, verbal instructions can be strengthened to increase student understanding by incorporating media such as videos and audio clips. Nonverbal communication is highly effective in reminding students of and reinforcing directions, explanations, and procedures. Gestures, facial expressions, body language, eye contact, and proximity are valuable tools for highlighting key information and reminding students of expectations and instructional steps. In addition, visual reminders around the classroom in the form of posters, charts, and presentation slides act as nonverbal reminders of processes and expectations to enhance understanding and allow for focused engagement in instruction.

SIGNIFICANCE OF EFFECTIVE COMMUNICATION SKILLS IN MEETING SPECIFIED GOALS

Effective communication skills are essential to successfully meeting learning goals across various contexts. When the teacher skillfully communicates desired outcomes in the instructional process and the steps to achieve them, students are able to meet learning goals because they have a focused understanding and purpose for learning. When communication is clear and free of distractions, students' engagement in instruction is enhanced, thus making it easier for them to achieve learning targets. In addition, using a variety of techniques to effectively communicate material across subject areas enhances understanding by providing multiple avenues for students to internalize, apply, and ultimately retain new information. Furthermore, when the teacher is conscientious of their communication, they become more attuned to students' individual learning needs and communication styles. This allows the teacher to effectively instill necessary supports and adjust communication to meet students' needs when meeting specified learning goals.

SIGNIFICANCE OF EFFECTIVE INTERPERSONAL SKILLS IN POSITIVE LEARNING ENVIRONMENT

Interpersonal relationships are a vital aspect of successful teaching and learning. When positive interpersonal skills are demonstrated and promoted, the teacher effectively establishes a supportive, inviting classroom environment in which students are empowered and motivated to learn. Strong interpersonal skills allow the teacher to build positive, respectful relationships with students, instilling in them a sense of confidence and engagement that fosters academic achievement. In understanding how to interact with students in a way that is relevant and meaningful to them, the teacher can enhance learning and achievement by tailoring instruction to students' unique interests and experiences. In addition, establishing a positive rapport with students enables the teacher to identify, address, and adapt instruction to students' individual learning needs, thus enhancing instruction to promote engagement and achievement.

VERBAL AND NONVERBAL COMMUNICATION

When developing and delivering instruction to meet specified goals across varying learning contexts, it is imperative that the teacher implement a variety of verbal and nonverbal communication techniques. **Verbal communication** methods, including repetition, providing explanations and examples, and changing the pace, tone, and inflection of speech are effective when introducing new, complex concepts and emphasizing key information to students. Incorporating videos and audio clips enhance verbal communication by providing an additional method for understanding when working to achieve learning goals. Incorporating clear **nonverbal communication** techniques is effective in reinforcing and reminding students of instructional targets and content. Body language, gestures, facial expressions, and eye contact highlight important information to support verbal communication and strengthen understanding when explaining new concepts or modeling new skills to students. In addition, visual aids such as posters, anchor charts, presentation slides, and images are tools for nonverbally restating procedures and concepts, as well as simplifying complex ideas to enable students to successfully reach specified learning goals.

ELECTRONIC COMMUNICATION

In an increasingly digital world, electronic communication has become integral in enhancing teaching and learning to efficiently meet specified goals across learning contexts. Digital resources improve clarity by providing teachers with multiple means of communicating learning targets, delivering instruction, and providing feedback. Electronic communication makes learning more accessible and comprehensible, as teachers can utilize it to deliver information and instruction in a variety of ways, according to students' individual learning needs, to meet desired outcomes. Digital communication platforms, such as virtual classrooms and interactive apps, promote interaction and participation that increase student engagement in the learning process. In addition, such platforms increase the efficiency of meeting specified learning goals by allowing for immediate communication and feedback between teachers and students throughout all stages of instruction. Such platforms also allow the teacher to provide instructional materials that students can easily reference to increase understanding. Electronic tools such as email, class websites, and communication apps establish open communication between teachers, students, and families that is beneficial in meeting learning goals by allowing the teacher to easily provide pertinent information that can be reinforced at home.

Effective Feedback and Self-Assessment

TIMELY FEEDBACK

Timely feedback improves the effectiveness of teaching and learning for enhanced student achievement. When the teacher consistently provides feedback on students' progress throughout all stages of instruction, it is more relevant, thus enabling students to effectively connect it to the context of their learning. Providing timely feedback also ensures that instructional content is at the forefront of students' minds, thus increasing the likelihood that students will effectively apply it for enhanced learning. Immediate feedback increases student motivation and allows for more focused instruction, as students are continuously aware of their strengths and areas for improvement. In addition, efficient feedback enables the teacher to quickly identify areas of misconception before advancing in instruction, thus ensuring student understanding before moving forward and avoiding the need for remediation. This allows the teacher to progress smoothly through instruction while ensuring comprehension to enhance student achievement.

APPROPRIATE LANGUAGE FOR PROVIDING FEEDBACK

The language of feedback influences its effectiveness in fostering student achievement. When providing students with feedback regarding their progress, the teacher must be mindful of their approach to ensure that it is properly received. It is important that the teacher consider students' **age** and **grade level** to tailor language accordingly and present feedback in a relevant and meaningful way. When the language of feedback is comprehensible to students, they are more effectively able to apply it to the context of their learning. The teacher's language must be respectful, positive, and encouraging while constructively suggesting areas for improvement so as to support students' self-concept and positive attitudes toward learning. This includes framing feedback with remarks that identify and reinforce students' strengths while offering support and guidance to enhance development. Language must be direct and specific to ensure understanding and that necessary changes are made as students progress through instruction. The teacher must also be attuned to students' individual characteristics in order to address them with language that is responsive and considerate of their needs. When the appropriate language is applied in presenting feedback, it increases student motivation, engagement, and ability to make improvements that enhance their learning experience.

EFFECTIVE FORMATS FOR FEEDBACK

Successful instruction is reliant on continuous feedback through a variety of **formats** to ensure that the teacher's guidance is accurate, constructive, substantive, and specific. Varying formats for providing formative and summative feedback are applicable and effective in different stages of the learning process. **Formative feedback** is often informal and occurs throughout instruction to guide student learning. Some methods include oral feedback in the form of asking students open-ended questions and providing suggestions for improvement, written comments on assignments, and peer-to-peer feedback in which students can offer one another support to build understanding. **Summative feedback** is often formal and occurs at the end of a lesson or unit to evaluate students' progress in achieving learning goals. **Rubrics** are a versatile tool for providing summative feedback, as they vary in complexity and the criteria within them can be tailored to specific learning objectives. This format is valuable for communicating expectations and clearly demonstrating the characteristics of quality work. In utilizing rubrics to provide feedback, the teacher can outline specific areas for evaluation, assign point values, and explicitly specify areas of strength and skills that need improvement.

SUBSTANTIVE FEEDBACK

When teachers provide **substantive feedback**, they ensure that students are given focused, useful, and relevant direction regarding their progress throughout the learning process. With such feedback, students receive **concrete information** regarding ways in which they can improve their performance in a given area that enables them to apply it to the context of their learning in a meaningful way. This ultimately strengthens students' connections between the teacher's substantive feedback and their work, thus enhancing understanding and success in learning. In addition, the nature of substantive feedback facilitates **personalized learning**, as it is tailored to address individual student progress and areas for improvement. This allows for student-centered instruction that enhances learning by addressing the needs of all students.

CONSTRUCTIVE FEEDBACK

Feedback on students' progress must always be **constructive** in nature to facilitate successful learning and development. Constructive feedback ensures students maintain a positive **self-concept** and attitude toward learning, which is integral to increasing self-motivation and engagement. When students are motivated and engaged, they are more likely to apply the teacher's suggestions to enhance their learning and understanding. When providing constructive feedback, it is important that the teacher consider the specific area in which the student needs improvement in order to provide effective guidance for enhancing comprehension and progress. In addition, the teacher must consider their approach to providing feedback to ensure that all suggestions are productive, encouraging, and helpful to the student. This includes presenting feedback through **positive** and **supportive language** that is free of negative connotations or inferences. The teacher should accompany feedback with comments that highlight students' **strengths** while offering **suggestions** and **guidance** on specific areas in which they can improve. Constructive feedback must include clear explanations on ways in which students can improve their performance, as well as establish how the teacher's suggestions will enhance their overall learning and growth.

SPECIFIC FEEDBACK

Specific feedback provides students with clarity regarding how to effectively improve their progress as they work toward achieving learning targets. When the teacher consistently delivers specific feedback, students are clear on expectations, can identify areas for improvement within their performance, and make necessary changes. Students are more likely to effectively apply feedback that specifies areas for development as they progress toward learning goals. If feedback is too vague, students may either disregard it or make incorrect, uninformed changes that hinder understanding and progress. Providing detailed suggestions and guidance enhances student engagement and motivation, as it increases their focus on particular areas for improvement to allow for success in learning. In addition, highlighting students' strengths through specific feedback encourages them to apply their abilities to other areas of instruction, thus enhancing student productivity and success in achieving learning targets.

PROMOTING USE OF FEEDBACK

Students' ability to utilize feedback is a valuable tool in enhancing their own learning for increased achievement. To develop this skill among students, the teacher must emphasize the value of feedback, demonstrate its applications in specific learning situations, and explain how implementing it is beneficial in improving academic performance. This notion can be reinforced by effectively **modeling** how to receive and apply feedback to enhance student understanding of the process. Feedback must always be constructive and highlight students' strengths to help them identify specific areas for improvement. By **checking** students' understanding of feedback frequently, the teacher ensures they know how to productively apply it for enhanced learning. This includes encouraging students to **respond** to given feedback by contributing their thoughts and asking for clarification as necessary. In addition, students are more likely to internalize and effectively apply feedback that is **timely** and provided throughout instruction, rather than at the end, thus fostering their ability to utilize it in guiding their own learning. This allows students to establish personal connections between feedback and their learning that strengthen their understanding and promote their academic success.

TEACHING STUDENTS TO USE SELF-ASSESSMENT

Developing students' **self-assessment** capabilities provides them with a sense of self-sufficiency for guiding and enhancing their own learning. To facilitate this, the teacher must establish a supportive **classroom environment** in which students feel comfortable and empowered to take risks and objectively evaluate their own progress as they seek areas for improvement. **Modeling** strategies for utilizing self-assessment to enhance learning and explaining its significance in supporting continued success are valuable strategies in enabling students to assess their own progress to guide and improve their learning. By guiding students with **open-ended questions** as they engage in learning, the teacher encourages students to assess their own progress and demonstrates how to implement effective questioning to seek areas for improvement within their own work. The teacher should include multiple outlets for self-assessment to facilitate the development of this skill, including **reflection** opportunities that enable students to evaluate their own understanding and guide their development as they engage in learning.

SIGNIFICANCE OF SELF-ASSESSMENT IN FACILITATING GROWTH AND ACHIEVEMENT

When students are able to objectively assess their own progress, they are equipped with the tools necessary to continuously seek areas for improvement that guide and enhance their learning. This empowers students with a sense of **ownership** and responsibility over their learning as they monitor their own performance to refine their skills for enhanced growth and achievement. Self-assessment and monitoring strengthen students' **personal connections** to their work, as they are able to relate their learning to their own prior knowledge and frames of reference. This ultimately makes learning more relevant, thus increasing motivation, productivity, and achievement. Students who regularly self-assess their work develop the independence necessary for engaging in **self-directed** learning, thus establishing a foundation for continued growth and success. In addition, continuously seeking areas for improvement allows students to develop a sense of confidence to take risks in their learning, as they understand how to overcome obstacles as they progress.

DEVELOPMENT OF REAL-WORLD LIFE SKILLS FOR FUTURE SUCCESS

The ability to effectively apply feedback and self-assessment for enhanced learning prepares students with the life skills necessary for future success in academic and real-world situations. Developing this skill instills within students the notion that there is always room for improvement in their performance. In addition, it develops their understanding of the characteristics of quality overcoming learning obstacles and the **self-motivation** required to take initiative that is integral to success. Students that frequently employ feedback and self-assessment have a strong sense of **independence** for and enhancing their own learning. In addition, this skill provides students with the **self-awareness** necessary to recognize their strengths and weaknesses, thus making them more inclined to continuously seek areas for increased understanding and improvement for maximized achievement. Students' communication and cooperation skills are enhanced when they learn to properly use feedback and self-assessment, as it develops their ability to appreciate constructive criticism and internalize multiple perspectives as they work to improve their performance.

SELF-ASSESSMENT THAT ENCOURAGES EVALUATION OF LEARNING AND CONTINUOUS IMPROVEMENT

Providing multiple strategies for self-assessment throughout instruction develops students' ability to monitor and evaluate their performance for continuous improvement. Self-assessment strategies can be formal or informal and can occur on an individual or whole-class basis. Teaching students how to set **SMART goals** (specific, measurable, attainable, relevant, time-bound) enables them to set learning goals, determine a path to achieve them, and reflect upon their performance to seek areas for improvement as they progress. Implementing strategies for students to indicate their level of comprehension is valuable in encouraging reflection on their own understanding and areas for improvement as they progress through the learning process. Such strategies include open-ended **questioning** to encourage reflection, color-coded **response cards** to signify understanding, or **whole-class activities** such as four corners. Graphic organizer activities such as **KWL charts** are beneficial in prompting students to consider prior knowledge and reflect on their progress after a lesson. This facilitates students in forming personal connections and determining areas in which they can extend and improve upon their learning. **Reflection** opportunities, such as exit tickets or learning logs, are also valuable for encouraging self-assessment, as they prompt students to consider areas in which they excelled, as well as potential room for improvement.

Characteristics of SMART Goals

S	Specific	The goal is clearly stated and narrowed down in scope. Details of the goal, including who, what, where, when, why, and how much, are explicitly outlined.
M	Measurable	The goal includes a quantifiable method of measuring progress toward achievement, such as reading twenty-five books in a year.
A	Attainable	The goal is challenging, yet realistic and within the realm of the individual's current abilities and skills.

Characteristics of SMART Goals

R	Relevant	The goal is meaningful to the individual and contributes toward personal improvement and the long-term goals.
T	Time-Bound	The goal sets a specific timeline for achievement. This helps the individual monitor progress and hold personal accountability.

Skilled Questioning to Support Learning

HIGHER-LEVEL QUESTIONING

Higher-level questioning that prompts students to **analyze**, **evaluate**, and **create** responses and solutions fosters effective student discussions by encouraging students to consider information beyond basic recollection. When students are asked to **explain**, **justify**, **predict**, and **provide examples**, they are encouraged to actively participate in learning, thus enhancing discussion. In addition, higher-level questioning increases the effectiveness of student discussion by promoting the use of higher-order and critical thinking skills to **consider alternatives**, **compare**, **contrast**, **discuss hypothetically**, and **develop** creative solutions to problems. Higher-level questioning encourages students to elaborate on their thinking and learning, thus allowing for productive discussions that strengthen the learning experience.

IMPACT OF STUDENT DISCUSSIONS ON OVERALL LEARNING EXPERIENCE

Student discussion is a valuable instructional strategy for deepening and enhancing the overall learning experience. When students have the opportunity to discuss new concepts in their own words, it increases their ability to internalize and retain information. Effective student discussions prompt students to relate information to their own experiences and create personal connections that enhance learning by making it relevant and meaningful. Likewise, in listening to and interacting with their peers, students gain insight on differing perspectives and can build on one another's background knowledge to increase understanding. Incorporating effective discussions into instruction also produces an interesting and engaging learning environment by encouraging active student participation. When students are asked to inquire and consider information on a complex level, explain and elaborate on their reasoning, and think critically about situations, they are given an active role that serves to deepen and enhance the learning experience.

IMPACT OF SKILLED QUESTIONING AND DISCUSSION

EXPLORATION OF CONTENT AND LEARNING

Skilled questioning and discussion are essential components in enhancing learning by establishing an engaging learning environment that promotes the exploration of content material beyond basic knowledge. By challenging students during discussions based upon their abilities through specific questioning, the teacher effectively prompts students to think critically about instructional content, devise new solutions to problems, and implement higher-order thinking skills that require further exploration of content material. Effective discussions encourage students to examine the nuances of subject matter and reflect upon others' perspectives to build upon their understanding. Furthermore, when students are provided with effective questions to promote interesting and engaging discussions, they become motivated to actively participate in their learning and explore instructional content on a deeper level.

EXTENDING STUDENTS' KNOWLEDGE ON INSTRUCTIONAL CONTENT

The implementation of skilled questioning when leading effective discussions is valuable in extending students' knowledge of instructional content. Skilled questioning activates higher-order thinking skills, as it prompts students to consider ideas and information on a more complex level.

94

When teachers skillfully craft questions on content material during discussions, they are able to extend students' knowledge on the instructional topic by creating specific, increasingly complex questions that build on students' capabilities. Effective questions during discussions also increase students' knowledge on content material by motivating them to seek further information and thoughtfully consider their answers to elaborate on and provide examples for their reasoning. Additionally, skilled questioning and discussions foster active participation in learning, giving students the opportunity to build and reflect upon other's knowledge and experiences. This ultimately increases their understanding of the instructional content by allowing them to integrate their frame of reference with others' perspectives.

FOSTERING ACTIVE INQUIRY

An interesting and engaging environment is necessary in fostering active curiosity and inquiry for learning among students. Through skilled questioning and effective student discussions, the teacher creates an atmosphere in which students must actively engage and participate throughout the learning process, thus providing them with a sense of self-motivation for active inquiry. In addition, skilled questioning challenges students to utilize higher-order thinking skills that require them to inquire about a discussion topic beyond basic information and seek new information to thoughtfully consider and elaborate on their responses. In the discussion setting, students are also engaged and encouraged to ask each other questions to deepen understanding. Effective questioning and student discussions enhance learning and productivity by creating an engaging, **inquiry-based** environment that provides students with a sense of ownership over their learning as they seek new information.

DEVELOPING HIGHER-ORDER THINKING SKILLS

Skillful questioning when leading student discussions is an effective method of developing **higher-order thinking** skills to strengthen understanding and enhance the learning experience. In thoughtfully proposing questions that challenge students based on their abilities, the teacher establishes a foundation of knowledge to build upon with increasingly rigorous skilled questioning. When students are asked to apply their learning to **analyze**, **evaluate**, and **create**, higher-order thinking skills are developed in that students must think deeply and critically about ideas, information, and situations beyond the basic recall of information. Effective questioning in discussions prompts students to think more complexly and synthesize previously learned information to craft and support new ideas, responses, and solutions. Students are thus required to take more time to evaluate their responses carefully, consider alternatives and differing perspectives of their classmates, and create personal connections by applying their own experiences to their learning.

INCREASING PROBLEM-SOLVING SKILLS

Incorporating skilled questions into class discussions fosters the development of problem-solving skills by eliciting students' critical thinking abilities to devise creative solutions. By asking complex, open-ended questions that prompt students to **hypothesize, predict**, and **consider alternative** methods of solving a problem, the teacher creates an engaging learning environment that promotes curiosity, exploration, and inquiry. Such questioning effectively develops problem-solving skills by increasing student motivation for seeking new solutions and analyzing their results. Thoughtfully crafted questions encourage students to **synthesize** and **apply** their own experiences and previously learned information when devising a solution to a problem. In addition, in proposing skilled questions when leading discussions, the teacher fosters students' abilities to apply knowledge, understanding, and reasoning methods from one learning context to another, thus developing real-world problem-solving skills. Effective class discussions encourage students to collaborate to build upon one another's experiences and knowledge when seeking solutions, as well as demonstrate the validity of multiple approaches to situations to develop students' overall problem-solving abilities.

PROMOTING POSITIVE, SUPPORTIVE INTERACTIONS TO ENHANCE THE LEARNING EXPERIENCE

In facilitating effective class discussions, the teacher must propose skillful questions that encourage positive and supportive interactions to ensure that all students feel respected when contributing. To achieve this, the teacher must lead discussions with open-ended questions that emphasize the validity of multiple responses and accompany students' responses with follow-up questions. Such skilled questioning fosters **prosocial** interactions by creating a safe and respectful learning environment that encourages students to collaborate, actively participate in discussion with one another, and appreciate varying perspectives. In addition, skillful questioning and effective discussions include appropriate wait time between questions and responses. This promotes supportive interactions by allowing students the opportunity to process their responses and by demonstrating the importance of active listening. In emphasizing this, students ultimately feel respected in their ideas and empowered to add to the discussion. When teachers effectively lead student discussions with thoughtfully crafted questions, they enhance the overall learning experience by creating a welcoming, respectful learning environment in which students feel confident to take risks and explore new ideas through discussion.

SIGNIFICANCE OF APPROPRIATE WAIT TIME IN EFFECTIVE STUDENT DISCUSSIONS

Appropriate wait time is an integral component in leading effective student discussions. When students are given a few seconds after questioning to consider their responses, they are able to effectively process and synthesize information to formulate and elaborate on their ideas. Wait time during discussions leads to more thoughtful responses, as students are given time to consider their learning on a more complex level. In addition, providing time between questions and discussion allows students to process one another's responses to contribute more effectively to the conversation and enhance the overall learning experience.

SIGNIFICANCE OF BLOOM'S TAXONOMY IN SKILLED QUESTIONING

Bloom's taxonomy is a framework for categorizing learning objectives with increasing levels of complexity to promote the development of higher-order thinking skills. Measures of ability are organized into **remembering**, **understanding**, and **applying** as lower-level benchmarks, and **analyzing**, **evaluating**, and **creating** as higher-level targets. Lower-level objectives are intended to build and evaluate student comprehension and ability to ultimately achieve higher-level targets intended to deepen understanding and develop higher-order thinking skills. Bloom's taxonomy is integral in engaging in skilled questioning. This model allows the teacher to develop specific, increasingly challenging questions, activities, and assessments that establish a foundation of knowledge and build upon it for the development of higher-order thinking skills. In addition, it

Lower level
remember
understand
apply

Higher level
analyze
evaluate
create

provides an outline for identifying students' cognitive abilities and allows the teacher to effectively develop appropriate questions that build and enhance understanding to foster success in learning.

Bloom's Taxonomy

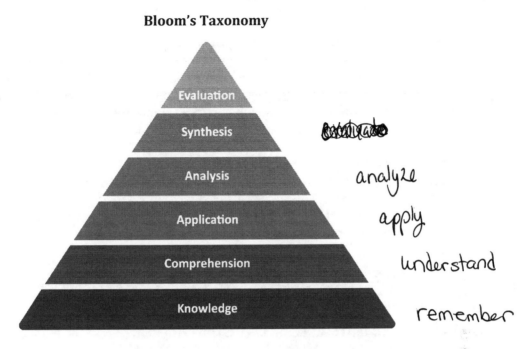

Assessment Methodology

ASSESSMENT METHODS

Effective teaching requires multiple methods of assessment to evaluate student comprehension and instructional effectiveness. Assessments are typically categorized as diagnostic, formative, summative, and benchmark, and are applicable at varying stages of instruction. **Diagnostic** assessments are administered before instruction and indicate students' prior knowledge and areas of misunderstanding to determine the path of instruction. **Formative** assessments occur continuously to measure student engagement, comprehension, and instructional effectiveness. These assessments indicate instructional strategies that require adjustment to meet students' needs in facilitating successful learning, and include such strategies as checking for understanding, observations, total participation activities, and exit tickets. **Summative** assessments are given at the end of a lesson or unit to evaluate student progress in reaching learning targets and identify areas of misconception for reteaching. Such assessments can be given in the form of exams and quizzes, or project-based activities in which students demonstrate their learning through hands-on, personalized methods. Additionally, portfolios serve as valuable summative assessments in allowing students to demonstrate their progress over time and provide insight regarding individual achievement. **Benchmark** assessments occur less frequently and encompass large portions of curriculum. These assessments are intended to evaluate the progress of groups of students in achieving state and district academic standards.

ASSESSMENT TYPES

- **Diagnostic:** These assessments can either be formal or informal and are intended to provide teachers with information regarding students' level of understanding prior to beginning a unit of instruction. Examples include pretests, KWL charts, anticipation guides, and brainstorming activities. Digital resources, such as online polls, surveys, and quizzes are also valuable resources for gathering diagnostic feedback.

- **Formative:** These assessments occur throughout instruction to provide the teacher with feedback regarding student understanding. Examples include warm-up and closure activities, checking frequently for understanding, student reflection activities, and providing students with color-coded cards to indicate their level of understanding. Short quizzes and total participation activities, such as four corners, are also valuable formative assessments. Numerous digital resources, including polls, surveys, and review games, are also beneficial in providing teachers with formative feedback to indicate instructional effectiveness.
- **Summative:** Summative assessments are intended to indicate students' level of mastery and progress toward reaching academic learning standards. These assessments may take the form of written or digital exams and include multiple choice, short answer, or long answer questions. Examples also include projects, final essays, presentations, or portfolios to demonstrate student progress over time.
- **Benchmark:** Benchmark assessments measure students' progress in achieving academic standards. These assessments are typically standardized to ensure uniformity, objectivity, and accuracy. Benchmark assessments are typically given as a written multiple choice or short answer exam, or as a digital exam in which students answer questions on the computer.

> **Review Video: Formative and Summative Assessments**
> Visit mometrix.com/academy and enter code: 804991

DETERMINING APPROPRIATE ASSESSMENT STRATEGIES

As varying assessment methods provide different information regarding student performance and achievement, the teacher must consider the most applicable and effective assessment strategy in each stage of instruction. This includes determining the **desired outcomes** of assessment, as well as the information the teacher intends to ascertain and how they will apply the results to further instruction. **Age** and **grade level** appropriateness must be considered when selecting which assessment strategies will enable students to successfully demonstrate their learning. Additionally, the teacher must be cognizant of students' individual differences and learning needs to determine which assessment model is most **accommodating** and reflective of their progress. It is also important that the teacher consider the practicality of assessment strategies, as well as methods they will use to implement the assessment for maximized feedback regarding individual and whole-class progress in achieving learning goals.

ASSESSMENTS THAT REFLECT REAL-WORLD APPLICATIONS

Assessments that reflect **real-world applications** enhance relevancy and students' ability to establish personal connections to learning that deepen understanding. Implementing such assessments provides authenticity and enhances engagement by defining a clear and practical purpose for learning. These assessments often allow for hands-on opportunities for demonstrating learning and can be adjusted to accommodate students' varying learning styles and needs while measuring individual progress. However, assessments that focus on real-world applications can be subjective, thus making it difficult to extract concrete data and quantify student progress to guide future instructional decisions. In addition, teachers may have difficulty analyzing assessment results on a large scale and comparing student performance with other schools and districts, as individual assessments may vary.

DIAGNOSTIC TESTS

Diagnostic tests are integral to planning and delivering effective instruction. These tests are typically administered prior to beginning a unit or lesson and provide valuable feedback for guiding and planning instruction. Diagnostic tests provide **preliminary information** regarding students' level of understanding and prior knowledge. This serves as a baseline for instructional planning that connects and builds upon students' background knowledge and experiences to enhance success in learning. Diagnostic tests allow the teacher to identify and clarify areas of student misconception prior to engaging in instruction to ensure continued comprehension and avoid the need for remediation. They indicate areas of student strength and need, as well as individual instructional aids that may need to be incorporated into lessons to support student achievement. In addition, these tests enable the teacher to determine which instructional strategies, activities, groupings, and materials will be most valuable in maximizing engagement and learning. Diagnostic tests can be **formal** or **informal**, and include such formats as pre-tests, pre-reading activities, surveys, vocabulary inventories, and graphic organizers such as KWL charts to assess student understanding prior to engaging in learning. Diagnostic tests are generally not graded as there is little expectation that all students in a class possess the same baseline of proficiency at the start of a unit.

FORMATIVE ASSESSMENTS

Formative assessments are any assessments that take place in the **middle of a unit of instruction**. The goals of formative assessments are to help teachers understand where a student is in their progress toward **mastering** the current unit's content and to provide the students with **ongoing feedback** throughout the unit. The advantage of relying heavily on formative assessments in instruction is that it allows the teacher to continuously **check for comprehension** and adjust instruction as needed to ensure that the whole class is adequately prepared to proceed at the end of the unit. To understand formative assessments well, teachers need to understand that any interaction that can provide information about the student's comprehension is a type of formative assessment which can be used to inform future instruction.

Formative assessments are often a mixture of formal and informal assessments. **Formal formative assessments** often include classwork, homework, and quizzes. Examples of **informal formative assessments** include simple comprehension checks during instruction, class-wide discussions of the current topic, and exit slips, which are written questions posed by teachers at the end of class, which helps the teacher quickly review which students are struggling with the concepts.

SUMMATIVE ASSESSMENTS

Summative assessment refers to an evaluation at the end of a discrete unit of instruction, such as the end of a course, end of a unit, or end of a semester. Classic examples of summative assessments include end of course assessments, final exams, or even qualifying standardized tests such as the SAT or ACT. Most summative assessments are created to measure student mastery of particular **academic standards**. Whereas formative assessment generally informs current instruction, summative assessments are used to objectively demonstrate that each individual has achieved adequate mastery of the standards in question. If a student has not met the benchmark, they may need extra instruction or may need to repeat the course.

These assessments usually take the form of **tests** or formal portfolios with rubrics and clearly defined goals. Whatever form a summative takes, they are almost always high-stakes, heavily-weighted, and they should always be formally graded. These types of assessments often feature a narrower range of question types, such as multiple choice, short answer, and essay questions to help with systematic grading. Examples of summative assessments include state tests, end-of-unit or chapter tests, end-of-semester exams, and assessments that formally measure student mastery of topics against a established benchmarks.

Project-based assessments are beneficial in evaluating achievement, as they incorporate several elements of instruction and highlight real-world applications of learning. This allows students to demonstrate understanding through a hands-on, individualized approach that reinforces connections to learning and increases retainment. **Portfolios** of student work over time serve as a valuable method for assessing individual progress toward reaching learning targets. Summative assessments provide insight regarding overall instructional effectiveness and are necessary for guiding future instruction in subsequent years but are not usually used to modify current instruction.

> **Review Video: Formative and Summative Assessments**
> Visit mometrix.com/academy and enter code: 804991
>
> **Review Video: Assessment Reliability and Validity**
> Visit mometrix.com/academy and enter code: 424680

BENCHMARK ASSESSMENTS

Benchmark assessments are intended to quantify, evaluate, and compare individual and groups of students' achievement of school-wide, district, and state **academic standards.** They are typically administered in specific intervals throughout the school year and encompass entire or large units of curriculum to determine student mastery and readiness for academic advancement. Benchmark assessments provide data that enable the teacher to determine students' progress toward reaching academic goals to guide current and continued instruction. This data can be utilized by the school and individual teachers to create learning goals and objectives aligned with academic standards, as well as plan instructional strategies, activities, and assessments to support students in achieving them. In addition, benchmark assessments provide feedback regarding understanding and the potential need for remediation to allow the teacher to instill necessary supports in future instruction that prepare students for success in achieving learning targets.

ALIGNMENT OF ASSESSMENTS WITH INSTRUCTIONAL GOALS AND OBJECTIVES

To effectively monitor student progress, assessments must align with **instructional goals** and **objectives**. This allows the teacher to determine whether students are advancing at an appropriate pace to achieve state and district academic standards. When assessments are aligned with specific learning targets, the teacher ensures that students are learning relevant material to establish a foundation of knowledge necessary for growth and academic achievement. To achieve this, the teacher must determine which instructional goals and objectives their students must achieve and derive instruction, content, and activities from these specifications. Instruction must reflect and reinforce learning targets, and the teacher must select the most effective strategies for addressing students' needs as they work to achieve them. Assessments must be reflective of content instruction to ensure they are aligned with learning goals and objectives, as well as to enable the teacher to evaluate student progress in mastering them. The teacher must clearly communicate learning goals and objectives throughout all stages of instruction to provide students with clarity on expectations. This establishes a clear purpose and focus for learning that enhances relevancy and strengthens connections to support student achievement.

CLEARLY COMMUNICATING ASSESSMENT CRITERIA AND STANDARDS

Students must be clear on the purpose of learning throughout all stages of instruction to enhance understanding and facilitate success. When assessment **criteria** and **standards** are clearly communicated, the purpose of learning is established, and students are able to effectively connect instructional activities to learning goals and criteria for assessment. Communicating assessment criteria and standards provides students with clarity on tasks and learning goals they are expected to accomplish as they prepare themselves for assessment. This allows for more **focused instruction** and engagement in learning, as it enhances relevancy and student motivation. Utilizing appropriate forms of **rubrics** is an effective strategy in specifying assessment criteria and standards, as it informs students about learning goals they are working toward, the quality of work they are expected to achieve, and skills they must master to succeed on the assessment. Rubrics indicate to students exactly how they will be evaluated, thus supporting their understanding and focus as they engage in learning to promote academic success.

RUBRICS FOR COMMUNICATING STANDARDS

The following are varying styles of rubrics that can be used to communicate criteria and standards:

- **Analytic:** Analytic rubrics break down criteria for an assignment into several categories and provide an explanation of the varying levels of performance in each one. This style of rubric is beneficial for detailing the characteristics of quality work, as well as providing students with feedback regarding specific components of their performance. Analytic rubrics are most effective when used for summative assessments, such as long-term projects or essays.
- **Holistic:** Holistic rubrics evaluate the quality of the student's assignment as a whole, rather than scoring individual components. Students' score is determined based upon their performance across multiple performance indicators. This style of rubric is beneficial for providing a comprehensive evaluation but limits the amount of feedback that students receive regarding their performance in specific areas.
- **Single-Point:** Single point rubrics outline criteria for assignments into several categories. Rather than providing a numeric score to each category, however, the teacher provides written feedback regarding the students' strengths and ways in which they can improve their performance. This style of rubric is beneficial in providing student-centered feedback that focuses on their overall progress.
- **Checklist:** Checklists typically outline a set of criteria that is scored using a binary approach based upon completion of each component. This style increases the efficiency of grading assignments and is often easy for students to comprehend but does not provide detailed feedback. This method of grading should generally be reserved for shorter assignments.

COMMUNICATING HIGH ACADEMIC EXPECTATIONS IN ASSESSMENTS

The attitudes and behaviors exhibited by the teacher are highly influential on students' attitudes toward learning. Teachers demonstrate belief in students' abilities to be successful in learning when they communicate **high academic expectations**. This promotes students' **self-concept** and establishes a **growth mindset** to create confident, empowered learners that are motivated to achieve. High expectations for assessments and reaching academic standards communicates to students the quality of work that is expected of them and encourages them to overcome obstacles as they engage in learning. When communicating expectations for student achievement, it is important that the teacher is aware of students' individual learning needs to provide the necessary support that establishes equitable opportunities for success in meeting assessment criteria and standards. Setting high expectations through assessment criteria and standards while supporting students in their learning enhances overall achievement and establishes a foundation for continuous academic success.

EFFECTIVE COMMUNICATION AND IMPACT ON STUDENT LEARNING

Communicating high academic expectations enhances students' self-concept and increases personal motivation for success in learning. To maximize student achievement, it is important that the teacher set high academic expectations that are **clearly** communicated through **age-appropriate** terms and consistently reinforced. Expectations must be reflected through learning goals and objectives, and **visible** at all times to ensure student awareness. The teacher must be **specific** in communicating what they want students to accomplish and clearly detail necessary steps for achievement while assuming the role of facilitator to guide learning and provide support. Providing constructive **feedback** throughout instruction is integral in reminding students of academic expectations and ensuring they are making adequate progress toward reaching learning goals. When high academic expectations are communicated and reinforced, students are empowered with a sense of confidence and self-responsibility for their own learning that promotes their desire to learn. This ultimately enhances achievement and equips them with the tools necessary for future academic success.

ANALYZING AND INTERPRETING ASSESSMENT DATA

Teachers can utilize multiple techniques to effectively analyze and interpret assessment data. This typically involves creating charts and graphs outlining different data subsets. They can list each learning standard that was assessed, determine how many students overall demonstrated proficiency on the standard, and identify individual students who did not demonstrate proficiency on each standard. This information can be used to differentiate instruction. Additionally, they can track individual student performance and progress on each standard over time.

Teachers can take note of overall patterns and trends in assessment data. For example, they can determine if any subgroups of students did not meet expectations. They can consider whether the data confirms or challenges any existing beliefs, implications this may have on instructional planning and what, if any, conclusions can be drawn from this data.

Analyzing and interpreting assessment data may raise new questions for educators, so they can also determine if additional data collection is needed.

USING ASSESSMENT DATA TO DIFFERENTIATE INSTRUCTION FOR INDIVIDUAL LEARNERS

By analyzing and interpreting assessment data, teachers can determine if there are any specific learning standards that need to be retaught to their entire classes. This may be necessary if the data shows that all students struggled in these specific areas. Teachers may consider reteaching these standards using different methods if the initial methods were unsuccessful.

Teachers can also form groups of students who did not demonstrate proficiency on the same learning standards. Targeted instruction can be planned for these groups to help them make progress in these areas. Interventions can also be planned for individual students who did not show proficiency in certain areas. If interventions have already been in place and have not led to increased learning outcomes, the interventions may be redesigned. If interventions have been in place and assessment data now shows proficiency, the interventions may be discontinued.

If assessment data shows that certain students have met or exceeded expectations in certain areas, enrichment activities can be planned to challenge these students and meet their learning needs.

ALIGNING ASSESSMENTS WITH INSTRUCTIONAL GOALS AND OBJECTIVES

Assessments that are congruent to instructional goals and objectives provide a **clear purpose** for learning that enhances student understanding and motivation. When learning targets are reflected in assessments, instructional activities and materials become more **relevant**, as they are derived from these specifications. Such clarity in purpose allows for more focus and productivity as students engage in instruction and fosters connections that strengthen overall understanding for maximized success in learning. Aligning assessments with instructional goals and objectives ensures that students are learning material that is relevant to the curriculum and academic standards to ensure **preparedness** as they advance in their academic careers. In addition, it enables the teacher to evaluate and monitor student progress to determine whether they are progressing at an ideal pace for achieving academic standards. With this information, the teacher can effectively modify instruction as necessary to support students' needs in reaching desired learning outcomes.

NORM-REFERENCED TESTS

On **norm-referenced tests**, students' performances are compared to the performances of sample groups of similar students. Norm-referenced tests identify students who score above and below the average. To ensure reliability, the tests must be given in a standardized manner to all students.

Norm-referenced tests usually cover a broad range of skills, such as the entire grade-level curriculum for a subject. They typically contain a few questions per skill. Whereas scores in component areas of the tests may be calculated, usually overall test scores are reported. Scores are often reported using percentile ranks, which indicate what percentage of test takers scored lower than the student being assessed. For example, a student's score in the 75th percentile means the student scored better than 75% of other test takers. Other times, scores may be reported using grade-level equivalency.

One advantage of norm-referenced tests is their objectivity. They also allow educators to compare large groups of students at once. This may be helpful for making decisions regarding class placements and groupings. A disadvantage of norm-referenced tests is that they only indicate how well students perform in comparison to one another. They do not indicate whether or not students have mastered certain skills.

CRITERION-REFERENCED TESTS

Criterion-referenced tests measure how well students perform on certain skills or standards. The goal of these tests is to indicate whether or not students have mastered certain skills and which skills require additional instruction. Scores are typically reported using the percentage of questions answered correctly or students' performance levels. Performance levels are outlined using terms such as below expectations, met expectations, and exceeded expectations.

One advantage of criterion-referenced tests is they provide teachers with useful information to guide instruction. They can identify which specific skills students have mastered and which skills need additional practice. Teachers can use this information to plan whole-class, small-group, and individualized instruction. Analyzing results of criterion-referenced tests over time can also help teachers track student progress on certain skills. A disadvantage of criterion-referenced tests is they do not allow educators to compare students' performances to samples of their peers.

WAYS THAT STANDARDIZED TEST RESULTS ARE REPORTED

- **Raw scores** are sometimes reported and indicate how many questions students answered correctly on a test. By themselves, they do not provide much useful information. They do not indicate how students performed in comparison to other students or to grade-level expectations.

- **Grade-level equivalents** are also sometimes reported. A grade-level equivalent score of 3.4 indicates that a student performed as well as an average third grader in the fourth month of school. It can indicate whether a student is performing above or below grade-level expectations, but it does not indicate that the student should be moved to a different grade level.
- **Standard scores** are used to compare students' performances on tests to standardized samples of their peers. Standard deviation refers to the amount that a set of scores differs from the mean score on a test.
- **Percentile ranks** are used on criterion-referenced tests to indicate what percentage of test takers scored lower than the student whose score is being reported.
- **Cutoff scores** refer to predetermined scores students must obtain in order to be considered proficient in certain areas. Scores below the cutoff level indicate improvement is needed and may result in interventions or instructional changes.

FORMAL AND INFORMAL ASSESSMENTS

Assessments are any method a teacher uses to gather information about student comprehension of curriculum, including improvised questions for the class and highly-structured tests. **Formal assessments** are assessments that have **clearly defined standards and methodology**, and which are applied consistently to all students. Formal tests should be objective and the test itself should be scrutinized for validity and reliability since it tends to carry higher weight for the student. Summative assessments, such as end-of-unit tests, lend themselves to being formal tests because it is necessary that a teacher test the comprehension of all students in a consistent and thorough way.

Although formal assessments can provide useful data about student performance and progress, they can be costly and time-consuming to implement. Administering formal assessments often interrupts classroom instruction, and may cause testing anxiety.

Informal assessments are assessments that do not adhere to formal objectives and they do not have to be administered consistently to all students. As a result, they do not have to be scored or recorded as a grade and generally act as a **subjective measure** of class comprehension. Informal assessments can be as simple as asking a whole class to raise their hand if they are ready to proceed to the next step or asking a particular question of an individual student.

Informal assessments do not provide objective data for analysis, but they can be implemented quickly and inexpensively. Informal assessments can also be incorporated into regular classroom instruction and activities, making them more authentic and less stressful for students.

USING VARIOUS ASSESSMENTS

The goal of **assessment** in education is to gather data that, when evaluated, can be used to further student learning and achievement. **Standardized tests** are helpful for placement purposes and to reflect student progress toward goals set by a school district or state. If a textbook is chosen to align with district learning standards, the textbook assessments can provide teachers with convenient, small-scale, regular checks of student knowledge against the target standard.

In order be effective, teachers must know where their students are in the learning process. Teachers use a multitude of **formal and informal assessment methods** to do this. Posing differentiated discussion questions is an example of an informal assessment method that allows teachers to gauge individual student progress rather than their standing in relation to a universal benchmark.

Effective teachers employ a variety of assessments, as different formats assess different skills, promote different learning experiences, and appeal to different learners. A portfolio is an example of an assessment that gauges student progress in multiple skills and through multiple media. Teachers can use authentic or performance-based assessments to stimulate student interest and provide visible connections between language-learning and the real world.

ASSESSMENT RELIABILITY

Assessment reliability refers to how well an assessment is constructed and is made up of a variety of measures. An assessment is generally considered **reliable** if it yields similar results across multiple administrations of the assessment. A test should perform similarly with different test administrators, graders, and test-takers and perform consistently over multiple iterations. Factors that affect reliability include the day-to-day wellbeing of the student (students can sometimes underperform), the physical environment of the test, the way it is administered, and the subjectivity of the scorer (with written-response assessments).

Perhaps the most important threat to assessment reliability is the nature of the **exam questions** themselves. An assessment question is designed to test student knowledge of a certain construct. A question is reliable in this sense if students who understand the content answer the question correctly. Statisticians look for patterns in student marks, both within the single test and over multiple tests, as a way of measuring reliability. Teachers should watch out for circumstances in which a student or students answer correctly a series of questions about a given concept (demonstrating their understanding) but then answer a related question incorrectly. The latter question may be an unreliable indicator of concept knowledge.

MEASURES OF ASSESSMENT RELIABILITY

- **Test-retest reliability** refers to an assessment's consistency of results with the same test-taker over multiple retests. If one student shows inconsistent results over time, the test is not considered to have test-retest reliability.
- **Intertester reliability** refers to an assessment's consistency of results between multiple test-takers at the same level. Students at similar levels of proficiency should show similar results.
- **Interrater reliability** refers to an assessment's consistency of results between different administrators of the test. This plays an especially critical role in tests with interactive or subjective responses, such as Likert-scales, cloze tests, and short answer tests. Different raters of the same test need to have a consistent means of evaluating the test-takers' performance. Clear rubrics can help keep two or more raters consistent in scoring.
- **Intra-rater reliability** refers to an assessment's consistency of results with one rater over time. One test rater should be able to score different students objectively to rate subjective test formats fairly.
- **Parallel-forms reliability** refers to an assessment's consistency between multiple different forms. For instance, end-of-course assessments may have many distinctive test forms, with different questions or question orders. If the different forms of a test do not provide the same results, it is said to be lacking in parallel-forms reliability.
- **Internal consistency reliability** refers to the consistency of results of similar questions on a particular assessment. If there are two or more questions targeted at the same standard and at the same level, they should show the same results across each question.

ASSESSMENT VALIDITY

Assessment validity is a measure of the relevancy that an assessment has to the skill or ability being evaluated, and the degree to which students' performance is representative of their mastery of the topic of assessment. In other words, a teacher should ask how well an assessment's results correlate to what it is looking to assess. Assessments should be evaluated for validity on both the **individual question** level and as a **test overall**. This can be especially helpful in refining tests for future classes. The overall validity of an assessment is determined by several types of validity measures.

An assessment is considered **valid** if it measures what it is intended to measure. One common error that can reduce the validity of a test (or a question on a test) occurs if the instructions are written at a reading level the students can't understand. In this case, it is not valid to take the student's failed answer as a true indication of his or her knowledge of the subject. Factors internal to the student might also affect exam validity: anxiety and a lack of self-esteem often lower assessments results, reducing their validity of a measure of student knowledge.

An assessment has content validity if it includes all the **relevant aspects** of the subject being tested—if it is comprehensive, in other words. An assessment has **predictive validity** if a score on the test is an accurate predictor of future success in the same domain. For example, SAT exams purport to have validity in predicting student success in a college. An assessment has construct validity if it accurately measures student knowledge of the subject being tested.

MEASURES OF ASSESSMENT VALIDITY

- **Face validity** refers to the initial impression of whether an assessment seems to be fit for the task. As this method is subjective to interpretation and unquantifiable, it should not be used singularly as a measurement of validity.
- **Construct validity** asks if an assessment actually assesses what it is intended to assess. Some topics are more straightforward, such as assessing if a student can perform two-digit multiplication. This can be directly tested, which gives the assessment a strong content validity. Other measures, such as a person's overall happiness, must be measured indirectly. If an assessment asserted that a person is generally happy if they smile frequently, it would be fair to question the construct validity of that assessment because smiling is unlikely to be a consistent measure of all peoples' general happiness.
- **Content validity** indicates whether the assessment is comprehensive of all aspects of the content being assessed. If a test leaves out an important topic, then the teacher will not have a full picture as a result of the assessment.
- **Criterion validity** refers to whether the results of an assessment can be used to **predict** a related value, known as **criterion**. An example of this is the hypothesis that IQ tests would predict a person's success later in life, but many critics believe that IQ tests are not valid predictors of success because intelligence is not the only predictor of success in life. IQ tests have shown validity toward predicting academic success, however. The measure of an assessment's criterion validity depends on how closely related the criterion is.
- **Discriminant validity** refers to how well an assessment tests only that which it is intended to test and successfully discriminates one piece of information from another. For instance, a student who is exceptional in mathematics should not be able to put that information into use on a science test and gain an unfair advantage. If they are able to score well due to their mathematics knowledge, the science test did not adequately discriminate science knowledge from mathematics knowledge.
- **Convergent validity** is related to discriminant validity, but takes into account that two measures may be distinct, but can be correlated. For instance, a personality test should distinguish self-esteem from extraversion so that they can be measured independently, but if an assessment has convergent validity, it should show a correlation between related measures.

PRACTICALITY

An assessment is **practical** if it uses an appropriate amount of human and budgetary resources. A practical exam doesn't take very long to design or score, nor does it take students very long to complete in relation to other learning objectives and priorities. Teachers often need to balance a desire to construct comprehensive or content-valid tests with a need for practicality: lengthy exams consume large amounts of instruction time and may return unreliable results if students become tired and lose focus.

ASSESSMENT BIAS

An assessment is considered biased if it disadvantages a certain group of students, such as students of a certain gender, race, cultural background, or socioeconomic class. A **content bias** exists when the subject matter of a question or assessment is familiar to one group and not another—for example, a reading comprehension passage which discusses an event in American history would be biased against students new to the country. An **attitudinal bias** exists when a teacher has a pre-conceived idea about the likely success of an assessment of a particular individual or group. A **method bias** arises when the format of an assessment is unfamiliar to a given group of students. **Language bias** occurs when an assessment utilizes idioms, collocations, or cultural references unfamiliar to a group of students. Finally, **translation bias** may arise when educators attempt to translate content-area assessments into a student's native language—rough or hurried translations often result in a loss of nuance important for accurate assessment.

AUTHENTIC ASSESSMENTS

An authentic assessment is an assessment designed to closely resemble something that a student does, or will do, in the real world. Thus, for example, students will never encounter a multiple-choice test requiring them to choose the right tense of a verb, but they will encounter context in which they have to write a narration of an event that has antecedents and consequents spread out in time—for example, their version of what caused a traffic accident. The latter is an example of a potential **authentic assessment**.

Well-designed authentic assessments require a student to exercise **advanced cognitive skills** (e.g., solving problems, integrating information, performing deductions), integrate **background knowledge**, and confront **ambiguity**. Research has demonstrated that mere language proficiency is not predictive of future language success—learning how to utilize knowledge in a complex context is an essential additional skill.

The terms "authentic" and "performance-based" assessments are often used interchangeably. However, a performance-based assessment doesn't necessarily have to be grounded in a possible authentic experience.

PERFORMANCE-BASED ASSESSMENTS

A performance-based assessment is one in which students demonstrate their learning by performing a **task** rather than by answering questions in a traditional test format. Proponents of **performance-based assessments** argue that they lead students to use **high-level cognitive skills** as they focus on how to put their knowledge to use and plan a sequence of stages in an activity or presentation. They also allow students more opportunities to individualize their presentations or responses based on preferred learning styles. Research suggests that students welcome the chance to put their knowledge to use in real-world scenarios.

Advocates of performance-based assessments suggest that they avoid many of the problems of language or cultural bias present in traditional assessments, and thus they allow more accurate assessment of how well students learned the underlying concepts. In discussions regarding English as a second language, they argue that performance assessments come closer to replicating what should be the true goal of language learning—the effective use of language in real contexts—than do more traditional exams. Critics point out that performance assessments are difficult and time-consuming for teachers to construct and for students to perform. Finally, performative assessments are difficult to grade in the absence of a well-constructed and detailed rubric.

TECHNOLOGY-BASED ASSESSMENTS

Technology-based assessments provide teachers with multiple resources for evaluating student progress to guide instruction. They are applicable in most formal and informal instructional settings and can be utilized as formative and summative assessments. Technology-based assessments simplify and enhance the efficiency of determining comprehension and instructional effectiveness, as they quickly present the teacher with information regarding student progress. This data enables the teacher to make necessary adjustments to facilitate student learning and growth. Implementing this assessment format simplifies the process of aligning them to school and district academic standards. This establishes objectivity and uniformity for comparing results and progress among students, as well as ensures that all students are held to the same academic expectations. While technology-based assessments are beneficial, there are some shortcomings to consider. This format may not be entirely effective for all learning styles in demonstrating understanding, as individualization in technology-based assessment can be limited. These assessments may not illustrate individual students' growth over time, but rather their mastery of an academic standard, thus hindering the ability to evaluate overall achievement. As technology-based evaluation limits hands-on opportunities, the real-world application and relevancy of the assessment may be unapparent to students.

ADVANTAGES AND DISADVANTAGES OF TECHNOLOGY-BASED ASSESSMENTS

Technology-based assessments can have many advantages. They can be given to large numbers of students at once, limited only by the amounts of technological equipment schools possess. Many types of technology-based assessments are instantly scored, and feedback is quickly provided. Students are sometimes able to view their results and feedback at the conclusion of their testing sessions. Data can be quickly compiled and reported in easy-to-understand formats. Technology-based assessments can also often track student progress over time.

Technology-based assessments can have some disadvantages as well. Glitches and system errors can interfere with the assessment process or score reporting. Students must also have the necessary prerequisite technological skills to take the assessments, or the results may not measure the content they are designed to measure. For example, if students take timed computer-based writing tests, they should have proficient typing skills. Otherwise, they may perform poorly on the tests despite strong writing abilities. Other prerequisite skills include knowing how to use a keyboard and mouse and understanding how to locate necessary information on the screen.

PORTFOLIO ASSESSMENTS

A **portfolio** is a collection of student work in multiple forms and media gathered over time. Teachers may assess the portfolio both for evidence of progress over time or in its end state as a demonstration of the achievement of certain proficiency levels.

One advantage of **portfolio assessments** is their breadth—unlike traditional assessments which focus on one or two language skills, portfolios may contain work in multiple forms—writing samples, pictures, and graphs designed for content courses, video and audio clips, student reflections, teacher observations, and student exams. A second advantage is that they allow a student to develop work in authentic contexts, including in other classrooms and at home.

In order for portfolios to function as an objective assessment tool, teachers should negotiate with students in advance of what genres of work will be included and outline a grading rubric that makes clear what will be assessed, such as linguistic proficiency, use of English in academic contexts, and demonstrated use of target cognitive skills.

CURRICULUM-BASED ASSESSMENTS

Curriculum-based assessments, also known as **curriculum-based measurements (CBM)**, are short, frequent assessments designed to measure student progress toward meeting curriculum **benchmarks**.

Teachers implement CBM by designing **probes**, or short assessments that target specific skills. For example, a teacher might design a spelling probe, administered weekly, that requires students to spell 10 unfamiliar but level-appropriate words. Teachers then track the data over time to measure student progress toward defined grade-level goals.

CBM has several clear advantages. If structured well, the probes have high reliability and validity. Furthermore, they provide clear and objective evidence of student progress—a welcome outcome for students and parents who often grapple with less-clear and subjective evidence. Used correctly, CBMs also motivate students and provide them with evidence of their own progress. However, while CBMs are helpful in identifying *areas* of student weaknesses, they do not identify the *causes* of those weaknesses or provide teachers with strategies for improving instruction.

TEXTBOOK ASSESSMENTS

Textbook assessments are the assessments provided at the end of a chapter or unit in an approved textbook. **Textbook assessments** present several advantages for a teacher: they are already made; they are likely to be accurate representations of the chapter or unit materials; and, if the textbook has been prescribed or recommended by the state, it is likely to correspond closely to Common Core or other tested standards.

Textbook assessments can be limiting for students who lag in the comprehension of academic English, or whose preferred learning style is not verbal. While textbooks may come with DVDs or recommended audio links, ESOL teachers will likely need to supplement these assessment materials with some of their own findings. Finally, textbook assessments are unlikely to represent the range of assessment types used in the modern classroom, such as a portfolio or performance-based assessments.

PEER ASSESSMENT

A peer assessment is when students grade one another's work based on a teacher-provided framework. **Peer assessments** are promoted as a means of saving teacher time and building student metacognitive skills. They are typically used as **formative** rather than summative assessments, given concerns about the reliability of student scoring and the tensions that can result if student scores contribute to overall grades. Peer assessments are used most often to grade essay-type written work or presentations. Proponents point out that peer assessments require students to apply metacognition, builds cooperative work and interpersonal skills, and broadens the sense that the student is accountable to peers and not just the teacher. Even advocates of the practice agree that students need detailed rubrics in order to succeed. Critics often argue that low-performing students have little to offer high-performing students in terms of valuable feedback—and this disparity may be more pronounced in ESOL classrooms or special education environments than in mainstream ones. One way to overcome this weakness is for the teacher to lead the evaluation exercise, guiding the students through a point-by-point framework of evaluation.

The Role of Assessment in Education

ROLES OF ASSESSMENT

INSTRUCTIONAL PLANNING FOR INDIVIDUALS AND GROUPS

Effective assessments provide valuable feedback to teachers on how to design and adjust instruction for individuals and groups. Both **formative** and **summative** assessments give insight into student understanding and needs before and after content material is taught. As instruction should be designed based on students' individual needs, assessment provides the information necessary to effectively do so. **Diagnostic** assessments provide teachers with pertinent information about students' individual background knowledge, experiences, and learning needs, thus allowing them to understand students' skills and abilities to focus and plan future instruction accordingly. Additionally, assessments provide teachers with feedback on student progress and areas of individual need that drive instructional planning in allowing teachers to more effectively plan curriculum that is tailored to students' individual needs, skills, and abilities. Assessments inform future instruction through highlighting concepts that students are not understanding for reteaching. Furthermore, it allows them to group students more effectively in future planning to provide scaffolding and ensure that all students are supported in achieving academic standards.

PROVIDING TEACHER ACCOUNTABILITY AND EVALUATING TEACHER EFFECTIVENESS

Teachers are responsible for ensuring that all students are properly supported in achieving lesson objectives, instructional goals, and state academic standards. Thus, they are responsible for effectively designing and implementing instruction, lessons, and activities that are tailored to meet individual students' needs as they work to achieve learning outcomes. Assessments provide feedback regarding student mastery of academic standards and are reflective of the effectiveness of the instructional practices and strategies implemented to support them in their achievement. Consequently, student achievement on assessments reflects and measures the effectiveness of the teacher in designing instructional materials that meet individual students' needs, foster engagement and understanding, and facilitate desired learning outcomes. When the teacher is evaluated based on student assessment results, they are held accountable for developing effective instruction and identifying areas for improvement in their teaching practice.

ASSESSMENT METHODS AND APPLICATIONS FOR ANALYZING STUDENTS' STRENGTHS AND NEEDS

Instructional assessment takes many forms, and each method has different applications and provides distinct feedback for analyzing students' strengths and needs. All forms of assessment should be incorporated in order to develop comprehensive instruction that is tailored to students' individual strengths and needs. **Formative assessments** are an informal, ongoing method of measuring student understanding throughout a lesson. They are valuable in allowing the teacher to adjust and adapt instructional practices and strategies to individual student needs as necessary as they move through a lesson. **Summative assessments** generally occur at the end of a lesson or unit and are intended to measure student achievement of a particular objective or instructional goal. These assessments allow teachers to identify students' individual strengths and needs, and influence future instruction by highlighting areas of understanding or misconception for reteaching. **Standardized assessments** reflect student mastery of state academic standards and illustrate whether students have met academic benchmarks for their grade level. The results of these assessments can be applied to identify students' strengths and needs to determine the starting point of future instruction and proper grouping of students based on skills, needs, and abilities.

USE OF STATE STANDARDS AND ASSESSMENTS
INSTRUCTION DEVELOPMENT

Effective instruction is driven by state standards and assessment. State academic standards serve as a framework for grade level academic benchmarks that students are expected to achieve during the school year. From these, teachers derive instructional goals and objectives, and ultimately, determine instruction, activities, and materials that will support students in academic achievement. Additionally, teachers use state standards as assessment criteria to monitor student progress and evaluate how successfully students are reaching them. These assessments provide feedback to teachers that influence future instruction through allowing them to identify areas of misconception that require reteaching or individual student need. State standardized assessments influence the development of instruction in that student achievement on these assessments indicates their level of success in meeting academic targets. They highlight areas of strength and need among students, providing teachers with a framework for effectively designing instruction to address these needs and support students in meeting academic goals.

EVALUATING STUDENT PROGRESS, STRENGTHS, AND NEEDS

State and classroom assessments provide data that allow the teacher to effectively analyze whole-class and individual student performance in meeting learning targets to determine further instructional planning. Whole-class achievement on assessments is indicative of the effectiveness of learning objectives, instructional strategies, and lesson activities in supporting students' achievement of academic standards. Whole-class assessments also provide insight on areas for improvement and reteaching. Individually, in analyzing where students fall on a bell curve for assessment, teachers can effectively identify specific strengths and needs of students to determine instructional planning. This information indicates student progress and where they may need additional support, which allows teachers to better meet students' individual needs in planning future instruction by implementing strategies which are tailored to their skills and abilities.

The Learning Environment

ESTABLISHING A POSITIVE, PRODUCTIVE CLASSROOM ENVIRONMENT
UNIQUE CHARACTERISTICS AND NEEDS OF STUDENTS AT VARYING DEVELOPMENTAL LEVELS

Students at each developmental level possess unique characteristics and needs that must be met in the classroom to ensure productivity and a positive classroom environment. For successful learning, the teacher must recognize the nuances of varying developmental levels to properly understand their students' abilities and design instruction accordingly. When the teacher is attuned to the distinct characteristics and needs of their students, they can align **curriculum, instructional strategies, activities,** and **assessments** in a way that is accessible and comprehensible to all students. This understanding enables the teacher to deliver instruction at a **pace** appropriate to students' developmental stage while ensuring they are challenged across domains based upon their ability for continuous whole-child development. In addition, knowledge of the general characteristics and needs of developmental stages enables the teacher to effectively identify and accommodate individual variances that occur within these stages for **student-centered** learning. When instruction is tailored to address the needs of varying developmental stages and individual differences, students feel supported in their learning. This ultimately fosters increased self-esteem, student engagement, and positive attitudes toward learning that contribute to an overall productive and successful classroom environment.

ADDRESSING DEVELOPMENTAL CHARACTERISTICS AND NEEDS OF YOUNGER STUDENTS

A positive and productive classroom environment for younger children requires the teacher to understand the intricacies of this developmental stage and implement strategies accordingly to promote success in learning. Younger students learn by **exploring** and **interacting** with the world around them and must be provided with multiple opportunities to do so. **Play** is integral to young students' development across domains. Therefore, both planned and free play should be incorporated throughout instruction. Play enables students to explore their environment and make connections that strengthen their learning while promoting the development of problem-solving and higher-order thinking skills. In addition, allowing frequent opportunities for play facilitates the acquisition of important social and emotional skills, such as cooperation, conflict resolution, and sharing. Likewise, incorporating frequent **movement** throughout lessons allows young students to explore their physical space and actively engage in learning for deeper understanding. Additionally, **cooperative learning** strategies encourage the development of necessary social and emotional skills and are important in teaching young children how to effectively work with others to solve a problem. When the teacher implements strategies appropriate to younger students' developmental levels, it enhances motivation, active engagement, and promotes positive attitudes toward learning for a productive classroom environment.

COLLABORATIVE OPPORTUNITIES IN ADDRESSING DEVELOPMENTAL CHARACTERISTICS AND NEEDS OF MIDDLE-LEVEL STUDENTS

Middle-level students experience significant developmental changes as they approach adolescence and therefore, have unique characteristics and needs that must be met to ensure a positive and productive learning environment. **Collaborative opportunities** are beneficial in supporting the development of cognitive, social, and emotional skills of middle-level students and should be implemented frequently. This strategy enables these students to work productively with others and promotes the development of positive **interpersonal** and **communication** skills. This is especially important in middle-level education, as students at this developmental stage begin forming their identities, attitudes toward learning, and influential peer relationships. Middle-level students build **self-confidence** through collaborative learning, as it enables them to develop positive leadership skills. Additionally, collaborative opportunities expose students to the varying backgrounds and perspectives of their classmates, thus fostering appreciation for individual differences and contributing to a positive classroom climate. Collaborative learning is also beneficial for **cognitive development**, as it allows students to build upon one another's background knowledge for enhanced learning and encourages critical and higher-order thinking while working together to solve a problem. Providing middle-level students with collaborative opportunities increases overall engagement for a positive and productive classroom environment, as well as develops necessary skills for successful transition into adolescence.

PROMOTING RESPECT FOR THE COMMUNITY AND PEOPLE IN IT AMONG OLDER STUDENTS

As older students prepare for adulthood, it is important that they develop a respect for their community and the people in it. Implementing strategies to facilitate this is vital in equipping older students with **real-world skills** necessary to become productive contributors to society. By self-educating and modeling respect for the community and its people, the teacher can influence students to adopt the same sentiment. Establishing a positive community within the classroom through such activities as class meetings, discussions, and cultural activities promotes respect for others that extends to real-world situations. Strategies that demonstrate connection to the community strengthen students' overall respect and responsibility for it. This can be achieved by incorporating **authentic materials**, including news stories, art, music, and relevant speakers, to develop students' understanding and insight regarding the characteristics and needs of the community. Encouraging students to bring items from home to share fosters appreciation for their community by exposing them to the backgrounds and perspectives within it. **Community service** projects such as fundraisers, food drives, and service field trips further promote students' respect for their community while demonstrating the real-world applications of their learning. This ultimately makes learning meaningful and contributes to a positive, productive learning environment.

POSITIVE CLASSROOM CLIMATE

Classroom climate refers to the overall atmosphere that the teacher establishes and is powerful in determining the nature of the learning experience. Students are most successful in their learning when the climate is positive, encouraging, and focused on creating a collaborative, supportive community. A positive classroom climate is **welcoming, inclusive**, and **respectful** of all individuals. Instruction is delivered in an engaging, comprehensible way in a structured, orderly, and safe environment. The atmosphere is **visually appealing** and stimulating, yet not overwhelming, and is physically arranged in a way that maximizes learning. **Collaboration** and **supportive interactions** are encouraged throughout the learning process to enhance engagement and develop positive social and emotional skills. Such an environment builds students' self-esteem and confidence by ensuring they feel safe and empowered to participate and work with others in the learning process. In addition, it encourages positive attitudes toward learning that are necessary for active student engagement and productivity. When the classroom climate is positive, students are more self-motivated, thus strengthening their learning and promoting academic achievement.

COLLABORATION AND SUPPORTIVE INTERACTIONS

Collaboration and **supportive interactions** are key components of a positive classroom climate and should be integrated throughout instruction to promote active engagement and success in learning for all students. To achieve this, the teacher must establish a classroom community focused on respect, inclusiveness, and open dialogue. This ensures students feel safe and empowered to express themselves and interact constructively. By teaching and **modeling** active listening skills, the teacher can demonstrate and influence respectful communication in the classroom. **Team-building activities**, including class meetings, games, and discussions, are valuable strategies for creating a community that encourages productive collaboration and supportive interactions. In addition, establishing **clear expectations** for positive communication and involving students in their creation instills a sense of personal responsibility to adhere to them when working with others. Once expectations are understood, students must be provided with multiple and varied **collaborative learning** opportunities to continuously practice developing positive interpersonal skills. As students participate in learning, the teacher must be sure to consistently praise cooperation and positive interactions to reinforce the standards of communication. When the teacher promotes collaboration and supportive interactions, they create a positive classroom climate that increases students' productivity and self-motivation to actively participate in learning for maximized achievement.

RESPECT FOR DIVERSITY AND INDIVIDUAL DIFFERENCES

An emphasis on respect for **diversity** and **individual differences** in the classroom is necessary to establish a positive, productive learning atmosphere. Teaching and modeling this sentiment to students instills the notion that everyone has unique and valuable experiences, perspectives, and characteristics to contribute to the classroom community. Emphasizing respect for all individuals ensures students feel validated and secure in their own identities while teaching them to appreciate diversities among their classmates. Such an environment promotes collaboration and supportive interactions, as it is built on a foundation of welcoming, inclusiveness, and acceptance that empowers students to confidently interact with peers as they engage in learning. When students feel respected, it increases their self-esteem and positive self-concept. Students that feel confident in the classroom are more likely to develop positive attitudes toward learning. This ultimately fosters a positive classroom climate in which students are motivated to actively engage in instruction and achieve academic success.

IMPACT OF INTERACTIONS ON CLASSROOM CLIMATE
TEACHER-STUDENT INTERACTIONS

Interactions between teachers and their students play a significant role in determining overall classroom climate and the quality of the learning experience. The way in which the teacher interacts with students influences their **social**, **emotional**, and **cognitive development**, as well as sets the tone for how students interact with each other. This ultimately shapes students' **self-esteem** and contributes to their level of engagement, attitude toward learning, and academic achievement. Therefore, it is important that the teacher ensure all interactions with students on a whole-class and individual level are positive, unbiased, encouraging, and respectful of each individual. Working to build relationships with students demonstrates a genuine interest in their lives that contributes to a positive, productive classroom climate in which students feel welcomed, accepted, and empowered to actively engage in learning. Positive interactions between the teacher and students support a healthy sense of self-esteem as well as positive social and emotional skills that contribute to cognitive development. Students with greater self-esteem are more likely to develop positive attitudes toward learning that foster increased self-motivation to actively participate in learning, thus contributing to enhanced academic achievement.

STUDENTS' INTERACTIONS WITH ONE ANOTHER

The classroom climate is dependent on the nature of **students' interactions** with one another. These interactions largely determine the quality of student learning as well as development across domains. Positive communication facilitates the development of healthy **social** and emotional skills that serve to enhance cognitive development. Students with strong social and **emotional skills** are often more motivated to actively participate in learning and are more productive in collaborative situations, as they can build upon one another's knowledge. Therefore, the teacher must implement a variety of strategies to ensure interactions among students are positive, respectful, and supportive to establish a classroom climate focused on productive learning. **Community building** exercises establish a climate built on positive and supportive communication while demonstrating the benefits of productive cooperation in achieving a goal. Teaching and **modeling** positive communication skills sets the tone and expectations for how students will interact with one another. Students should be given **frequent opportunities** to interact both during and outside of instructional time to promote the development of necessary interpersonal skills for healthy social development. In addition, **strategic student groupings** during collaborative work and consistent monitoring help ensure maximized productivity and that the standards for communication are reinforced.

COMMUNICATING AN ENTHUSIASM FOR LEARNING
ESTABLISHING ENVIRONMENTS PROMOTING POSITIVE ATTITUDES TOWARD LEARNING

The nature of the classroom environment is reliant on the **efforts**, **behaviors**, and **attitudes** of the teacher. The teacher is responsible for setting the tone of the classroom, which determines the overall climate and has significant impacts on the quality and effectiveness of the learning experience. The classroom environment influences students' engagement, positive communication, and attitudes toward learning, which contribute to their overall academic achievement. Successful teaching and learning require the teacher to intentionally take measures to establish a welcoming, accepting, and encouraging classroom environment that promotes excitement and positive attitudes toward learning. Teachers must model genuine respect for their students and enthusiasm for learning, as well as present instruction in a way that is engaging, comprehensible, and responsive to students' needs and interests. The physical classroom must be arranged in such a way that is visually appealing, safe, and facilitative of productive learning. It is also important that the teacher establish and consistently reinforce structured routines, procedures, and behavioral expectations to contribute to an overall positive climate and ensure students feel secure and willing to participate in learning. When the classroom environment is exciting, positive, and engaging, it encourages positive attitudes toward learning that increase motivation to succeed.

INFLUENCE ON STUDENTS' MOTIVATION, PRODUCTIVITY, AND ACADEMIC ACHIEVEMENT

Modeling is perhaps one of the most powerful strategies in influencing students' attitudes, behaviors, and actions in the classroom. As students spend a great deal of time with their teachers, the level of enthusiasm for learning demonstrated by the teacher inevitably influences their own excitement in the classroom. Therefore, the teacher must conscientiously model enthusiasm for teaching and learning to positively influence students' internal motivation for productivity, learning, and achievement. Students are highly perceptive, and as such, if the teacher appears unmotivated in their practice or disinterested in the content, students will likely adopt the same sentiment and become disengaged or apathetic toward learning. The enthusiasm modeled by the teacher must be **authentic** to elicit the same genuine interest in learning from students. When the teacher demonstrates sincere excitement about the content they are teaching, it prompts curiosity for learning among students that enhances their motivation and attitudes toward learning. In addition, modeling enthusiasm for teaching and learning enhances the relationship between the teacher and students, thus contributing to a positive classroom climate that makes students excited to learn. When students have a positive attitude toward learning, they are more motivated to productively engage in learning and achieve academic success.

METHODS AND IMPACT ON CLASSROOM CLIMATE AND STUDENT ENGAGEMENT

Communicating sincere enthusiasm for teaching and learning is essential to establishing a positive, productive classroom climate focused on student engagement and achievement. Students' interest and excitement for learning are directly reflective of the sentiments exhibited by the teacher. As such, it is important that the teacher intentionally and consistently communicate excitement for their practice and content. To achieve this, the teacher must ensure that their **behaviors**, **actions**, **language**, **tone of voice**, and **interactions** with students are positive in nature. By working to build positive **interpersonal relationships** with students and demonstrating genuine interest in their lives, experiences, interests, and needs, the teacher can effectively communicate enthusiasm for their practice that motivates students to engage in learning. This is further reflected in the physical **classroom arrangement**. A classroom that is visually appealing, stimulating, and reflective of students' interests and achievements illustrates the teacher's enthusiasm and promotes a positive classroom climate in which students are excited and motivated to engage in learning.

CONVEYING HIGH EXPECTATIONS FOR ALL STUDENTS

SIGNIFICANCE IN PROMOTING PRODUCTIVITY, ACTIVE ENGAGEMENT, AND SUCCESS IN LEARNING

Communicating **high academic** and **behavioral expectations** is necessary for establishing a classroom climate focused on productivity, active engagement, and achievement. Students are heavily influenced by the teacher's expectations for them, and therefore, when high learning standards are set, students will more likely strive to achieve them. High expectations increase the **relevancy** of learning by focusing instruction and providing a clear purpose that motivates students to participate. In addition, by conveying high expectations, the teacher demonstrates a **belief in their students' abilities** to overcome personal challenges and achieve success. This notion promotes a **growth mindset** among students, which is the belief that intelligence is not inherent, but rather, can be attained and consistently improved upon. This enhances students' self-esteem and confidence, which promotes positive attitudes toward learning that foster active engagement, productivity, and success. Communicating high expectations while providing necessary supports motivates students to challenge themselves academically and gives them a sense of self-responsibility over their learning that encourages them to work to their highest potential. This ultimately creates a positive classroom climate in which students feel supported and empowered to productively engage in learning and achieve success.

STRATEGIES AND IMPACT ON CLASSROOM CLIMATE AND STUDENT ACHIEVEMENT

Communicating **high academic** and **behavioral expectations** is most effective when done so through a variety of means. This ensures that students are aware of the teacher's expectations of them and consistently reinforces high standards to establish a positive classroom climate focused on student motivation, productivity, and achievement. Expectations must always be **clear** and **visible** in the classroom, and the teacher must frequently remind students by restating them throughout instruction. Establishing learning goals and objectives that are challenging, yet attainable based on students' abilities effectively communicates high expectations and the teacher's belief that students can achieve them. This is further iterated when students encounter challenges and rather than lowering expectations, the teacher maintains the same high standards while providing necessary supports for achievement. The teacher can also communicate high expectations by ensuring they provide students with timely, clear, and constructive **feedback** on their progress and ways in which they can improve to meet them. Frequent **communication with families** is beneficial in reinforcing academic and behavioral expectations at home to ensure student awareness and maximize their effectiveness in the classroom.

LITERACY-RICH ENVIRONMENT

A **literacy-rich** classroom focuses on the development of all literacy components by immersing students in reading, writing, speaking, and listening skills across subject areas. While all students benefit from such an environment, it is especially important for **ELL students** and students with **developmental disabilities** in acquiring the literacy and language skills necessary for success. In a literacy-rich environment, the teacher provides multiple opportunities to engage in teacher-led and student-selected reading, writing, speaking, and listening activities in all areas of instruction. Students may be asked to solve word problems in math, write a report on a famous artist in art, or keep an observation log in science to encourage literacy development across content areas. Students are provided with multiple print and digital literacy materials on a variety of topics with varying levels of complexity to accommodate individual developmental levels while encouraging reading, vocabulary acquisition, and listening skills. Additionally, the teacher surrounds students with **print-rich** materials, including posters, word walls, labels, and bulletin boards on a variety of topics to further promote literacy development. A literacy-rich environment continuously promotes and emphasizes the importance of literacy skills in all areas of life that serve as a necessary foundation for academic and real-world success.

> **Review Video: Importance of Promoting Literacy in the Home**
> Visit mometrix.com/academy and enter code: 862347
>
> **Review Video: Characteristics of Literacy-Rich, Content-Area Classrooms**
> Visit mometrix.com/academy and enter code: 571455

SAFE, NURTURING, AND INCLUSIVE CLASSROOM ENVIRONMENT

A safe, nurturing, and inclusive classroom environment focuses on meeting students' emotional needs for healthy development in this domain. The overall climate in such an environment is welcoming and emphasizes **respect**, **acceptance**, and **positive communication** among the teacher and students. The classroom is brightly decorated and reflective of students' diversities, interests, and achievements to promote a sense of security and inclusivity that motivates active participation in learning. Instructional activities are also reflective of students' differences, learning styles, and interests, with necessary supports instilled to accommodate individual learning needs. This establishes an **equitable environment** that ensures all students feel respected, nurtured, and supported both academically and emotionally. Such an environment is **structured** and orderly with clear expectations, procedures, and routines to foster a sense of security as students engage in learning. Collaboration and supportive interactions among students are encouraged to create a positive, productive classroom community in which students feel confident to express themselves and participate in learning. A classroom environment that is safe, nurturing, and inclusive develops students' sense of self-concept that contributes to positive communication, relationships, and attitudes necessary for emotional development.

DEVELOPING STUDENTS' EMOTIONAL INTELLIGENCE

Emotional intelligence refers to the ability to recognize and regulate one's own emotions as well as identify and empathetically respond to the emotions of others. Developing this skill through a variety of strategies is integral to successful development across other domains. By **modeling** such skills as empathy and active listening, the teacher can influence students' abilities to identify and properly respond to their own and other's emotions. Teaching **coping strategies**, including journaling, breathing, or counting techniques, promotes students' self-regulation to manage emotions when faced with a conflict or challenge. Teaching emotional intelligence can also be integrated throughout instruction, such as prompting students to describe the feelings of a character in a book, or discuss emotions evoked from a painting. Students with strong emotional intelligence are likely to develop positive interpersonal relationships for healthy social development. This contributes to improved cognitive development in that when students collaborate productively, they build upon one another's knowledge. Emotionally intelligent students are also likely to have positive attitudes toward learning, as they have the capacity to self-regulate when faced with obstacles and properly engage in instruction for enhanced cognitive development.

MEETING AND RESPECTING STUDENTS' EMOTIONAL NEEDS, INDIVIDUAL RIGHTS, AND DIGNITY

Successful learning and **whole-child** development are reliant on the degree to which students' emotional needs, individual rights, and dignity are met and respected in the classroom. This establishes the tone of the overall classroom climate that determines students' sense of safety, nurturing, and inclusion when interacting with others and engaging in learning. By taking measures to prioritize students' emotional needs and create a respectful, accepting classroom community, the teacher establishes a positive learning atmosphere that promotes cognitive, social, and emotional growth for whole-child development. When students feel emotionally supported and respected in their identities, they develop a healthy sense of self-esteem that positively influences their attitude toward learning and motivation to participate. This ultimately impacts **cognitive development**, as students that actively and confidently engage in learning are more likely to be academically successful. These students are also more effectively able to develop important interpersonal communication skills necessary for healthy **social development**, as students that feel secure and accepted are more likely to be supportive of others. By meeting students' emotional needs and respecting their individual rights and dignities, the teacher effectively prepares students with the skills necessary for academic and real-world success.

Classroom Routines and Procedures

CLASSROOM ROUTINES AND PROCEDURES
INFLUENCE ON CLASSROOM CLIMATE, PRODUCTIVITY, STUDENT BEHAVIOR, AND LEARNING

A well-managed classroom focused on productivity, positive behavior, and success in learning relies on the effectiveness and consistency of **routines** and **procedures** instilled for daily activities. By implementing these at the beginning of the school year and continuously reinforcing them throughout, the teacher establishes an orderly, efficient classroom that facilitates students' ability to productively engage in learning. Classroom management, and therefore, student behavior and productivity, is enhanced by structured routines and procedures, as students that are clear on expectations are more inclined to follow them. Such structure provides students with a sense of predictability and security in their environment that contributes to their willingness to participate in learning. Routines and procedures simplify daily tasks and allow for smooth transitions between activities. This minimizes opportunities for student distraction or disruption, thus promoting positive behavior, increasing instructional time, and enhancing students' ability to focus on learning in an orderly, productive classroom climate.

> **Review Video: Classroom Management - Rhythms of Teaching**
> Visit mometrix.com/academy and enter code: 809399

CONSIDERATIONS REGARDING AGE-APPROPRIATENESS TO ENSURE EFFECTIVENESS

Classroom procedures and routines must reflect the characteristics and capabilities of the students' **age group**. It is important that the teacher understand and apply their knowledge of students' **developmental levels** across domains when considering which routines and procedures to establish in their classroom. In doing so, the teacher ensures that expectations are age-appropriate, realistic, and effective in creating an orderly, productive environment. Procedures and routines must always be clear, succinct, and limited in number to avoid overwhelming students. However, in communicating them, the teacher must use comprehensible language relative to students' age-group. The nature of learning must be considered when determining age-appropriate routines and procedures. For young children, procedures for cleaning up toys after playtime is appropriate, whereas procedures for turning in homework and taking assessments applies to older students. The degree to which students are expected to perform routines and procedures independently must also be considered and reflective of their capabilities. Young children may need a great deal of assistance, whereas older students can perform certain tasks independently. Consequences for not following expectations must be appropriate to students' age group. Losing free play time may be appropriate for young children, whereas parent communication may be effective for older students.

EXAMPLES OF AGE-APPROPRIATE ROUTINES AND PROCEDURES

Young children: Young children can reasonably be expected to perform **basic daily routines** independently, although they likely will need frequent reminders. Daily procedures may include having young children hang up their coats, put away lunchboxes, and unpack their backpacks at the beginning of the day as they prepare to begin morning work. Similarly, young children can be expected to independently follow end-of-day procedures and routines, such as packing up their backpacks, cleaning up learning materials, and lining up at the door for dismissal. Young children should be able to follow simple behavioral procedures as well, such as keeping hands to themselves, responding to attention signals from the teacher, and cleaning up learning materials before transitioning between activities. Young children also benefit from being assigned classroom "jobs," such as line leader, paper collector, or teacher assistant, as these routines instill a sense of accountability and self-responsibility.

Middle-level: Middle-level students can be expected to follow a variety of routines and procedures with **increasing levels of independence**. These students can reasonably be expected to enter the classroom on time and prepared with necessary learning materials. In addition, middle-level students can be held responsible for independently turning in homework according to the procedures for doing so and beginning their morning work. Middle-level students should be able to follow procedures for accessing learning materials, transitioning to cooperative learning activities, cleaning up their own materials before moving to a new activity, and non-instructional tasks, such as sharpening pencils, using the restroom, or throwing away trash with minimal reminders from the teacher.

High school: Routines and procedures in the high school classroom should **reflect** students' level of **maturity and increasing capabilities for independence** as they approach adulthood. These students can reasonably be expected to independently come to class on time, prepared, and follow procedures for turning in homework and beginning morning work. In addition, high school students can be expected to follow procedures for direct instruction, cooperative learning activities, and independently transitioning between activities. High school students can be held to a greater degree of accountability regarding grading procedures, tardiness and attendance, and procedures for turning in late assignments.

FACILITATING AN ORGANIZED, PRODUCTIVE ENVIRONMENT THAT MAXIMIZES STUDENT LEARNING

Clear routines and procedures for daily classroom activities are necessary to create an organized, productive environment that maximizes student learning. In order to be effective, routines and procedures must be reflective of the teacher's **instructional** and **classroom management** style, explicitly stated, and consistently reinforced. This ensures expectations are relevant, realistic, and that students are continuously aware of them as they engage in learning. Procedures for entering and exiting the classroom, as well as how students will begin and end their day, establish a structured, **predictable** routine that enhances focus on instruction. Smooth **transition procedures** maintain order and enhance efficiency when moving between activities, as they eliminate idle time, minimize student distraction, and allow for increased time dedicated to productive teaching and learning. Such transition procedures include how and when to access and clean up materials, move from independent to collaborative group work, or move between learning stations. The teacher must also consider procedures for performing non-instructional activities, such as sharpening pencils or going to the restroom, as these further avoid disruptions to instructional time. Procedures and routines establish organization and efficiency in the classroom by simplifying tasks to allow for increased productive instructional time and enhanced student learning.

Procedures and routines are necessary for establishing a well-managed and productive classroom environment. While the specifics of routines may vary depending upon the teacher's classroom management style and students' learning needs, many common procedures and routines share similar guidelines.

- **Entering the classroom/morning routine:** A procedure for the beginning of class ensures that students enter the room in an orderly manner with a clear understanding of what is expected of them. This routine should include entering the room quietly, unpacking necessary items for class, turning in homework, and working on an opening activity while the teacher takes attendance.

- **Leaving the classroom/packing up routine:** A procedure for packing up and leaving the classroom at the end of class or the school day ensures that students have all of their necessary materials, leave the room clean and organized, and exit in an orderly manner. Such a routine may include cleaning up learning materials, putting away assignments or papers, straightening desks, throwing away trash, packing up backpacks, and lining up by the door prior to dismissal. Students may be assigned specific jobs for cleaning up and organizing the room.
- **Turning in work:** Procedures for turning in classwork and homework allow for smoother transitions between activities and limit interruptions to instruction. This should occur at a specific time during the class period and can include designating a "turn in" box in the classroom for students to hand in assignments, or having students pass their papers to the front in a specific order. A student may be designated to collect papers at the end of an activity as well.
- **Using the restroom:** Restroom procedures limit student distraction and interruptions to instruction. Restroom breaks should generally not occur during direct instruction, and students should be permitted to go one at a time to avoid misbehavior. Students should be given a restroom pass, sign out before leaving the room, and sign back in upon returning to ensure that the teacher is always aware of students' whereabouts. Specific hand signals in which students can silently request permission to use the restroom are beneficial in further minimizing disruptions.
- **Transitions between activities:** Procedures for transitions allow for an orderly learning environment in that they indicate to students when and how to move between activities in the classroom. These procedures should include an attention signal and a clear explanation of the steps for transitioning, such as cleaning up materials from the previous activity, and a signal to indicate when students are permitted to move. Students should be expected to transition between activities quickly, quietly, and without disruption.
- **Non-instructional tasks:** Procedures for non-instructional tasks limit interruptions to instructional time for more focused learning. Activities such as getting a tissue, sharpening pencils, and throwing away trash should occur during specific times when the teacher is not directly instructing and should be done quietly and without disruption.
- **Managing student behavior:** Clear procedures for misbehavior establish a predictable, orderly learning environment. These procedures should be explicit, consistent, and follow a logical sequence. They may include a verbal warning, seating change, loss of privileges, or communication with home.
- **Accessing and using materials, supplies, and technology:** Procedures for these activities are beneficial in limiting disruption, maintaining organization, and avoiding interruptions to instruction. Such procedures indicate when and how to access and use materials, supplies, and technology in a respectful and orderly manner. The teacher should clearly communicate expectations for access and use, as well as utilize a specific signal to indicate when students are permitted to move. These procedures should also include methods for proper cleanup at the end of the activity.
- **Finishing work early:** A procedure for finishing work early minimizes idle time and limits student disruption. Students that finish early may be permitted to work on other assignments or read quietly, or the teacher can dedicate an area of the room for extra practice and review activities for students to work on if they finish early. The teacher may also permit early finishers to assist other students in applicable learning situations.

- **Emergency drills:** Procedures for emergency drills ensure that students know how to complete them in a safe, orderly manner. When the drill begins, students should immediately stop what they are doing, leave all materials on their desks, and line up by the door in an organized fashion. Students should exit the room with the teacher and move quickly and quietly through the hallways to the designated drill location. For emergency drills that occur inside the classroom, students should move quickly and quietly to a previously designated location within the room and remain there until the drill is over.
- **Attention signal:** A dedicated signal to capture students' attention indicates that they need to stop what they are doing, focus, and listen quietly to the teacher for further information or instructions. This signal could be in the form of a hand signal, call and response, phrase, or sound and should be used consistently.
- **Direct instruction:** A procedure for direct instruction is beneficial in maintaining students' focus on learning. This should include steps for active listening, including sitting up straight, facing the teacher, maintaining eye contact, and refraining from distracting neighboring classmates. Students should have clear steps regarding how to ask questions, such as raising their hand or utilizing color-coded cards to indicate levels of understanding, and how to take notes, when applicable.
- **Independent work:** An independent work procedure limits distractions and promotes students' ability to focus. This should include communicating expectations for quiet time during this period, including refraining from talking to neighboring peers, working at and remaining in assigned seats, and engaging in the proper procedure if a student finishes early. If a student needs assistance, he or she can indicate it by raising a hand, or utilizing a dedicated signal to request help, such as color-coded cards.
- **Collaborative work:** A procedure for collaborative work indicates to students how to move from independent to group activities. This includes moving to a group setting without disruption, maintaining a normal volume, communicating respectfully, and cleaning up materials when finished before moving back to assigned seats in an orderly manner.

NON-INSTRUCTIONAL DUTIES AND INSTRUCTIONAL ACTIVITIES MAXIMIZING EFFICIENCY

Many non-instructional duties, such as taking attendance, grading papers, and facilitating communication, can be coordinated with instructional activities when effective **routines** and **procedures** are instilled to accomplish them. This enhances overall efficiency in the classroom, as time is not lost on completing administrative tasks, allowing more dedicated time to instruction for maximized student learning. Taking attendance, for example, can be incorporated into students' morning work routine, as they can mark their own presence as part of the procedure for entering the classroom and beginning the day. Grading and communication with colleagues or families can take place during independent work, assessments, or recreational time. The teacher can also observe, monitor, and assess students' progress as they engage in learning. Student **self-correction** in lieu of formal grading can be beneficial in allowing students to reflect on their performance, seek areas for improvement, and strengthen their understanding, while integrating grading as an instructional activity. In addition, a variety of **digital resources** are available that allow for immediate student feedback and communication with families throughout instruction. In utilizing such resources, the teacher can efficiently coordinate administrative duties with instructional activities to maximize time for student learning.

EFFECTIVE TIME MANAGEMENT

Practicing effective time management is beneficial in establishing an efficient, orderly classroom environment focused on productivity and maximizing student learning. By instilling specific **procedures** for managing daily routines such as transitioning, accessing materials and supplies, and using technology, the teacher can ensure that these tasks are completed in a timely manner while minimizing time lost on non-instructional activities and student distraction. This allows more time to be focused on instruction and student learning. To achieve this, procedures for such tasks must be **explicit** and consistently reinforced. Prior to transitioning between activities, accessing materials, or using technology, the teacher must provide a clear, detailed explanation of each step of the procedure, as well as expectations for how students will complete it. Modeling the procedure is beneficial in providing a visual example to ensure student understanding. In order to be effective, each procedure must include a specific **signal** to indicate when students can begin, and the teacher must consistently monitor to ensure students are completing the task correctly. When students have a clear understanding on how to accomplish daily activities, they can do so quickly, effectively, and without disruption. This increases overall efficiency in the classroom and maximizes time dedicated to student learning.

USING TECHNOLOGY TO PERFORM ADMINISTRATIVE TASKS

Technology resources are widely available to assist teachers in accomplishing a variety of administrative tasks, and therefore, are highly beneficial in establishing a **well-managed**, **organized**, and **productive** learning environment. Completing such tasks as taking attendance, maintaining gradebooks, or facilitating communication through technology allows the teacher to do so more **efficiently**. This allows for more time dedicated to productive teaching and learning, as well as smoother transitions between activities, as time is not lost on completing such duties. Increased efficiency in completing administrative duties is beneficial in sustaining students' attention, engagement, and productivity in learning, as it minimizes idle time that could lead to distraction or disruption. In addition, utilizing technology to perform administrative duties enhances overall organization, as all tasks performed digitally can be stored in a single area on the device used for easy access and recall of information. Through email, digital apps, or class websites, the teacher can efficiently communicate with colleagues and students' families to update them regarding important events, assignments, and individual progress. This creates a sense of connectedness between the teacher and community that contributes to a positive, productive classroom climate.

VOLUNTEERS AND PARAPROFESSIONALS
ENHANCING AND ENRICHING INSTRUCTION

Paraprofessionals and **volunteers** are highly valuable in enhancing and enriching the overall learning experience, as their efforts contribute to an organized, positive, and productive classroom environment. These aides collaborate with the teacher throughout planning and instruction to implement best practices in meeting students' learning needs. Paraprofessionals and volunteers can lead small groups of students as they engage in instruction for a more focused, **student-centered** learning experience. They can also provide additional support to struggling students while the teacher engages in whole-class instruction. Specifically, paraprofessionals are typically licensed in the educational field and are qualified to provide **individual accommodations** to students with individual learning needs to create an inclusive learning environment. In addition, working with paraprofessionals and volunteers is beneficial in creating an efficient, organized classroom that enhances student learning, as they can assist with **non-instructional duties** that allow for smooth transitions during instruction, such as preparing learning materials, handing back papers, or grading assignments. **Classroom management** is also enhanced when paraprofessionals and volunteers are present, as they can assist in reinforcing expectations and monitoring behavior to ensure all students are positively and productively engaging in learning.

MONITORING THEIR PERFORMANCE IN THE CLASSROOM

Paraprofessionals and volunteers are invaluable resources for creating a positive, productive classroom environment. However, to ensure the contributions of these aides are consistently beneficial in meeting students' needs and maximizing learning, it is important to continuously monitor their performance in the classroom. Paraprofessionals and volunteers are typically interviewed by administration prior to entering the classroom to determine whether their qualifications are aligned with meeting students' needs to enhance instruction. The administration is also often responsible for monitoring their performance throughout the school year. Specifically, paraprofessionals are licensed in the field of education, and therefore, are often formally evaluated against specific **performance measurement tools**. **Observations** by administration can either be scheduled or conducted as an informal "walk-through" to assess how the paraprofessional or volunteer interacts with the teacher and students and their effectiveness in contributing to a productive learning environment. The teacher can also monitor the performance of volunteers and paraprofessionals in their classroom. By analyzing **students' progress** when working with these aides and eliciting **feedback** from students, the teacher can determine their effectiveness in enhancing the learning experience. Frequently communicating with paraprofessionals and volunteers provides valuable insight regarding whether they contribute to a positive classroom climate focused on student learning.

Classroom Organization

PHYSICAL CHARACTERISTICS OF A SAFE AND PRODUCTIVE LEARNING ENVIRONMENT

A classroom environment that is **safe** and facilitates **productivity** in learning is essential to fostering student motivation, engagement, and achievement. The physical space must be **clean, well-organized**, and **orderly**. All equipment, furniture, and materials must be in usable condition, well-maintained, and free of damage. This ensures that students are safe when engaging with the learning environment, as well as provides an appealing space that encourages participation. Furniture and equipment must be arranged in a way that facilitates safety and ease of movement as students transition between activities. Likewise, all furniture, materials, and equipment must be appropriate to the students' **age group** in terms of level of difficulty, height, and size to enable students to properly interact with them for productive learning. Students must have access to a **variety** of learning materials to promote interest and engagement for productive learning, including areas for individual and collaborative learning. The classroom should be decorated in such a way that is welcoming, stimulating without being overwhelming, and reflective of students' diversities and interests. When the physical environment is inviting, safe, and tailored to students' developmental levels, it creates a positive classroom climate in which students are motivated to productively engage in learning.

SIGNIFICANCE OF EFFECTIVE CLASSROOM ARRANGEMENT

A thoughtfully arranged classroom has significant and positive impacts on the nature of the learning atmosphere. Effective classroom arrangement creates an inviting learning environment in which students are motivated to engage in learning actively and productively. The manner in which the teacher organizes furniture, equipment, and learning materials influences students' **focus, access** to resources, and **behavior**, as well as the teacher's ability to effectively implement **classroom management** strategies. An organized, orderly classroom in which necessary resources are easily accessible enables students to properly focus on instruction, thus promoting active engagement and productivity in learning. This reinforces positive behavior, as students are less likely to be disruptive when their learning environment is free of unnecessary distractions. The classroom arrangement determines the flow and ease of movement and should be strategically planned to facilitate productive learning while enabling the teacher to easily monitor and assist all students for effective classroom management. Effective arrangement allows the teacher to control the level of student movement and prevent potential distractions while ensuring students can easily transition from one learning activity to the next to promote efficiency, active engagement, and productivity.

ESTABLISHING SAFE, PRODUCTIVE, AND SUCCESSFUL LEARNING ENVIRONMENTS

Establishing a safe, productive, and successful learning environment requires the teacher to thoughtfully consider several factors when determining the most effective classroom arrangement for meeting desired learning outcomes and students' needs. Students' **age group, size**, and **developmental levels** influence which arrangement best facilitates safety and productivity in learning. For example, younger students learn through interaction with their environment and therefore need ample space for movement and play to support their development. A more structured arrangement that enables direct instruction while also facilitating hands-on, collaborative learning meets the needs of middle-level and older students. In addition, students' **individual needs** must be considered when determining classroom arrangement in order to ensure equitable access to instruction and learning materials. The teacher must also consider the **size** and **layout** of the classroom, including the location of learning resources such as the projector screen, computers, and chalkboard. With this in mind, teachers must determine the **style** of teaching and learning taking place, how they want students to move, what information must be visible, as well as which materials must be accessible to create a safe, productive learning environment that meets students' needs in achieving learning outcomes.

CONSIDERATIONS FOR DESK ARRANGEMENT

There are numerous possibilities for desk arrangements in the classroom, each with advantages and limitations that must be considered and addressed. **Desired learning outcomes**, as well as the style of teaching and learning, influence which arrangement is most effective. Arrangements that facilitate individual focus, limited distraction, and clear teacher-student visibility are suited to **direct instruction**. However, these arrangements often limit collaborative learning. To address this, the teacher can designate an area in the classroom for group work, utilize common areas such as the library, or move students' desks for collaborative activities. Variations of group arrangements facilitate **collaborative learning**, as students can easily face one another and work together. However, grouped seating may cause student distraction during individual work and limit teacher-student visibility. It is therefore important that the teacher establish clear expectations and frequently monitor students' progress to ensure they remain on task. The **classroom size** must be considered, as the space may not allow for certain desk arrangements and still facilitate ease of movement, visibility, and student learning. **Individual learning needs** must also be considered when determining seating arrangements. Some students require specific accommodations, such as preferential seating, an individual learning space for limited distractions, or a physical accommodation.

Various types of seating arrangements are described below:

- **Stadium Seating**—Desks in this classroom are situated in lines at a slight angle with the students facing directly toward the teacher. This seating method is useful for lectures and individual work, as the teacher can easily monitor whether each student is on task. This arrangement is generally unsuited for group work, as students are not able to easily face one another, and may limit the teacher's ease of movement between students to provide individual assistance.

- **Cluster Seating**—Desks in this classroom are arranged in groups of 3-5 throughout the classroom. This method is beneficial for supporting collaborative work and pairing students that need support with others that can provide scaffolding. However, this arrangement may be distracting during individual work and limit teacher-student visibility.

- **Rows and Columns**—Desks are individually spaced apart with the students facing directly toward the teacher and front of the room. This arrangement is useful for presentations, direct instruction, and individual work, as it limits distractions from other students. The teacher can easily see whether individual students are on task. However, this arrangement is not facilitative of group work, as students cannot easily face each other. This arrangement also limits the teacher's ability to move between students to provide assistance.

- **Horseshoe**—Desks in this classroom are arranged in a large "U" shape with students facing the teacher at the front of the room. This arrangement is useful for individual instruction, as it ensures teacher-student visibility and equal view of the chalkboard and projector screen during direct instruction. This method also facilitates whole-class discussions. However, this arrangement inhibits students' ability to work collaboratively in groups and, depending on classroom size, may limit ease of teacher and student movement.

- **Miniature Horseshoes**—Desks in this classroom are arranged in 2-5 miniature horseshoes with students facing the front of the room. This arrangement is beneficial for both individual and collaborative work, as the teacher can clearly monitor whether students are on task and can move between groups to provide individual assistance, while enabling students to easily face one another for group activities. However, this method may lend itself to student distraction during individual work, and the physical size of the classroom may limit the possibility for this arrangement.

- **Pairs**—Desks in this classroom are arranged two-by-two in rows with students facing the front of the classroom. This arrangement is useful for partner work and pairing students that need support with others that provide scaffolding, while limiting distractions during individual work. This method is not suitable for group work or whole-class activities, as students cannot easily face each other, and movement may be limited.

- **Combination**—This classroom incorporates a variety of desk arrangements, including individual seats, pairs, groups, and the "horseshoe" arrangements. This method is useful for accommodating varying learning styles and needs, as it can facilitate individual and collaborative work. However, this arrangement utilizes a great deal of space and may impede ease of movement and visibility for the teacher and students.

- **Flexible**—This classroom provides students with a variety of options for seating choices throughout the classroom, such as bean bag chairs, exercise balls, or floor seating. This option is beneficial for supporting students' individual learning needs, as they can choose to sit where they learn best. Flexible seating also supports collaborative learning and contributes to a welcoming, positive classroom climate. However, unstructured seating may lend itself to student distraction and limit student-teacher visibility during direct instruction.

- **Runway**—Desks in this classroom are arranged in rows on either side of the room with students facing the center, leaving the middle space clear for the teacher. This is useful for direct instruction, as students can easily see the teacher and class presentations, and the teacher can monitor whether each student is on task. This method also facilitates whole-class discussions. This arrangement is generally not suited for collaborative work, as students cannot easily face those seated near them, and it may limit the teacher's ability to provide individual assistance.

- **Conference**—All desks in this classroom are arranged in a large, two-by-two rectangle situated in the middle of the room with students facing one another. This arrangement is beneficial for collaborative work, whole-class activities, and class discussions, as students can easily face one another. The teacher can generally provide individual assistance and can easily monitor whether students are on task. However, the physical size of the classroom may not facilitate this arrangement. In addition, this method may lead to student distraction during individual work.

CLASSROOM SEATING ARRANGEMENTS

Miniature Horseshoes

Pairs

Combination

Flexible

Runway

Conference

CLASSROOM ORGANIZATION ENSURING ACCESSIBILITY AND FACILITATES LEARNING

Strategic classroom organization is necessary to ensure physical accessibility for all students and facilitating learning across instructional contexts. Students' **height, size**, and **special needs** must be considered and addressed when determining physical classroom arrangement. All furniture, equipment, and necessary materials must be equally accessible and facilitate ease of movement for all students as they participate in learning activities. Some students may require individualized **physical accommodations** to support their learning, such as preferential seating, special furniture arrangements to enable physical accessibility, or access to technology. By instilling these supports into the organization of the classroom, the teacher establishes an equitable environment that supports learning across instructional contexts. The classroom must be arranged to ensure all students have **visibility** and access to the teacher, as well as pertinent instructional information and resources, including the projector screen, chalk board, and computers. The physical environment must be aligned to and facilitative of the style of instruction taking place while supporting students' individual needs in achieving learning goals. When the teacher ensures that the classroom environment is physically accessible to all students, they empower students to engage in learning across instructional contexts successfully.

Behavior Management Theory

MANAGING AND MONITORING STUDENT BEHAVIOR
BEHAVIORISM AND CONDITIONING

The theoretical school of **behaviorism** was established by John B. Watson and further developed by Ivan Pavlov and B.F. Skinner. Behaviorism emphasizes the role of environmental and experiential learning in the behavior of animals and humans. Simply put, if a person experiences a desirable result from a particular behavior, that person is more likely to perform the behavior in pursuit of the result. Likewise, undesirable results cause a person to avoid performing an associated behavior. This process of **reinforcing** or rewarding good behaviors and **punishing** unwanted behaviors is known as conditioning. Behaviorists use the terms positive and negative to refer to the mode of conditioning. The term **positive** refers to an added stimulus, such as giving a child a treat as positive reinforcement or giving added homework as positive punishment. **Negative**, on the other hand refers to removing a stimulus, such as taking recess away as a negative punishment, or taking away extra classwork as negative reinforcement for students performing their homework independently. In the classroom, the teacher has the opportunity to help students learn to meet specific behavioral expectations. The tools of behaviorism may be carefully employed in the classrooms through positive and negative punishments and rewards. Classroom rules and expectations should be made clear as soon as possible and reinforced through verbal praise, prizes, or special privileges. Likewise, negative behaviors should be discouraged through verbal warnings, loss of privileges, and communication with the family or administrators when necessary.

CHOICE THEORY

Choice theory, developed by **William Glasser**, states that behavior is chosen, either consciously or unconsciously, to meet the **five basic needs** of survival, love and belonging, power, freedom, and fun. Rather than implement positive and negative reinforcements to drive behavior, the teacher must aim to teach students self-responsibility for their actions. This includes encouraging students to reflect and consider the reasons for their actions and attempt to rectify any misbehavior. This method relies on the notion that if students understand how their desire to meet certain needs impacts their actions, they are more likely to engage in positive behavior. In the classroom, the teacher focuses on meeting students' **five basic needs** to encourage positive behavior by creating a classroom climate that emphasizes **communication, relationship building**, and **self-reflection**.

This includes establishing positive relationships with students, holding class discussions, and teaching conflict resolution skills to create a safe, welcoming learning environment. Instructional activities are tailored to individual needs, and students have a great deal of choice in their own learning with the intention of promoting positive behavior by meeting their needs for power and freedom.

ASSERTIVE DISCIPLINE THEORY

The **Assertive Discipline theory** was developed by **Lee** and **Marlene Canter**. This theory states that the teacher is in charge of **instruction, the classroom**, and **students' behavior**. The expectation is that the teacher establishes clear behavioral standards that protect their right to teach and students' right to learn without distraction or disruption. Negative consequences for unwanted behavior are instilled to deter students from deviating from behavioral expectations. This theory argues that if teachers are viewed as firm and consistent, students will have a greater respect for them and ultimately engage in positive behavior. In the classroom, the teacher is in control of **establishing** and **consistently reinforcing** standards for student behavior. This establishes a sense of predictability, as students are clear on what is expected of them as they engage in learning. Students are expected to comply with the teacher's expectations, and a system of **negative consequences** are in place to discourage unwanted behavior. Positive behavior is rewarded to further reinforce desired behavior. The teacher in this classroom believes that creating such an environment enhances students' ability to focus on learning without disruption.

STUDENT-DIRECTED LEARNING THEORY

The **Student-Directed Learning theory**, or the idea of the **Democratic Classroom**, was founded by **Alfie Kohn** and emphasizes the importance of **student choice** and **classroom community** in influencing behavior. This includes having students contribute to the development of behavioral expectations, as this helps students understand their purpose while instilling a sense of ownership and accountability. Instructional activities are tailored to accommodate students' individual interests and natural curiosity while emphasizing cooperation to foster an engaging learning environment that promotes positive behavior. This theory focuses on eliciting students' intrinsic motivation to engage in positive behavior, rather than relying on positive and negative reinforcements. In the classroom, students primarily direct their own learning based upon their **natural curiosity** while the teacher acts as a **facilitator**. Students contribute to the development of behavioral expectations that are instilled to promote respect and focus on learning. **Active engagement**, **cooperation**, and **collaborative learning** are emphasized over direct instruction. Students may be engaging in differing activities simultaneously as the teacher moves around the classroom to monitor progress and assist as necessary.

SOCIAL LEARNING THEORY AND BEHAVIOR MANAGEMENT

The **Social Learning theory**, developed by **Albert Bandura**, asserts that one's **environment** and the **people** within it heavily influence behavior. As humans are social creatures, they learn a great deal by **observing** and **imitating** one another. This theory is also rooted in the importance of **self-efficacy** in achieving desired behavior, as students must be motivated and confident that they can effectively imitate what they observe. In the classroom, the teacher establishes behavioral expectations and focuses on **modeling** positive behaviors, attitudes, and interactions with the intention of encouraging students to do the same. The teacher recognizes and praises positive behavior from students to elicit the same behavior from others. The teacher also emphasizes a growth mindset in the classroom to promote students' sense of self-efficacy.

BEHAVIOR STANDARDS AND EXPECTATIONS FOR STUDENTS AT DEVELOPMENTAL LEVELS

Behavioral standards that emphasize respect for oneself, others, and property are necessary in creating a safe, positive, and productive learning environment for students of all ages. However, as students at varying developmental levels differ in their capabilities across domains, behavioral expectations must be **realistic**, **applicable**, and reflect an **awareness** of these **differences** while encouraging growth. Young children, for example, are learning to interact with others and function in a group setting. Behavioral expectations must be attuned to this understanding while promoting the development of positive interpersonal skills. Young children also require ample opportunities for active movement and cannot reasonably be expected to sit still for long periods of time. Middle level students are at a unique transitional period in their development and often exhibit characteristics of both young children and adolescents. Behavioral standards for these students must recognize the significant social, emotional, cognitive, and physical changes occurring at this stage by emphasizing self-control, emotional regulation, and positive interactions. As older students prepare for adulthood, they can generally be expected to conduct themselves with a degree of maturity and responsibility in a variety of settings. Appropriate behavioral standards for these students emphasize self-responsibility, respectful interactions, and independently completing necessary tasks.

EFFECTIVE MANAGEMENT OF STUDENT BEHAVIOR

MANAGEMENT PROCEDURES AND SIGNIFICANCE IN POSITIVE, PRODUCTIVE, AND ORGANIZED LEARNING ENVIRONMENT

Promoting **appropriate behavior** and **ethical work habits** while taking specific measures to **manage student behavior** creates a safe, organized, and productive classroom. Such an environment is beneficial for students' motivation, engagement, and ability to focus on learning. This is achieved by communicating and consistently reinforcing **high**, yet **realistic behavioral expectations** for all students. This, when combined with **relationship building** strategies, establishes a positive rapport between the teacher and students that encourages appropriate behavior and ethical work habits. Students are more inclined to adhere to expectations for behavior and work habits when their relationship with the teacher is founded on mutual understanding and respect. In addition, students that feel they are a part of developing academic and behavioral expectations feel a greater sense of **ownership** and responsibility to follow them, and, therefore, it is beneficial to include students in this process. Encouraging students to **self-monitor** their behavior and utilize conflict resolution strategies furthers this sense of accountability, as it prompts students to positively manage their own actions and work habits. Misbehavior must be addressed appropriately and in a timely manner, and consequences must follow a logical sequence, such as a verbal warning, followed by loss of privileges or communication with family.

> **Review Video: <u>Student Behavior Management Approaches</u>**
> Visit mometrix.com/academy and enter code: 843846
>
> **Review Video: <u>Promoting Appropriate Behavior</u>**
> Visit mometrix.com/academy and enter code: 321015

STRATEGIES

Proactively implementing effective behavior management strategies is beneficial to establishing and maintaining a positive, productive learning environment. The **physical environment** should be arranged in such a way that facilitates ease of movement while limiting the amount of free space that could encourage student disruption. Planning for **smooth transitions** from one activity to the next further discourages behavioral disruptions. Desks should be arranged so that students can easily view the teacher, projector, chalkboard, or other information pertinent to learning.

Expectations for behavior, procedures, and routines, including consequences, should be predictable, consistent, succinct, and visible at all times. Allowing students to participate in the development of classroom procedures and routines is valuable in providing students with a sense of personal accountability that increases the likelihood that they will follow them. Students also often respond well to incentives for modeling appropriate behavior, such as a **PBIS reward system**, verbal praise, or a positive phone call home. Nonverbal strategies are valuable in subtly managing student behavior throughout instruction, such as hand gestures, proximity, or eye contact. Misbehavior should be addressed discreetly and privately so as to avoid embarrassing the student or encouraging further disruption.

IMPORTANCE OF CONSISTENCY

Standards for behavior must be enforced consistently in order to establish a well-managed classroom in which students can focus on learning. This includes communicating **clear expectations**, holding all students equally accountable with specific **positive and negative consequences**, and **following through** on implementing them. In doing so, the teacher ensures that students are always aware of the behavior expected from them, and what will happen if they do not adhere to the standards. When students are clear regarding behavioral expectations and assured that they will be enforced, they are more inclined to demonstrate appropriate conduct. This creates a predictable, secure environment that promotes student motivation, engagement, and focused productivity in learning. Consistently enforcing behavior standards gives the teacher a sense of credibility among students, and therefore, students are more likely to respect and adhere to these expectations. In addition, holding all students to the same high behavioral standards contributes to a positive classroom climate in which all students feel they are treated fairly.

Materials and Resources

MATERIALS AND RESOURCES THAT ENHANCE STUDENT LEARNING AND ENGAGEMENT
INSTRUCTIONAL MATERIALS AND RESOURCES

The careful selection of instructional materials and resources for lesson plans is an integral component of enhancing student engagement and the overall learning experience. Lesson materials should be relevant to students' interests so as to facilitate personal connections to learning and ultimately, deepen understanding. In building positive relationships with students by educating themselves on students' backgrounds and interests, teachers can effectively locate and implement varied instructional materials and resources that are relevant to students and foster motivation for learning. Additionally, interactive materials, such as manipulatives or other hands-on learning resources, enhance learning and engagement through encouraging participation. Similarly, cooperative learning materials encourage student participation, and therefore, engagement, through fostering collaboration. Teachers can also enhance learning experiences through incorporating authentic materials that are relevant to instruction such as maps, brochures, historical documents, or similar materials that enhance student engagement and learning.

TECHNOLOGICAL RESOURCES

Technology is integrated in nearly every aspect of life as a tool to enhance and assist in daily activities. This notion also applies in the classroom, as technological resources are an excellent method of increasing student engagement and interest, supporting students in their individual learning needs, and ultimately, enhancing learning. The use of computers, tablets, smartphones, and other technological resources serve to improve understanding of classroom instruction, foster relevancy and personal connections, and scaffold instruction to address diverse learning styles and needs. Additionally, teachers have myriad digital resources available in the form of interactive websites, videos clips, and apps that can be implemented to enrich lessons and increase development across all subject areas. Often, these resources accommodate students' individual learning needs through providing increasingly challenging activities based on individual skill level, and therefore, the teacher can utilize these resources to tailor instruction to address individual student needs. Technological resources can also add authenticity to learning experiences, making them more engaging and enhancing student learning. Virtual field trips or science experiments can provide real-world connections to instruction by recreating authentic learning experiences without students having to leave the classroom.

COMMUNITY RESOURCES

Community resources are beneficial in enriching instruction to foster engagement and enhance student learning. They provide students the opportunity to connect and apply what they learn in the classroom with the real world. This ultimately makes learning more authentic, as students are able to see the relevancy of what they are learning, and therefore, enhances learning by making it more engaging. Through field trips, teachers can incorporate community resources such as museums, art exhibits, science centers, and even local areas such as parks or historical sites into curriculum to accompany material learned in class. Additionally, if access to field trips is limited, teachers can take advantage of community outreach programs that bring learning experiences to classrooms. Reaching out to members of the community that are relevant to topics being covered in class, such as scientists or local historians, can be beneficial in allowing students to understand how what they are learning is applicable outside of the classroom. Locating and implementing community resources enhances student learning and engagement through making learning authentic, relevant, and applicable in the real world.

DEVELOPMENTALLY APPROPRIATE MATERIALS AND RESOURCES

To create engaging and effective learning experiences, instructional materials and resources must be developmentally appropriate. Teachers must have a solid understanding of the general cognitive, physical, social, and emotional developmental levels of their students, as well as individual differences in skills and abilities to properly select developmentally appropriate materials. The age and developmental level appropriateness of instructional resources can be determined by considering the material's size, height, and level of difficulty for students. Whether materials accommodate individual differences in skill level, ability, or interest can be determined by their versatility. If a resource can be used in multiple ways, it will appeal to a variety of learning needs and interests and support development across domains. Developmentally appropriate materials are reflective and considerate of students' diversities. Teachers can determine this by using their knowledge of students' backgrounds to select materials that incorporate and are sensitive to their students' cultural differences to support development by fostering personal connections to learning.

Instructional Technologies

CURRENT TECHNOLOGY, SYSTEMS, AND OPERATIONS
TERMS AND CONCEPTS

As technology resources advance, it is important that the teacher understands basic terms and is informed on recent developments. **Hardware** refers to the physical components of technology systems and operations, including computers, keyboards, mice, monitors, and projectors. Recently, tablets, smart boards, and smart phones have been incorporated into classrooms as well. **Software**, such as word processors, internet browsers, games, applications, and social media, are programs run within the computer, and are valuable resources in planning, delivering, and evaluating instruction. **Input devices** allow users to enter information into the computer to complete tasks or display information. These devices include the keyboard, mouse, microphone, camera, and touch screen. **Output devices**, such as screens, speakers, headphones, and printers, display information in a comprehensible format as well as communicate with users or other devices. A **network** is a group of computers or devices that communicate with one another. In education, networks allow multiple schools within a district to communicate, enables colleagues to share resources, and provides internet access for locating information. **Basic design** principles, in regard to instruction, refers to the components of creating content that is visually appealing, clear, and accurate.

Electronic Information

Effectively Locating on Networks and Application in Instruction

The ability to proficiently utilize networks for harnessing electronic information enhances the planning, organization, delivery, and evaluation of instruction. The **internet** is perhaps the most common network that teachers employ when locating information to apply to their practice. Therefore, teachers must know how to efficiently navigate this resource to maximize productivity and instructional effectiveness. Several **search engines** are available that enable teachers to locate and acquire a multitude of information to apply it to all aspects of instruction. To properly use a search engine, teachers must consider the information they are seeking and determine specific key terms that will garner the best results. Search results must then be filtered for accuracy, credibility, and relevancy before integrating them into the instructional process. Once the desired information is located, teachers can refine their search by utilizing results to locate additional or more detailed information. Additionally, schools within the same district are often connected on a common network, thus allowing teachers to utilize it for sharing and locating information and resources to apply to the planning, organization, delivery, and evaluation of instruction. Once information is sufficiently compiled and reviewed, teachers can determine where it is most applicable and beneficial in enhancing the instructional process.

Secondary Storage and Remote Devices

Secondary storage devices are useful tools for preserving and reinforcing files and data. Secondary storage can either exist as **hardware devices**, such as USB or external hard drives, or **remote devices**, including a cloud or online repository. The procedures for accessing information on secondary storage devices are dependent on the nature of the device. Remote devices allow the user to retrieve stored files from any location, by using a web browser to access a file storing service or by using the file explorer feature on a computer. They also allow the user to easily share information within the files with others. Information on hardware secondary storage devices is only retrievable when the device is connected to the computer, as this gives the user access to the information stored on the device through the file explorer. Once the information is accessible, the user can then manipulate it to acquire, analyze, and evaluate electronic information. The user can then save any changes made to the information and continue to store it in the secondary device.

Utilizing Online Help and Documentation

Employing the assistance of online resources and documents when acquiring, analyzing, and evaluating electronic information enhances the teacher's ability to create and provide accurate, valid, and relevant instruction. **Online resources**, including electronic communities, tutorials, forums, chat services, and consultations, are valuable in educating the teacher on effective practices for locating, refining, and determining the credibility, relevancy, and usefulness of electronic information to integrate into instruction. In addition, these resources are beneficial in helping the teacher understand how to access, analyze, and evaluate digital information to incorporate into instruction using secure procedures that protect their own and students' safety and privacy. **Online documents** in the form of PDFs, articles, or journals allow the teacher to research and gather information to utilize as reference tools for effectively acquiring, analyzing, and evaluating electronic information. When teachers utilize online resources and documentation to improve their knowledge and effectiveness in the acquisition, analysis, and evaluation of electronic information, they ensure students receive high-quality instruction that safely facilitates success in learning.

EVALUATING ELECTRONIC INFORMATION

The availability of digital information and resources has been transformative in enhancing teaching and learning. While it is a valuable tool, there are several considerations the teacher must make when evaluating the merits of electronic information. All material found online must be determined as **accurate**, **reliable**, and **valid** prior to integrating it into the instructional process. This is achieved by assessing multiple sources related to a given topic to ensure that the information provided is factual. In addition, the teacher must evaluate the **credibility** and expertise of the creator to ascertain the legitimacy of their content. Electronic information must be current, relevant to desired learning outcomes, and comprehensible to effectively engage and support students in the learning process. Digital material must also be **culturally sensitive** and representative of multiple perspectives to prevent bias, as this is imperative in creating an inclusive learning environment that encourages students to consider information from varying points of view. Evaluating electronic information prior to utilizing it is integral to planning, organizing, and delivering effective instruction, as it ensures students are provided with high-quality materials for successful learning.

RELEVANT TOOLS AND PROCEDURES FOR SYNTHESIZING KNOWLEDGE AND INFORMATION

Utilizing the proper technology resources and tools for the synthesis of knowledge and information serves to increase overall efficiency and effectiveness when planning, organizing, delivering, and evaluating instruction. Such tools as **word processing programs**, **slide shows**, and other **multimedia presentations** allow the teacher to synthesize various pieces of information and knowledge within one location, thus allowing them to compile multiple resources for lesson planning, organization, and delivery of instruction. Additionally, these tools often allow for collaboration, as multiple individuals can contribute to the compilation of knowledge and resources. When analyzing and evaluating instruction, **spreadsheet** documents are beneficial for combining several elements of related information to examine results and make informed decisions regarding how to proceed with instruction. Similarly, **graphic tools**, including charts, diagrams, and tables, enable the teacher to identify trends and correlations related to their instructional process in order to recognize areas for improvement or adjustment to meet students' learning needs.

CREATING AND MODIFYING SOLUTIONS IN PROBLEM-SOLVING AND PROJECT-BASED SITUATIONS

Implementing task-appropriate technology resources throughout the instructional process improves one's ability to create and modify solutions in problem-solving and project-based situations. To effectively apply these tools, the teacher must evaluate the aspects of the given task or problem to determine which digital resource, such as a **word processing** document, **spreadsheet**, **graph**, or **database**, will be most useful in creating a solution or product. These tools encompass a multitude of features that allow the user to navigate, manipulate, and devise solutions within them that can be modified as the information or the nature of the task evolves or as necessary. The vast availability of technology resources provides the user with multiple methods to engage in problem-solving and project-based learning activities. This ultimately enhances productivity when creating solutions and products, as well as efficiency when modifying them.

TOOLS AND PROCEDURES FOR EVALUATING RESULTS

Technology resources for quantifying data and evaluating results enhance the teacher's ability to plan, organize, and deliver instruction. When the teacher determines the nature of the information they are seeking, they can effectively choose such task-appropriate tools as **spreadsheets**, **databases**, or **graphs** to enter data and evaluate results for application in instruction. These resources enable the teacher to organize multiple data sets in relation to one another in a relevant, logical manner to accurately evaluate results, identify correlations, and make informed instructional decisions based upon their findings. The features within these tools allow the teacher to modify information as desired results change or as necessary. Properly implementing task-appropriate tools and procedures for evaluating results supports the teacher in determining instructional effectiveness, comprehension, and student needs to make adjustments as necessary, thus enhancing the learning experience.

ELECTRONIC COMMUNITIES

Collaboration with colleagues is an integral component of developing and refining one's instructional practice. Electronic communities provide teachers from different locations and levels of experience the opportunity to interact with one another as learners, initiators, and contributors within the realm of education. In this space, teachers can develop their knowledge and skills in planning, organizing, delivering, and evaluating instruction by participating in discussions with other educators, as these communities provide access to multiple perspectives, experiences, and authentic insights. This enables teachers to build upon one another's strengths and abilities to improve their overall practice. Additionally, electronic communities serve as a space in which teachers can share and work together in creating instructional resources, materials, lesson plans, and ideas. Collaborating in online communities enhances the efficiency and quality of the instructional process, as teachers can borrow relevant materials from one another to enrich their curriculum, and multiple individuals can participate in the development of instructional materials by contributing their unique ideas and perspectives.

PRODUCTIVITY TOOLS FOR COLLABORATING AND COMMUNICATING INFORMATION

Digital productivity tools increase the efficiency of collaboration and communication in the classroom to enhance instruction. Resources, such as **slideshows**, **multimedia presentations**, and **word processing applications**, allow students to upload, edit, and collaborate on assignments in real-time for more productive and interactive learning. In addition, these tools allow the teacher to review and communicate immediate feedback on assignments as students work to ensure understanding and allow them to make necessary changes before moving on. When delivering instruction, digital productivity tools enhance efficiency by enabling the compilation of multiple pieces of information in a centralized resource for presentation. These tools are also valuable in communicating updates and pertinent information to teachers, students, and families. Whole-class participation apps provide the teacher with immediate feedback on student understanding that enables them to adapt and improve instruction as necessary to meet students' needs. Through **newsletters**, **digital applications**, and **social media platforms**, teachers can distribute learning materials, as well as quickly communicate important dates, events, and assignments to students and families for enhanced instruction.

METHODS FOR PUBLISHING INFORMATION

Publishing information through a variety of methods ensures clear, efficient, and consistent communication for successful teaching and learning. In the classroom, publishing information through several mediums enables the teacher to deliver multifaceted content that reinforces and enhances instruction by addressing the needs of varying learning styles to ensure comprehension. When delivering pertinent information regarding classroom updates, events, or assignments to students and families, utilizing multiple means of publication ensures accessibility and efficiency of communication for all recipients. **Printed publication** materials, including handouts, flyers, pamphlets, or newsletters, enable the teacher to provide students and families with hard copies of important information and updates. **Digital publication** outlets allow for immediate communication and modification of information, including displaying information on a monitor, slide show, internet documents, classroom website, and social media platforms. Additionally, several digital applications are available that allow students and families to join a digitally connected group to receive immediate communication updates from the teacher regarding important classroom information.

CONSISTENT KNOWLEDGE ON CURRENT TECHNOLOGIES

When teachers are knowledgeable on current technologies and their application in the classroom, they are more equipped to effectively plan, organize, deliver, and evaluate instruction. Teachers must consistently educate themselves on new technologies to incorporate into their practice to foster student engagement and success in learning. By participating in **continuing education**, in the form of professional development trainings, technology courses, workshops, and conferences, teachers can stay informed on new and relevant digital resources to enhance instruction. Additionally, teachers can **collaborate** with colleagues or mentors either in person or through electronic communities to share information and gain insight on current technologies and how to implement them in the classroom. **Self-education** is a valuable tool for learning about technological developments and how to utilize them in instruction. When teachers take initiative to conduct their own research about recent advancements and personally engage with new digital resources, they can determine how to effectively incorporate them into instruction to enhance teaching and learning.

Technology Use in the Classroom

SIGNIFICANCE OF TECHNOLOGY IN INSTRUCTION

Rapid advancements in technology systems and operations require the teacher to actively educate themselves on new developments to effectively plan, organize, deliver, and evaluate instruction. Most students are **digital natives**, meaning they have grown up accustomed to using technology in their daily lives and are familiar with its functions. As such, the teacher must be proficient with current technology and how to effectively incorporate it into daily instruction to create a relevant, interesting, and engaging learning environment. Understanding how to utilize and implement new technology resources improves a teacher's effectiveness in planning, organizing, and delivering differentiated instruction, as it enables them to derive material from a multitude of resources that appeal to students' individual needs and interests. In addition, it improves the teacher's ability to collaborate with other teachers for instructional planning and communicate with students, families, and colleagues. This ultimately enhances the learning experience by providing individualized, student-centered, and interactive instruction to promote engagement and support academic success. Additionally, understanding the functions of current technology systems and operations enhances the planning, organization, and evaluation of instruction by enabling the teacher to effectively utilize relevant digital productivity tools.

INCORPORATION INTO DAILY CLASSROOM ACTIVITIES

Numerous educational technology resources are available to enhance all aspects of daily instruction. Digital tools can be highly beneficial in increasing student engagement, participation, and understanding, as well as addressing a variety of learning needs. Technology resources such as presentation slides, video clips, or audio books, can be used to introduce new topics or supplement instruction. Teachers can also create an **online classroom** in which they deliver instruction as well as provide students opportunities to collaborate in a digital workspace, ask questions, participate in discussions, turn in assignments, and receive feedback. Online activities such as WebQuests or digital scavenger hunts are valuable in allowing students to explore new concepts or research information while interacting with authentic digital resources. Teachers can also incorporate **total participation activities** to conduct formative assessments using technology resources, such as online surveys, polls, games, or word clustering games. In addition, students can prepare for assessments by utilizing resources such as online flashcards, quizzes, or review games. **Educational experiences** can also be supplemented using technology resources. For example, digital science experiments can reinforce concepts learned in the classroom. Additionally, virtual field trips allow students to explore locations they may otherwise be unable to visit.

SAFE AND APPROPRIATE USE OF TECHNOLOGY

ISSUES THAT MAY BE ENCOUNTERED

Technology provides valuable learning tools, yet the teacher must be mindful of issues that may arise regarding safety and appropriateness when planning, organizing, delivering, and evaluating instruction. When using the internet, social media, and digital resources, students may be vulnerable to inappropriate or unsafe content. The teacher must assess all digital material when planning and organizing instruction to ensure that content, advertisements, and search engine results are **safe, instructionally applicable**, and respectful of **students' privacy**. Student misuse of technology is a common issue that may be exacerbated when students are permitted to bring their own devices to class. **Misuse** includes using technology for off-task activities, accessing inappropriate websites, apps, or social media, and engaging in cyberbullying. It is important that the teacher establish clear expectations for the use of personal devices and take proper measures to block access to non-instructional material to ensure students engage with technology appropriately. Students may encounter individuals online that subject them to harmful or inappropriate communication. In addition to ensuring that students remain on task, the teacher must frequently monitor students' technology use to ensure they are not engaging with individuals or materials that may ask them to divulge personal details or compromise their safety.

IMPORTANCE OF EDUCATING STUDENTS ON APPROPRIATE TECHNOLOGY USE

Educating students on appropriate technology use establishes a focused, engaged, and safe learning environment. When the teacher **models** and **instructs** students on appropriate and responsible practices, they develop an awareness of the immediate and future implications of their online behavior. This ultimately teaches students to make informed decisions that protect their safety and privacy when using digital resources both within and outside of the classroom. Establishing clear procedures and expectations for technology discourages misuse, as it helps ensure that students are focused, on task, and engage appropriately with technology as a learning tool to enhance instruction. In addition, it teaches students how to interact with others online safely and responsibly using proper **digital citizenship**, as well as how to respond if they encounter inappropriate content or behavior. When the teacher effectively educates students on proper technology use, it becomes an efficient and valuable instructional resource that enhances the overall learning experience.

PRIVACY GUIDELINES

To establish a safe learning environment in which all students are protected, it is imperative that the teacher consistently adhere to strict privacy guidelines. The teacher must ensure that all of their actions and practices within and outside of the classroom align with **FERPA**, as well as state and district laws regarding student privacy. Additionally, the teacher must be well informed on and follow the privacy policies of their individual school. Students' **personal information**, including grade history, attendance and discipline records, medical history, special needs, address, birthday, and any other sensitive details must remain confidential. In an increasingly digital learning environment, it is important that the teacher make sure photographs, video recordings, or names of students are not shared online or on social media without proper consent. When students interact with digital resources in the classroom, their data is often collected and recorded. Therefore, the teacher must be cognizant of what information is shared and select technology resources appropriately, as well as instruct students not to divulge any personal information about themselves online. Following strict privacy guidelines is necessary in protecting all students' rights to confidentiality.

COPYRIGHT LAWS

When creating, planning, and delivering instruction, the teacher must consider copyright laws before selecting or distributing materials and resources to ensure they do not infringe upon the creator's rights. While teachers are often given flexibility regarding the **Copyright Law** under the **Fair Use Doctrine**, they must be mindful to ensure that accessing, copying, and utilizing unpurchased materials, content, resources, or images falls under this doctrine to avoid copyright infringement. Teachers must make certain that all resources are used explicitly for instructional purposes and avoid reproducing and distributing entire works for individual student use, but rather copy or display excerpts. To avoid potential copyright infringement when planning and delivering instruction, the teacher can either ask the creator for permission to use their work, or ask their school, district, or individual students to purchase the material. Teachers can further protect themselves by citing the source of all retrieved and distributed content. Utilizing free instructional material that is not covered under the Copyright Law, including facts and resources within the **public domain** or **Creative Commons**, as well as government records, pictures, and maps, allows teachers to avoid copyright infringement when creating, planning, and delivering instruction.

FAIR USE DOCTRINE, PUBLIC DOMAIN, AND CREATIVE COMMONS

Fair Use Doctrine	<ul><li>The Fair Use Doctrine allows educators to use, reproduce, and redistribute copyrighted materials for educational purposes so long as they adhere to specified guidelines. These guidelines are typically categorized as:</li><li>**Purpose**: Materials must be used for educational, nonprofit purposes to achieve a specific learning objective</li><li>**Nature**: Refers to the type of copyrighted work being reproduced (fictional/nonfictional, consumable)</li><li>**Amount**: Reproduction and redistribution must be limited to a small portion of the creator's work, such as an excerpt from a book</li><li>**Effect**: Reproduction and redistribution may not interfere with the creator's ability to substantially profit from their work in the future</li></ul>
Public Domain	Materials in the public domain are not protected under copyright laws and are free for use, reproduction, or redistribution. This includes government or historical documents, speeches, ideas, or facts, or works published before March 1, 1989 that do not have an official copyright license. Copyrighted works in the United States enter the public domain seventy years after the death of the original creator.
Creative Commons	Creative Commons is an organization in which creators can reserve partial copyrights to their original works while relinquishing others to allow for public use, reproduction, and redistribution. This organization is intended to provide educators with access to learning materials, resources, and original works to incorporate into their classroom.

ACCEPTABLE USE POLICIES

Acceptable use policies are integral to establishing a classroom environment in which all students and staff engage with technology safely and appropriately. An acceptable use policy is an **agreement** between students, families, the school, and the district to ensure users are **accountable** for their use of technology and online behavior. These policies outline specific guidelines and **expectations** to make users aware of safe and responsible practices regarding technology use in the classroom and help to prevent inappropriate behavior by defining clear **consequences** for violating the terms. In addition, acceptable use policies are beneficial in informing students, staff, and families of the actions taken to protect students' privacy and safety when using technology in the classroom, such as blocking access to inappropriate or non-instructional websites. When acceptable use policies are successfully implemented and followed, students, teachers, and families are protected while interacting with digital materials in the classroom, ensuring a safe and appropriate learning environment.

> **Review Video:** <u>**Benefits of Technology in the Classroom**</u>
> Visit mometrix.com/academy and enter code: 536375

DIGITAL ETIQUETTE

Digital etiquette refers to a set of guidelines for **appropriate** and **responsible** interaction with technology and individuals online. These guidelines emphasize the importance of engaging with individuals online politely and respectfully in a considerate manner, just as they would in face-to-face communication. This includes using appropriate language, respecting others' opinions, and avoiding engaging in harmful interactions or content online. In addition, digital etiquette outlines how to adjust communication style based on one's audience to ensure proper and professional interactions. Digital etiquette also defines proper measures for protecting oneself and others when engaging online. This includes avoiding potentially harmful situations such as providing personal information about oneself or others, communicating with individuals whom one does not know, and carefully considering the present and future implications of one's online behavior. As a teacher, following and instilling these guidelines in students is integral to establishing a positive learning environment in which students safely and responsibly interact with technology. Digital etiquette provides teachers and students with a framework for acceptable technology use and online behavior that is necessary for success in an increasingly digital world.

EFFECTIVE INCORPORATION OF TECHNOLOGY IN INSTRUCTION PROCESS

To enhance the quality of the overall instructional process, the teacher must thoughtfully consider a variety of aspects regarding which technology resources will be most valuable in increasing efficiency and effectiveness. The teacher must determine **desired learning outcomes** and evaluate which technologies will be most beneficial in planning, organizing, delivering, and evaluating instruction. They must evaluate the **efficacy** of the resource in supporting students as they achieve learning targets. This includes ensuring that technology resources are current, relevant, and effective in enhancing the delivery of comprehensible and engaging instruction. When determining which technologies to implement for student use, the teacher must assess **developmental appropriateness**, as well as whether the resources are **adaptable** to individual differences, learning needs, and interests. Additionally, it is important that the teacher ensure that technology resources foster **interaction** and **active learning** among students, so as to support curiosity and engagement in learning. As **equity** issues regarding technology may exist within the classroom, the teacher must consider what supports may need to be implemented to properly support students in achieving learning targets. Students' safety and privacy when utilizing technology is paramount. Therefore, the teacher must be certain that selected digital resources protect students from harmful content.

DEVELOPMENTALLY APPROPRIATE SELECTION OF TECHNOLOGY FOR INSTRUCTION

Student learning and achievement is maximized when the teacher applies knowledge of **developmentally appropriate** practices, activities, and materials to selecting technology resources that enhance instruction. Understanding the characteristics and needs of developmental stages, across domains relative to students' age group and individual learning differences, when planning and delivering instruction enables the teacher to implement technology that supports achievement. Effectively applying this knowledge requires the teacher to incorporate digital resources that provide **age** and **individually appropriate** challenges to facilitate developmental growth. This includes integrating technology that supports instruction by stimulating engagement, curiosity, and exploration. Developmentally appropriate technology provides appropriate levels of difficulty, interaction, and active learning opportunities based upon students' developmental stage while accommodating individual needs, interests, and abilities. Additionally, in developmentally appropriate practice, the teacher integrates technology resources to accompany instructional activities for a length of time that is beneficial to students relative to their developmental stage to maximize learning benefits.

INTEGRATING TECHNOLOGY TO PROMOTE CREATIVITY AND INNOVATION

The availability of digital resources allows the teacher to provide students with multiple opportunities to develop their creativity and innovation in all areas of instruction. When integrated to accompany learning, technology is highly beneficial in allowing students to navigate new ways to **construct knowledge**, **generate ideas**, and **create products**. Effectively incorporating technology for these purposes requires the teacher to consider the instructional topic, specific skills they intend to develop, desired learning outcomes, and students' individual needs and interests. This knowledge enables the teacher to determine which digital resources are most engaging, applicable, and beneficial in providing a learning environment that enhances creativity and innovation among students. For example, digital storytelling resources are effective in enhancing creative writing in language arts, virtual labs can enhance science instruction, and digital drawing apps can enrich artistic creativity for creating new ideas and products. During instruction, assuming the role of facilitator while allowing flexibility for appropriate student choice is an effective strategy for allowing the expression of creativity as students manipulate digital tools for the development of knowledge, ideas, and products. It is important to note, however, that technology in the classroom must be used intentionally to enhance, rather than replace, instruction.

The effective integration of technology into instruction is invaluable to promoting creative thinking and innovation among students when constructing and generating knowledge, new ideas, and products. With the vast array of available technology for instructional use, the teacher can select from a multitude of resources on a variety of topics to enhance instruction and accommodate students' varying learning styles, needs, and interests. The incorporation of technology facilitates the creative and innovative process while promoting **critical thinking** and **problem-solving** abilities by allowing students to explore, manipulate, and learn the functions of digital tools in a way that is relevant to them. This encourages students to employ **higher-order thinking** skills as they make connections between the capabilities of digital resources and their application in solving problems and creating new ideas and products. Using technology to support instruction increases engagement and enhances the overall learning experience. Students' understanding is deepened as they construct knowledge using technology resources.

EQUITY ISSUES IN THE CLASSROOM RELATED TO THE USE OF TECHNOLOGY

The integration of technology to enhance learning is a valuable and increasingly prevalent component of instruction. However, equity issues related to the use of technology pose significant impacts on teaching and learning. Schools in **rural** or **socioeconomically disadvantaged** districts may lack the necessary funding to provide all students with technology devices for classroom use. Economically underprivileged students may lack internet access, as well as computers and digital devices at home or access to a public library, thus impeding their ability to complete assignments outside of class that require technology use. During instructional activities that require students to bring personal digital devices for participation, students without their own devices face inequity that hinders their ability to engage in learning. In addition, students that lack access to digital resources often face challenges in the classroom, as they may not have developed the same knowledge regarding technology use and functions as classmates with more experience. Equity issues related to technology access and use can negatively impact academic achievement. Therefore, it is imperative that the teacher is mindful of potential inequities that exist within their classroom when planning instruction to properly address them and support student success.

IDENTIFYING AND ADDRESSING ISSUES

As technology becomes increasingly integrated into daily life, inequities among students are more apparent and pose significant impacts to achievement. Identifying disparities related to technology is integral to applying equitable practices to ensure that students are supported. To properly identify digital equity issues, the teacher must recognize some of the **causal factors**, including socioeconomic status, race, and geographic location, and determine the presence of these factors in their district. Additionally, the teacher must be aware of individual students' backgrounds and needs to identify potential inequities regarding technology. Applying **equitable practices** to address these issues ensures all students have equal academic opportunities. It cannot be assumed that all students have devices or access to computers and the internet at home. Therefore, the teacher should avoid requiring technology use outside of the classroom when possible. If the school is financially able, students can be issued equipment such as devices and hotspots to establish equity. The teacher can also provide alternative, paper assignments that achieve the same outcomes as the technology-based version if school devices are unavailable. In the classroom, the teacher can provide time during, before, and after the school day for technology use, as well as provide available school-issued devices for activities.

EFFECTIVELY ADDRESSING EQUITY ISSUES

Access to technology and familiarity with its functions is vital for success in the modern-day classroom. Therefore, implementing appropriate measures for addressing inequities among students regarding technology use is imperative to supporting and facilitating academic achievement. By consciously applying **equitable practices**, teachers and staff ensure that all students are provided with the necessary support for access to technology and digital resources for instructional use. In addition, promptly identifying and addressing equity issues ensures that students are able to keep pace with their peers in regard to understanding how to utilize digital resources to maximize their learning. Applying equitable practices to support students that lack access to technology helps close the achievement gap by providing all students with equal opportunities for academic achievement.

Chapter Quiz

Ready to see how well you retained what you just read? Scan the QR code to go directly to the chapter quiz interface for this study guide. If you're using a computer, simply visit the bonus page at **mometrix.com/bonus948/oaeapkma** and click the Chapter Quizzes link.

The Professional Environment

Transform passive reading into active learning! After immersing yourself in this chapter, put your comprehension to the test by taking a quiz. The insights you gained will stay with you longer this way. Scan the QR code to go directly to the chapter quiz interface for this study guide. If you're using a computer, simply visit the bonus page at **mometrix.com/bonus948/oaeapkma** and click the Chapter Quizzes link.

Legal and Ethical Use of Resources

LEGAL AND ETHICAL REQUIREMENTS FOR USING RESOURCES AND TECHNOLOGIES

The legal and ethical requirements regarding the use of educational resources and technologies serves as an important frame of reference for teachers when selecting learning materials. Understanding these guidelines is beneficial in effectively determining which resources and technologies are **safe**, **secure**, **appropriate**, and **legal** for classroom use. This helps to protect the data and privacy of both teachers and students when interacting with instructional materials. In addition, this ensures that teachers and students are aware of what constitutes acceptable use of technology resources to protect their safety when engaging online. It is also important to be cognizant of legal and ethical standards in relation to the **reproduction** and **redistribution** of learning materials and technologies. Doing so ensures teachers understand how to properly adhere to copyright laws so as not to infringe upon the original creator's ability to profit from their work.

COPYRIGHT ACT

When selecting educational resources and technologies to implement in the classroom, it is important that teachers consider the guidelines of the **Copyright Act**. The Copyright Act protects creators by prohibiting the unauthorized use, reproduction, or redistribution of their original works. This extends to digital resources as well, including photographs, video clips, website articles, or online learning materials. While the **Fair Use Doctrine** permits teachers to utilize copyrighted materials for educational purposes, they must be mindful of its restrictions and take the proper precautions to avoid **copyright infringement**. When using copyrighted resources or technologies, teachers can obtain permission directly from the creator, purchase the materials or licenses for use themselves, or ask their school, district, or students to purchase them. In addition, when using, reproducing, or distributing lesson materials, teachers should always cite the appropriate source in order to give credit to the original creator.

FAIR USE DOCTRINE

Under the **Fair Use Doctrine**, teachers are permitted to utilize, reproduce, and redistribute copyrighted materials for educational purposes. However, this doctrine includes limitations that teachers must adhere to when selecting educational resources and technologies to implement in the classroom. The **purpose** of utilizing copyrighted materials must be strictly educational and intended to achieve specific objectives. Teachers must also consider the **nature** of all copyrighted resources and technologies to determine whether they meet the requirements of the Fair Use Doctrine. All copyrighted materials must be used for informational purposes, and typically should be limited to published, nonfiction works. The **amount** of copyrighted material that is reproduced or redistributed must be limited to small excerpts rather than the entire work, and teachers must appropriately cite the original source. In addition, teachers must consider the effect of their use of

142

copyrighted resources and technologies on the future **potential market**. Use of copyrighted materials must not interfere with the creator's ability to profit from their work.

DATA SECURITY

Teachers, staff, and students engage with numerous digital resources for a variety of administrative and educational purposes. As such, protecting **data security** when interacting with these materials is increasingly important in establishing a safe, secure learning environment. When selecting educational technologies, such as student information systems (SIS) or digital learning tools, it is imperative that teachers ensure they are aligned with legal and ethical standards regarding data security. All resources must adhere to the requirements outlined by the **Family Educational Rights and Privacy Act (FERPA)** regarding the disclosure of students' sensitive or personally identifiable information. Teachers must also observe their **district and school's policies** regarding the implementation of educational technologies to ensure they are approved for use. In addition, many education technology companies collect students' data as they interact with digital resources with the intention of utilizing it to inform future educational decisions. It is therefore important that teachers consider the nature of the technology they are implementing to ensure that the data collected from students is used strictly for educational purposes. Taking measures to protect students' data when interacting with educational technology resources ensures their safety both within and outside of the classroom.

PRIVACY

Protecting students' privacy when interacting with educational resources and technologies is paramount to ensuring their safety both within and outside of the classroom. Prior to selecting learning materials, teachers must ensure that they follow all legal and ethical requirements regarding student privacy. This includes determining whether the resources and technologies in question follow the standards outlined by the **Family Educational Rights and Privacy Act (FERPA)** and the **Children's Online Privacy Protection Act (COPPA)**. In doing so, teachers ensure that students' sensitive and personally identifiable information, such as academic, behavioral, or medical records, are secure when interacting with instructional materials. This is necessary to protecting students from encountering potentially harmful situations or individuals that could compromise their privacy and cause long-term negative impacts.

ACCEPTABLE USE POLICIES

Acceptable use policies to govern the use of educational technologies are integral to ensuring a safe, secure learning environment. These documents give guidelines for **acceptable behavior** when interacting with digital resources under the school network, as well as outline **consequences** for violating the terms. Acceptable use policies also inform teachers, staff, students, and families of the measures in place to protect **data security** and **privacy** within the school, such as only allowing individuals with the proper credentials to access the network. Acceptable use policies are beneficial in discouraging users from engaging in inappropriate behavior by outlining standards for responsible use to ensure that sensitive information remains secure. This helps to prevent interaction with potentially harmful individuals or situations that could threaten the safety and privacy of students, teachers, staff, or families, as well as the security of the school network.

Legal and Ethical Obligations Surrounding Student Rights

LEGAL REQUIREMENTS FOR EDUCATORS

SPECIAL EDUCATION SERVICES

Establishing an inclusive, equitable learning environment for students with disabilities requires educators to adhere to strict legal guidelines regarding special education services. According to **IDEA (Individuals with Disabilities Education Act)**, educators must provide students with disabilities a **free and appropriate public education (FAPE)** in the **least restrictive environment (LRE)**. To do this effectively, educators are required to fully comply with students' **IEP (Individual Education Plan)** at all times. This includes providing students requiring special education services with the necessary supports, accommodations, and modifications according to their IEP throughout all stages of instruction. Educators must also document the academic and behavioral progress of these students in relation to the goals outlined in their IEP to report to the designated case manager. In addition, the specifics of students' special education services must be kept confidential in order to protect their privacy. Adhering to these legal requirements promotes equity in the classroom by ensuring that the unique needs of students with disabilities are met, thus allowing them to effectively participate and engage in learning.

> **Review Video: Medical Conditions in Education**
> Visit mometrix.com/academy and enter code: 531058

FERPA

Understanding and observing the legal requirements related to students' and families' rights is integral to maintaining their confidentiality and establishing a safe, secure learning environment. Educators are required to follow the guidelines of **FERPA (Family Educational Rights and Privacy Act)** regarding students' education records and personally identifiable information. According to FERPA, educators may not release students' education records or personally identifiable information except in authorized situations, such as when the student enrolls in another school, or the information is requested by a financial aid institution in which the student has applied. In all other instances, the educator must have written permission to disclose this information. FERPA also provides students' parents or legal guardians the right to access their child's education records and request that the education records be amended. While educators may not disclose personally identifiable information, they are permitted to release directory information regarding the student, including their name, phone number, or student identification number. However, educators must provide an appropriate amount of time to allow for the refusal of such disclosure. It is also important to note that the rights guaranteed under FERPA become applicable only to the student once they have turned 18 or begun postsecondary education.

DISCIPLINE PROCEDURES AND STUDENT CODE OF CONDUCT

Adhering to legal requirements regarding student discipline procedures is necessary to ensure a safe, orderly, and unbiased learning environment. School districts are responsible for developing a **student code of conduct** to distribute among teachers, staff, students, and families. This document outlines expectations for student behavior, as well as specific consequences for varying degrees of infractions that may occur on school grounds. Educators must strictly adhere to the guidelines stated in the student code of conduct when enacting disciplinary measures. This includes ensuring that consequences for student misbehavior align with the nature of the action and do not interfere with the student's right to a free public education. Disciplinary actions must be free of bias, and must not endanger the student's physical, mental, or emotional health. In addition, the educator must document instances of student discipline, and keep these records confidential to protect the student's right to privacy. Extended suspensions and expulsions must be reserved for instances in which all other disciplinary measures have been exhausted. In such cases, the student is entitled to a hearing at the board of education, and teachers must provide adequate instructional materials for the time that the student is out of the classroom.

Guidelines for acceptable student behavior on school property are outlined in a student code of conduct. Providing students with this reference helps to ensure that the school functions in a safe, orderly, and productive manner so as to create and maintain an environment focused on learning. This document typically addresses a number of topics related to **daily school procedures**, including student dress code standards, acceptable use policies for the internet and digital devices, attendance, grading policies, and academic integrity. Student codes of conduct also address **potential behavioral issues**, such as acceptable conduct while riding school buses, the use of illegal substances on school property, and harmful or disruptive behavior, including bullying, harassment, or fighting. The expectations iterated in student codes of conduct are typically accompanied by an ascending matrix of classroom, administrative, and district-level **consequences** that coincide with the severity and frequency of student infractions.

ESTABLISHING AN EQUITABLE LEARNING ENVIRONMENT FOR ALL STUDENTS

An **equitable environment** is one in which students receive the individual support necessary to facilitate their success in learning. Establishing such an environment requires educators to adhere to several legal guidelines to ensure all students are provided with fair access to learning opportunities. Educators must be sure that all students are included in the educational program, and therefore, may not discriminate based upon students' race, religion, gender, background, disability, or any other differentiating characteristics. All students must be provided with equal access to learning materials, resources, technologies, and supports. In addition, educators must fully comply with all accommodations outlined in students' **IEPs**, **504 plans**, and **Behavior Intervention Plans (BIP)**, and implement all required supports to provide them with equitable access to learning.

> **Review Video: 504 Plans and IEPs**
> Visit mometrix.com/academy and enter code: 881103

CHILD ABUSE

One of the primary responsibilities of an educator is to ensure the safety of all students. In order to do so, it is important that educators understand and follow all legal requirements related to child abuse. Within the classroom, educators are responsible for establishing a safe, secure learning environment. All interactions with students must be appropriate and refrain from harming students' **physical**, **mental**, or **emotional health**. Educators must also recognize the signs of potential **child abuse** or **neglect** among their students. If any abuse or neglect is suspected, educators are legally required to report it immediately to the proper agency according to their state and local laws, regardless of whether there is concrete evidence, as waiting to report it may place the student in continued danger. Reports of potential child abuse or neglect must be **confidential** so as to protect the students' privacy. Depending on the protocols established by individual school districts, educators may be required to notify their school's administration and resource officer of the report.

SIGNIFICANCE OF UNDERSTANDING AND ADHERING TO LEGAL REQUIREMENTS

Understanding the legal requirements for educators ensures that teachers know what is expected of them to maintain professionalism and establish a safe, secure learning environment. This avoids misconception regarding the teacher's **roles** and **responsibilities** within the educational program so teachers understand how to adhere to legal guidelines properly. When teachers are aware of the legal requirements they must follow, they are more effectively able to implement the appropriate protocols for addressing specific education-related situations. This includes instances related to establishing an equitable learning environment, providing special education services, interacting appropriately with students, colleagues, and families, as well as protecting students' privacy. In addition, understanding the legal requirements for educators ensures that they are aware of their own professional rights and how to protect themselves in various education-related situations.

ETHICAL GUIDELINES
CONFIDENTIALITY

Adhering to ethical guidelines in relation to confidentiality is an important part of demonstrating professionalism as well as protecting the privacy of students, their families, and others in the school building. Teachers are required to follow all standards outlined by **FERPA** regarding student and family privacy. This includes preserving the confidentiality of all **personally identifiable information** about students, such as grades, medical history, discipline records, or special education services, except in authorized situations. By following these guidelines, teachers ensure that they do not release any information that may compromise the safety of students or their families. In addition, when students and families feel their personal information is kept confidential, they are more likely to seek necessary supports from the educational program without the fear of being stigmatized. Similarly, teachers must follow ethical guidelines to protect the privacy of their colleagues. Any knowledge about a colleague's personal information must be kept confidential so as to establish positive, professional relationships founded on mutual trust. Doing so facilitates productive collaboration among colleagues to benefit student success in learning.

INTERACTIONS WITH STUDENTS AND OTHERS IN THE SCHOOL COMMUNITY

The daily interactions among students, teachers, staff, and administration largely determine the quality of the school environment. A positive, safe, and professional school community is one in which educators adhere to ethical guidelines regarding interactions with one another and students. Communication with colleagues must be respectful of one another's privacy and confidentiality. This includes avoiding gossiping situations and ensuring that all discussions about colleagues are factual, neutral, and professional in nature. In addition, interactions with members of the school community must **avoid discrimination** of any sort. Similarly, all interactions with students must be inclusive, accepting, and respectful of differences. In addition, educators must maintain proper **boundaries** when communicating with students. This includes avoiding communication outside of the school setting except in authorized situations and ensuring that all interactions maintain professionalism. Any interactions with students must avoid compromising their **physical or mental health**, **safety**, or **ability to learn**. By adhering to these ethical guidelines, educators can ensure that all communication with students and members of the school community contribute to establishing and maintaining a safe, appropriate, and professional learning environment.

Teacher's Role as an Advocate

ADVOCATING FOR STUDENTS

The teacher's role as an advocate is invaluable in ensuring students receive the necessary support to facilitate their achievement. As teachers spend most of the school day with students, they are equipped with an understanding of how to best meet the unique needs within their classroom. Teachers will inevitably encounter situations in which advocacy for students is integral to providing equitable learning opportunities. Students with **physical, social, emotional**, or **learning disabilities** need teachers to advocate on their behalf to ensure special education services or accommodations are implemented. Teachers may also need to advocate for **underprivileged students** to ensure they have equitable access to the learning materials, resources, and technologies necessary for success. Additionally, students experiencing **bullying** may need teachers to ensure the appropriate measures are taken to resolve the issue and maintain a safe learning environment. Effective advocacy requires teachers to listen and communicate with students to determine their needs and seek the appropriate avenues for support. Teachers must also communicate with colleagues, administration, and families to collaborate in addressing students' needs. In some instances, teachers may need to contact the board of education or education advocacy organizations specific to students' needs to ensure they are provided with adequate support.

ADVOCATING FOR THE EDUCATIONAL PROFESSION

Teachers offer valuable perspectives regarding ways to enhance the quality of the education profession. As such, it is important that teachers advocate for themselves in order to help ensure they have the **conditions**, **resources**, and **support systems** necessary to facilitate student success. This includes advocating for equitable allocation of funding, learning materials, technology resources, and professional development opportunities that would help teachers more effectively meet students' learning needs. Teachers can advocate for the profession in a variety of ways. **Communicating frequently** with students, families, and administration allows teachers to discuss their needs and ways to improve the education system. Attending **PTA meetings, public forums**, or **school board meetings** allows teachers to voice their concerns and offer potential solutions. Teachers can also contact **state legislators** to influence their decisions regarding education policies that would impact the quality of the profession. In addition, there are numerous **education advocacy organizations** that teachers can join to connect with one another and influence such decisions. Taking measures to advocate for the education profession is an important part of creating a positive, productive school climate focused on supporting student achievement.

Roles and Responsibilities within the Local Education System

DEPARTMENT CHAIRPERSONS

Department chairpersons are appointed to act as **leaders** within their subject area. These individuals are responsible for a variety of instructional and administrative duties to ensure the **efficacy** of their academic department in supporting the goals and mission of the school. This includes contributing to curriculum development, communicating instructional expectations from administration to their colleagues, and ensuring that daily instruction within the department aligns with campus and district academic standards. Department chairpersons also serve as **resources** for their team, including collaborating with them to design instructional activities and assessments, offering support, and facilitating positive communication with administration. When working with administration, department chairpersons discuss the progress of their department in meeting academic goals, collaborate to develop strategies for assisting faculty in supporting student learning, and ensure their colleagues have the support, materials, and resources necessary for effective instruction. In addition, department chairpersons are often responsible for coordinating department activities and programs that promote student achievement and contribute to creating a positive school community.

SCHOOL PRINCIPAL

The primary role of the **principal** is establishing and maintaining a **school culture** that supports students, teachers, staff, and families in the educational program. This role comprises a multifaceted array of responsibilities that extend to nearly every aspect of the school. The principal is responsible for supervising the **daily operations** of the school to ensure a safe, orderly environment in which teachers, staff, and students are working in alignment with the school's mission. To achieve this, the principal must communicate expectations for a positive, productive school community, ensure academic and behavioral policies are followed by staff and students, and assign staff members specific duties to facilitate an organized, efficient learning environment. In addition, it is important that the principal support staff, students, and families by engaging in frequent, open communication, addressing concerns, and providing resources necessary to promote growth and achievement. The principal is also responsible for ensuring that the school's educational program is effective in supporting teachers, staff, and students in the achievement of academic standards. This includes overseeing curriculum, monitoring instructional practices, measuring their school's performance in relation to district academic standards, as well as communicating the progress and needs of the school to the board of education.

BOARD OF TRUSTEES

Each school within a district is overseen by a **board of trustees** responsible for making decisions to ensure that the educational program supports students' learning needs for academic achievement. The board of trustees is comprised of a group of **elected individuals** that are typically members of the community in which they serve. As such, they have an understanding of the educational needs of the students within the community and can apply this knowledge to make effective decisions regarding the learning program. Members within a board of trustees are responsible for creating an educational program in alignment with students' needs, as well as setting goals and developing strategies that support students in achieving them. This includes determining a **budget plan, allocating resources**, and making **administrative decisions** that benefit the school. In addition, board members are responsible for analyzing assessment data to make informed decisions regarding strategies to best support individual schools within the district and ensuring that measures are being implemented to effectively meet students' learning needs.

CURRICULUM COORDINATORS

Curriculum coordinators are responsible for the **development** and **implementation** of curriculum that is aligned with campus and district academic goals. These individuals work closely with teachers and administrators to analyze student progress in relation to the educational program, primarily through **assessment scores**, to determine the overall effectiveness of the curriculum in supporting students' achievement. Analyzing student progress enables curriculum coordinators to identify strengths and areas for improvement within the curriculum to make adjustments that best meet students' learning needs as they work to achieve learning targets. Ensuring that curriculum aligns with academic standards and students' learning needs facilitates more effective teaching and learning. Doing so provides teachers with a clear understanding of how to adequately prepare students for success, thus allowing them to design focused instruction and implement necessary supports to promote the achievement of campus and district academic standards.

SCHOOL TECHNOLOGY COORDINATORS

Incorporating technology into the classroom is highly valuable in diversifying instructional strategies to promote student learning and engagement. School **technology coordinators** facilitate this integration to enhance teaching and learning, as they are responsible for the **organization, maintenance**, and **allocation** of available technology resources within the school building. This includes ensuring that all technology is functional, updated, properly stored, and accessible to teachers. These individuals are also responsible for **staying current** on developing digital resources that could be implemented to improve the learning experience, as well as communicating with the board of education regarding **acquiring** technology resources for their school. Doing so

148

ensures that teachers have the materials necessary to best support students' learning. In addition, technology coordinators **educate** teachers and staff on the uses of technology resources, as well as strategies to implement them in the classroom for more effective instruction.

SPECIAL EDUCATION PROFESSIONALS

Special education professionals work with students of various disabilities, their teachers, and families to provide an equitable, inclusive environment that supports learning and development. These individuals are responsible for creating an educational plan that is tailored to support the unique needs of disabled students and ensuring that this plan is followed in all areas of the school. Special educators develop **individualized education programs** (IEPs) according to students' areas of need, develop academic and behavioral goals, as well as provide supports and modifications to accommodate students in achieving them. Special education professionals work with teachers to educate them on the proper implementation of individualized accommodations to ensure all students have the support necessary to successfully engage in learning. This includes collaborating with teachers to adapt and modify curriculum, instructional activities, and assessments to meet the individual needs of students with disabilities. In addition, special educators may work alongside classroom teachers in a team-teaching setting or provide individualized instruction as necessary. Students' academic and behavioral progress is monitored over time, and special educators communicate this information to families in order to collaborate in developing future goals and strategies to support achievement.

ROLES AND RESPONSIBILITIES OF PROFESSIONALS WITHIN THE EDUCATION PROGRAM

The roles and responsibilities of various professionals within the educational program are described as follows:

- **Principal**—The principal is responsible for ensuring that the daily operations of the school function in a safe, orderly manner that aligns with the goals of the educational program. This includes delegating tasks to staff, enforcing academic and behavioral policies, ensuring instructional practices support student achievement, and communicating with students, staff, and families to establish a positive learning environment.
- **Vice Principal**—The vice principal's role is to assist the principal in supervising the daily operations of the school to create a safe, orderly, and productive learning environment. They are responsible for working with teachers, staff, students, and families to support them in the educational program. This includes enforcing academic and behavioral policies, addressing concerns, facilitating communication, and ensuring instructional practices support student achievement of campus and district academic goals.
- **Board of Trustees**—The board of trustees is responsible for developing an educational program that reflects the learning needs of students within the community. This includes developing educational goals, strategies to support students in achieving them, and ensuring that schools within the district are in alignment with the educational program. The board of trustees is also responsible for such administrative decisions as developing a budget plan and allocating resources to schools within the district according to students' needs.
- **Curriculum Coordinator**—Curriculum coordinators are responsible for developing a curriculum that aligns with campus and district academic goals, and ensuring it is implemented properly to support student achievement. This includes working with teachers and administrators to measure student progress within the curriculum and adjusting instructional strategies as necessary to support student success.

- **Assessment Coordinator**—Assessment coordinators schedule, disperse, and collect standardized assessments and testing materials within the school building. They are responsible for educating teachers on proper assessment protocols to ensure that all practices align with district policies, collaborating with them to develop strategies that support student achievement, and ensuring all students are provided with necessary accommodations according to individual need.
- **Technology Coordinator**—Technology coordinators facilitate the integration of digital resources into the curriculum. They are responsible for acquiring, organizing, maintaining, and allocating technology within the school. These individuals also work with teachers and staff to educate them on ways to utilize technology resources to enhance instruction.
- **Department Chair**—Department chairpersons act as leaders among the teachers within their content area. Their responsibilities include contributing to curriculum development, facilitating communication between administration and their colleagues, and ensuring instructional practices align with the educational program. They also collaborate with members of their team to develop instructional practices that best support student achievement of campus and district academic goals.
- **Teacher Assistant**—The teacher assistant's role is to support the classroom teacher in both instructional and non-instructional duties. This includes assisting with the preparation, organization, and cleanup of lesson materials, working with small groups of students, managing student behavior, and ensuring the classroom functions in a safe, orderly manner.
- **Paraprofessional**—Paraprofessionals are licensed within the field of education and are responsible for assisting the teacher with daily classroom operations. This includes working with individual or small groups of students to provide instructional support, assisting with the preparation of lesson plans and materials, managing student behavior, and completing administrative duties.
- **Speech-Language Pathologist**—Speech-Language pathologists are special education professionals that work with students that have varying degrees of language and communication difficulties. They are responsible for evaluating and diagnosing disabilities related to speech and language, as well as developing individualized treatment programs. Speech-language pathologists then work with these students to remedy language and communication disabilities, as well as collaborate with teachers, staff, and families regarding ways to support their progress.
- **ESL Specialist**—ESL (English as a second language) specialists work with students for whom English is not their native language. They are responsible for evaluating students' levels of English language proficiency across the domains of reading, writing, speaking, and listening, determining necessary linguistic supports, and working with teachers to develop strategies that support English language acquisition. ESL specialists also work with individual or small groups of students to monitor progress and develop English language proficiency skills.
- **Guidance Counselor**—The role of guidance counselors is to support students' social, emotional, academic, and behavioral needs. This includes providing counseling services, mediation, and for upper grade level students, advice regarding course selection and career choices. These individuals communicate with teachers, staff, and families to develop and implement plans to support students' personal growth and academic achievement.

- **School Nurse**—The school nurse is responsible for providing a range of healthcare to students and staff in the school building. This includes evaluating the physical, mental, and emotional health of students and staff, as well as delivering general first-aid treatments. School nurses are also responsible for organizing and dispersing prescribed medications to students in accordance with their healthcare plan and educating teachers and staff regarding best practices for ensuring students' health and safety. School nurses may work with special education professionals to assess students' needs in the development of an individualized education program.

- **Building Service Worker**—Building service workers are responsible for the general maintenance of the school building and outside campus. This includes ensuring that all areas, equipment, and furniture are clean, functional, and safe for student and staff use. These individuals are also responsible for transporting heavy equipment and furniture throughout the school building.

- **Secretary**—The school secretary is responsible for assisting the principal, vice principal, and other office personnel in daily administrative duties. This individual assumes a variety of responsibilities to ensure the efficient function of daily operations within the school. Their responsibilities include communicating with students, families, and other office visitors, directing phone calls to the appropriate location, handling financial matters, and coordinating the school calendar.

- **Library/Media Specialist**—Library and media specialists coordinate the organization, maintenance, and allocation of all library and media resources within the school building. They are responsible for educating students regarding the proper use of library and media resources to locate information, including how to navigate the internet safely and appropriately for educational purposes. Library and media specialists also direct students toward reading material aligned with their literacy skills and provide teachers with learning materials to incorporate into instruction.

- **Instructional Leadership Team (ILT)**—An instructional leadership team is comprised of individuals responsible for educating teachers regarding current and relevant instructional philosophies and practices to enhance student learning. These individuals collaborate with teachers to educate them regarding how to implement instructional strategies, activities, and assessments to effectively meet students' learning needs and support their achievement of campus and district academic goals.

- **School Resource Officer**—The role of the school resource officer is to maintain a safe, orderly environment for teachers, staff, and students. They are responsible for ensuring the physical security of the school, handling legal infractions within the school, and addressing conflicts among students. The school resource officer also works with administration and staff to develop emergency drill procedures.

- **Pupil Personnel Worker (PPW)**—Pupil personnel workers are responsible for addressing issues that hinder the academic achievement of at-risk students. These individuals communicate with teachers, administration, staff, and families to ensure these students are supported both within and outside of the school building. This includes addressing issues related to behavior, crisis intervention, attendance, and home lives. Pupil personnel workers direct families toward school and community support resources and collaborate with teachers to implement supports that facilitate success in learning.

Local, District, and State Educational Structure

MAINTAINING ACCURATE STUDENT RECORDS

Maintaining accurate **instructional** and **non-instructional** records is imperative for providing a comprehensive representation of students' academic and behavioral progress within the education program. Records pertaining to such matters as students' **academics**, **behavior**, **attendance**, **medical history**, and **special education services** must be well-organized and updated frequently in order to establish a safe, orderly environment that best supports their learning needs. Most school districts and campuses provide specific requirements regarding the procedures for maintaining accurate student records. This includes the frequency in which grades and attendance must be updated, as well as the processes for documenting behavioral progress and information related to goals outlined in students' IEPs, BIPs, and 504 plans. Educators must strictly adhere to these policies at all times in order to gain accurate insight regarding students' progress in relation to reaching academic and behavioral goals. This allows educators to make informed instructional decisions, seek the proper supports, and adjust their practices as necessary to meet students' learning needs. In addition, maintaining accurate records is also beneficial for communicating productively with students' families to develop and implement plans to support their achievement.

PROCEDURES FOR ADMINISTERING STATE AND DISTRICT MANDATED ASSESSMENTS

State and district mandated assessments measure students' progress in relation to reaching academic benchmarks. Properly administering these assessments requires the consistent adherence to strict procedures to ensure confidentiality, equity, and accuracy. Only authorized test **proctors** may administer these tests. These individuals are responsible for preparing the testing room and testing materials prior to the assessment. For digital exams, they must ensure all students have the proper credentials. Proctors must follow all testing instructions, including the procedures for administering test materials and reading directions aloud exactly as they are written. All students with IEPs must receive the proper **accommodations** for an equitable testing environment. Students must receive the same allotted time to complete the assessment unless IEP accommodations permit extra time. The testing environment must be free of any materials unrelated to the exam, and the proctor must observe students throughout the test to ensure they follow the correct procedures. After the test, proctors must collect and organize all answer sheets and booklets. For digital assessments, proctors must ensure students log off properly. Testing materials must be packaged according to the instructions and stored in a secure area until they are sent to the testing agency for scoring.

IMPORTANCE OF ADHERING TO PROCEDURES

State and district mandated assessments are intended to measure students' progress in relation to achieving academic benchmarks, and the results are used for a variety of purposes. Assessment results influence decisions regarding the allocation of funding and resources among schools, changes to curriculum, and adjustments to the education program to more effectively meet students' learning needs. These results are also used to identify and address achievement gaps among various populations to increase equity. Therefore, the strict adherence to all required procedures for administering state and district mandated assessments is imperative to producing an **objective** and **accurate** representation of student achievement. Doing so ensures the same degree of **uniformity** in regard to testing conditions, operations, and materials across schools, as well as ensures all students are provided the necessary accommodations to ensure an **equitable** testing environment. Adhering to these procedures is also important in maintaining student **confidentiality** both during and after the assessment by preventing the sharing or reproduction of testing materials and ensuring students' completed exams are properly organized and stored in a secure area.

SEEKING INFORMATION AND ASSISTANCE
UNDERSTANDING THE STATE EDUCATION SYSTEM STRUCTURE

State education systems are organized in a **tiered** structure, and each component is responsible for varying aspects of the education program. The **state department of education** is responsible for overseeing and establishing standards to regulate the operations of all school districts within the state. This includes allocating funds for individual districts, providing professional certifications, as well as developing comprehensive polices to govern curriculum, academic standards, and assessments at the district level. **School districts** are responsible for implementing the policies established by the state department of education. Each district is governed by a board of trustees elected by members of the community to oversee the operations of all public schools within the district. This includes hiring staff members, determining a budget plan for individual schools, and developing an education program aligned with state policies. **School campuses** within a district are tasked with maintaining the daily operations within the building. This includes addressing matters related to students, staff, and the community, as well as ensuring instructional practices are aligned with the educational program created by the district. Recognizing the roles of the varying components within the education system is beneficial in understanding the proper avenues to take when seeking information or assistance.

UNDERSTANDING THE PROFESSIONAL ROLES OF INDIVIDUALS WITHIN THE SCHOOL CAMPUS

The school campus is comprised of a complex network of professional roles that work together to establish an efficient, orderly, and productive learning environment focused on student achievement. Each professional within the building is responsible for specific duties to maintain the daily operations of the school campus and meet students' learning needs. Understanding the nature and responsibilities of these varying roles, including how they work together in supporting the education program, is beneficial in effectively navigating the school campus when seeking information or assistance. This knowledge is important for determining which individual or department will be most helpful in addressing specific situations or providing support, as well as the proper procedures for doing so.

AVAILABLE RESOURCES AT THE CAMPUS, LOCAL, AND STATE LEVEL

Understanding the structure of the education system is beneficial in determining the proper avenues for seeking information and assistance related to specific situations at the campus, local, and state level. Professionals within the **school campus** serve as valuable support resources for a variety of matters, including those related to students, families, staff, and academics. For example, principals and administrators can provide information and assistance regarding the daily operations of the school building. Guidance counselors and other specialists are important resources for student and family matters, special education services, and support programs. Mentors, department chairs, and colleagues can provide support in relation to instructional practices. At the **district level**, members of the board of trustees can provide information and assistance regarding the education program, such as budget and resource allocation, assessments, curriculum development, and transportation. Additionally, varying departments within the local board of education are beneficial resources for information pertaining to human resource matters, professional development opportunities, and community support services. The **state department of education** is comprised of several factions that provide a variety of services, including information and assistance regarding professional certification, continuing education, updates to education policies, as well as grants and funding for schools.

Professional Development

AVAILABLE RESOURCES AND SUPPORT SYSTEMS

Effective educators continuously seek professional development opportunities to refine their teaching practice. There are multiple resources and support systems that teachers can utilize to develop their professional knowledge and skills. Within the school building, mentors are available to offer ideas, advice, and support in developing teaching practices and strategies to implement in the classroom for effective teaching and learning. The school's **instructional leadership team** (ILT) is also a valuable resource for educating teachers regarding current instructional practices to enhance student engagement and learning. Teachers can continue their professional education by enrolling in university courses or participating in state-initiated programs to stay informed on relevant pedagogical theories and practices. Service centers are also available that offer workshops, training, and conferences on a variety of topics related to education to support teachers' professional development. In addition, numerous digital support resources are available that allow teachers to enroll in courses, participate in informational webinars, and collaborate with other educators in professional learning communities to build and enhance their teaching practice.

EXAMPLE OPPORTUNITIES THAT CAN ENHANCE TEACHING PRACTICE

Professional development opportunities are available to address a variety of needs for refining one's practice and developing pedagogical knowledge. Professional development trainings can serve to educate teachers on how to utilize and incorporate current technologies into the classroom, as well as teach strategies for implementing relevant and engaging instructional techniques, materials, and resources into the classroom. These opportunities can also be beneficial in teaching educators how to demonstrate cultural competency and skills for productive collaboration with colleagues to enhance student learning. Teachers can also seek professional development opportunities to learn best practices for addressing a variety of student needs, such as intellectual, physical, social, or emotional disabilities, or linguistic needs of ELLs. Actively seeking and participating in professional development trainings helps to ensure teachers stay current on pedagogical theories that can serve as a framework for their instructional practice.

EFFECTIVELY UTILIZING RESOURCES AND SUPPORT SYSTEMS

The field of education is multifaceted and continuously evolving. As such, it is important that teachers of all experience levels engage in the vast array of **available resources** and **support systems** to develop and refine their professional skills. Doing so enhances students' learning, as teachers that actively seek professional development are more current on pedagogical theories and practices, as well as instructional strategies, resources, and technologies to incorporate in the classroom. This allows teachers to design and implement more effective instruction, as it provides them with an increased range of knowledge and tools to enhance student engagement and understanding. In addition, as students' individual needs are diverse, participating in resources and support systems allows teachers to educate themselves on how to properly accommodate them to enhance the learning experience. Utilizing resources and support systems also enables teachers to learn from and collaborate with other educators in professional learning communities to continuously develop new skills, ideas, and instructional methods that enhance student learning.

TEACHER APPRAISALS
CHARACTERISTICS, GOALS, AND PROCEDURES

Teacher appraisals are a method of evaluation intended to provide the teacher with continuous feedback regarding their **performance** and areas in which they can improve their professional skills to enhance student learning. Feedback is provided periodically throughout the school year and derives from classroom **observations** typically conducted by the principal or grade-level administrator. Observations can either be **formally** scheduled and last the duration of a lesson, or can be in the form of shorter, informal **walk-through** evaluations. In both instances, the observer watches and collects information as the teacher delivers instruction, directs learning activities, and interacts with students. The teacher's performance is then measured against **criteria** across several domains pertaining to planning, preparing, and delivering instruction. This score is used to provide the teacher with detailed feedback in post-observation meetings regarding their strengths and specific areas in which they can improve their practice to more effectively meet students' learning needs. Feedback is used to support the teacher in developing specific **professional goals** and strategies for improving their teaching skills.

BENEFITS OF APPRAISAL RESULTS IN IMPROVING PROFESSIONAL SKILLS

The results of teacher appraisals are beneficial in providing educators with **specific feedback** regarding areas in which they can improve their professional skills. Effective teachers understand the value of continuously **refining their practice** to enhance student learning, and therefore, actively seek opportunities to do so. However, it may prove difficult for teachers to objectively assess their own efficacy in the classroom. Appraisal results communicate feedback from the outside perspective of the observer for a comprehensive evaluation of their performance, thus providing teachers with clarity regarding their strengths and areas for growth. This allows educators to effectively develop **professional goals** to improve their skills in targeted areas and **strategies** to achieve these goals successfully.

WORKING WITH SUPERVISORS, MENTORS, AND COLLEAGUES
ENHANCING PROFESSIONAL KNOWLEDGE AND SKILLS

When teachers collaborate with supervisors, mentors, and other colleagues, it facilitates a productive **professional learning community** that supports the continuous development of knowledge and skills related to education. Doing so provides teachers with the opportunity to work with educational professionals of varying backgrounds, experiences, and expertise. This exposes teachers to a wide range of **perspectives**, **approaches**, and **philosophies** that they can learn from to build and enhance their practice. In such a setting, teachers can interact with other professionals within the school community to share ideas, support one another, and collaborate productively in developing strategies to improve their efficacy in the classroom. Additionally, actively engaging with supervisors, mentors, and colleagues facilitates the open communication necessary for productive collaboration in effectively addressing issues to enhance the school community.

ADDRESSING ISSUES AND BUILDING PROFESSIONAL SKILLS

Productive collaboration with supervisors, mentors, and colleagues is essential to addressing issues related to the educational program and continuously developing professional practices. There are multiple opportunities for such collaboration within the school community that accommodate varying purposes. By participating in **professional learning communities**, members of the educational program can collaborate and support one another in addressing concerns and building professional skills. In subject-area **department** or **team meetings**, educators can work together to share ideas, strategies, and resources related to their content area for more effective instruction. Working with supervisors and mentors in **post-observation conferences** provides teachers with valuable feedback regarding their strengths and areas for improvement. Such collaboration is beneficial in creating specific goals and strategies for professional growth. Additionally, engaging in collaborative **professional development opportunities**, including workshops, conferences, programs, and courses, is beneficial in allowing educators to build upon one another's experiences, backgrounds, and expertise to enhance professional practices.

PROFESSIONAL DEVELOPMENT RESOURCES

The various professional development resources available to teachers and staff are discussed below:

- **Mentors/Support Systems**: Mentors and other dedicated support resources within the school system are intended to provide teachers with guidance to enhance their professional knowledge, skills, and expertise. These individuals are typically highly experienced and work with teachers to develop effective instructional strategies, classroom management techniques, and learning materials to improve their teaching skills.
- **Conferences**: Education conferences are multifaceted events in which teachers can learn about current developments in their field to improve their professional knowledge, pedagogical skills, and technical expertise. Conference events are comprised of numerous professional development opportunities, including presentations on current pedagogical theories and practices, collaborative workshops, and training sessions regarding the implementation of new instructional strategies and technology resources. At these events, teachers can also network with one another to connect and share resources, ideas, and strategies that enhance their teaching practice.
- **Professional Associations**: Education associations provide teachers with access to numerous professional development opportunities for improving knowledge, pedagogical skills, and technical expertise. These associations can be related to general education or content specific, and offer information regarding education conferences, workshops, training opportunities, and courses to enhance teaching practices. Professional education associations also allow teachers the opportunity to network with one another to build professional knowledge by sharing ideas, resources, and strategies to implement in the classroom.
- **Online Resources**: Numerous online resources, including websites, blogs, webinar trainings, and discussion forums are available to support teachers in enhancing their professional knowledge, skills, and technical expertise on a variety of topics. Teachers can utilize these resources to learn current pedagogical theories and practices, instructional and classroom management strategies, as well as relevant technology resources to implement in the classroom for enhanced student learning. Online resources are also valuable for collaborating with other teachers in building professional knowledge and sharing ideas, learning materials, and resources that improve instructional practices.
- **Workshops**: Workshop training sessions provide teachers the opportunity to build professional knowledge, skills, and expertise by educating them on current instructional strategies, classroom management techniques, and digital resources in a hands-on setting. Workshops are typically dedicated to a specific pedagogical topic and allow teachers to collaborate with one another in learning how to implement it in their classroom.
- **Journals**: Education journals publish newly researched information regarding pedagogical theories and practices teachers can utilize to enhance their professional knowledge. These journals include scholarly articles and case studies regarding topics such as instructional strategies and practices, classroom management techniques, and the implementation of digital resources. Education journals allow teachers to stay current on pedagogical developments in order to continuously improve their teaching skills.

- **Coursework**: Engaging in coursework is beneficial in continuing formal professional education to enhance knowledge, pedagogical skills, and technical expertise. Doing so allows teachers to learn from other experienced educators regarding current educational theories, practices, instructional strategies, and technology resources. By participating in formal coursework, teachers can continuously build upon their teaching skills and stay current regarding developments in their field.

REFLECTION AND SELF-ASSESSMENT
IMPROVING TEACHING PERFORMANCE AND ACHIEVING PROFESSIONAL GOALS

Just as students are encouraged to reflect upon their academic performance, it is important that teachers **reflect** on and **self-assess** their own efficacy in the classroom. Doing so is integral for improving professional knowledge and skills to enhance student learning. Effective teachers continuously self-evaluate their performance to ensure they are providing engaging, relevant instruction that effectively meets students' learning needs for success. Frequently reflecting upon and assessing the effectiveness of their lesson plans, instructional strategies, assessments, and approaches to classroom management is beneficial in providing teachers with insight regarding their **professional strengths** as well as specific **areas for growth**. With this insight, teachers can identify the knowledge, skills, and strategies they need to improve upon to deliver more effective instruction. This ultimately allows teachers to set relevant professional goals to enhance their teaching practice and determine the steps they need to take in achieving them.

METHODS

Continuous reflection and self-assessment through a variety of methods is beneficial in providing teachers with insight into the effectiveness of their teaching practice. **Reflecting on lessons** after they are finished allows teachers to self-assess their instruction by identifying specific elements that were successful, as well as components that can be improved in the future to enhance student learning. By eliciting **student feedback**, teachers can evaluate whether their instructional strategies, lesson activities, and assessments promote student engagement and understanding. Working with **mentors** and **colleagues** to discuss the effectiveness of lessons, instructional approaches, and classroom management techniques is also valuable in facilitating self-evaluation of teaching practices to seek areas for improvement. In addition, teachers are typically provided the opportunity to **respond to post-observation feedback** prior to attending an appraisal conference. This provides teachers with the opportunity to reflect on their overall performance and prepare to collaborate with the observer in developing professional goals.

Team Teaching and Professional Collaboration

TEAM TEACHING

Team teaching refers to the collaboration of two or more teachers, paraprofessionals, instructional aides, or special education workers in planning and delivering instruction and assessments. There are **several structures** to this approach to accommodate varying teaching styles and student needs. One teacher may provide direct instruction while another engages in lesson activities or monitors student progress. Similarly, one teacher may instruct while another observes and collects information to improve future planning. Students may be grouped with teachers according to their needs to provide differentiation, or teachers may participate simultaneously and equally in all aspects of the learning process. The intention of this approach is to create a **student-centered environment** focused on enhancing and deepening the learning experience. Team teaching is beneficial in allowing increased **individualized instruction** that more effectively meets students' learning needs. Additionally, when multiple teachers are present, students have access to varying

ideas and **perspectives** that strengthen their understanding. Team teaching also benefits teachers, as it enables them to utilize one another's strengths for improved instruction. There are, however, limitations to this approach. Differences in **classroom management** styles, **teaching practices**, and **personalities**, when not addressed properly through respectful communication and flexibility, hinder the effectiveness of team teaching.

VERTICAL TEAMING

Communication and collaboration among teachers of varying grade levels is integral to effective instruction that supports students' learning and development. Through **vertical teaming**, content specific teachers **across grade levels** have the opportunity to work together in discussing and planning curriculum, instruction, assessments, and strategies that prepare students for achievement. Teachers of lower grade levels are often unsure of what students in upper grade levels are learning. As a result, these teachers may be uncertain of the skills and abilities their students need to be adequately prepared for success as they transition through grade levels. Likewise, teachers of upper grade levels are often unsure of what students have learned in previous grades, thus hindering their ability to adequately plan instruction and implement necessary learning supports. Vertical teaming facilitates the communication necessary for teachers across grade levels to collaborate in **establishing expectations for preparedness** at each grade level and developing a common curriculum path. This enhances teaching and learning, in that teachers are more effectively able to plan instruction that is aligned with learning targets and prepare students with the necessary knowledge, tools, and supports for continued academic success.

HORIZONTAL TEAMING

Horizontal teaming refers to the collaboration of **same-grade level** teachers and staff that work with a common group of students. These teams may comprise teachers within a **single subject area** or **across disciplines** and may also include special education workers, grade-level administrators, paraprofessionals, and guidance counselors. Horizontal teaming is beneficial in facilitating the **coordinated planning** of curriculum, instruction, and assessments, as well as discussion regarding students' progress in the educational program. In addition, this method of teaming provides teachers and staff the opportunity to work together in developing educational goals, addressing areas of need, and implementing strategies to support students' success in learning. Horizontal teaming is also beneficial in encouraging teachers and staff to cooperate with one another in alignment with the goals and mission of the school to create a positive learning community focused on promoting student achievement.

BENEFITS OF MENTORS IN ENHANCING PROFESSIONAL KNOWLEDGE AND SKILLS

Mentors within the school community are typically experienced teachers that are available to offer support, guidance, and expertise to new teachers. As these individuals typically have a great deal of experience as educators, they are highly valuable resources in increasing professional knowledge and improving teaching skills. Mentors can provide **strategies, tools**, and **advice** for planning and delivering instruction, classroom management, and meeting students' learning needs to promote achievement. This includes suggesting ideas and resources for lesson activities and assessments, as well as techniques for differentiating instruction, enhancing student engagement, and promoting positive behavior. In addition, mentors can offer insight on how to effectively **navigate the school community**, including how to interact appropriately with colleagues and superiors, complete administrative duties, and communicate effectively with students' families. Regularly working with mentors in the school building ensures that new teachers are supported in developing the knowledge and skills necessary to become effective educators.

INTERACTION WITH PROFESSIONALS IN THE SCHOOL COMMUNITY

In order for an educational community to function effectively, professionals in the building must work together cohesively on a daily basis to support the school's mission and student learning. The nature of these interactions significantly determines the climate and culture of the school environment. Appropriate, professional interactions are important in facilitating the productive collaboration necessary to create a positive school community that promotes student success in learning. All interactions must therefore be **respectful**, **constructive**, and **sensitive** to the varying backgrounds, cultures, and beliefs among professionals in the school community. This includes using **appropriate language**, practicing **active listening**, and ensuring that discussions regarding colleagues, superiors, students, and other individuals in the building remain positive. When interacting in a team setting, it is important to maintain open dialogue and support one another's contributions to the educational program. All professionals in the school building must understand one another's roles and appreciate how these roles function together to support the educational program. Doing so ensures that collaboration is productive, purposeful, and aligned with enhancing students' learning experience.

SUPPORTIVE AND COOPERATIVE RELATIONSHIPS WITH PROFESSIONAL COLLEAGUES
SUPPORTS LEARNING AND ACHIEVEMENT OF CAMPUS AND DISTRICT GOALS

Effective collaboration among school staff and faculty members is reliant on establishing and maintaining supportive, cooperative professional relationships. Doing so facilitates a sense of **mutual respect** and **open communication** that allows colleagues to work together constructively in developing educational goals, plans to support students in achieving them, and strategies to address areas of need within the educational program. Mutual support and cooperation are also beneficial in fostering the **coordinated planning** of curriculum, learning activities, assessments, and accommodations to meet students' individual needs for academic achievement. Such professional relationships allow for more effective teaching and learning, as students are supported by a school community that works together cohesively to promote learning and the achievement of campus and district academic goals.

STRATEGIES FOR ESTABLISHING AND MAINTAINING RELATIONSHIPS

Building and maintaining professional relationships founded on mutual support and cooperation is integral in creating a positive, productive school community focused on student achievement. **Frequent communication** with colleagues in a variety of settings is an important factor in establishing and sustaining such professional relationships. Maintaining continuous and open communication allows professional colleagues in the school building to develop the respect for and understanding of one another necessary to establish a strong rapport. By participating together in **school activities**, **events**, and **programs**, teachers and staff members can build connections while contributing to enhancing the school community and climate. **Community building** strategies, such as participating in activities or games that require teamwork, are also valuable opportunities for developing supportive and cooperative professional relationships among colleagues. In addition, **collaborating** with one another in regard to curriculum, lesson planning, and promoting student achievement, contributes significantly to developing positive professional relationships. There are multiple avenues for such collaboration, including participating in professional learning communities (PLC's), department meetings, vertical or horizontal teaming, or engaging in team teaching. Doing so provides teachers and staff the opportunity to communicate and develop mutual goals that support the educational program and student learning.

Participating in the Local Educational Community

IMPACT OF VOLUNTEERING ON POSITIVE EDUCATIONAL COMMUNITY

Participating in school activities, events, and projects positively impacts the nature of the school community and culture. When teachers and staff members volunteer their time to contribute in such a way, it strengthens **connections** to the school community that foster positive attitudes toward it. By actively engaging in activities, events, and projects, teachers and staff have the opportunity to collaborate in making **positive contributions** to the school community. This facilitates the development of relationships among colleagues that enhance their ability to work cooperatively in creating a positive learning atmosphere that benefits students and the educational program. Students are more supported in such an environment, and therefore, develop positive attitudes toward learning and strong relationships with their teachers that enhance the overall school **climate**. In addition, as students are influenced by the behaviors, actions, and attitudes modeled by adults in the building, contributing positively to the school community encourages them to do the same.

PARTICIPATION OPPORTUNITIES

Participating in school activities, events, and projects is valuable in integrating oneself into the school community while making positive contributions. Such participation can occur through a variety of avenues, both within and outside of the school campus. Teachers can assist in school fundraisers, food and clothing drives, or field trips, as well as serve as tutors, lead school clubs or other extracurricular activities. By attending school sporting events, recitals, concerts, or plays, teachers can participate in the school community while supporting students. Events such as open-house and parent teacher nights, as well as public forum meetings, are also valuable opportunities to participate in the school community in a way that positively contributes to students' learning.

ENHANCING THE EDUCATIONAL COMMUNITY

As teachers work closely with students, colleagues, and administration, their contributions to the school and district are integral in enhancing the school community. Teachers provide valuable insight regarding the needs of the educational program and ways to improve the school environment. As such, their participation in the school and district is beneficial in helping to ensure the needs of staff and students are adequately met to create a positive educational community. In addition, active participation in the school and district facilitates the collaboration necessary for establishing relationships among colleagues that contribute to a positive school culture and climate. Teachers can contribute to building such an educational community in a variety of ways. By participating in **school activities**, **events**, and **projects**, teachers can work cooperatively to create a positive learning atmosphere. Teachers can also attend **school meetings** and serve on focused **committees** to solve problems and influence decisions that improve the nature of the school environment. At the district level, teachers can communicate with members of the board of education and participate in **public forums** to express ideas, discuss concerns, and offer input regarding ways to enhance the educational community.

Family Involvement and Collaboration

EFFECTIVELY WORKING AND COMMUNICATING WITH FAMILIES

Utilizing multiple means of communication when working with students' families ensures information is **accessible** to and **inclusive** of all involved family members. As students' home lives are dynamic, conveying information through several avenues allows families in various situations to participate in their child's education. This is invaluable in establishing and maintaining the positive relationships necessary between students' families and schools for effective teaching and learning. General classroom information, including concepts being taught, important dates, assignments, or suggestions for activities to do at home that reinforce learning in the classroom, can be communicated both digitally and in written form. Newsletters, calendars, or handouts can be both printed and included on a class website to ensure accessibility for all families. Updates regarding individual students can be communicated electronically, through writing, or in person. Email, digital communication apps, and the telephone allow for frequent communication to address students' progress, express concerns, or offer praise. Teachers and families can also communicate through handwritten notes, progress reports, or students' daily agendas. In-person communication, such as during a scheduled conference, is beneficial for discussing individual students' progress and goals related to the education program in depth, as well as ways to support their success in learning.

BUILDING POSITIVE RELATIONSHIPS THAT ENHANCE OVERALL LEARNING

Students are more supported and learn more effectively when the relationships between their teachers and families are founded on **mutual respect**, **understanding**, and **cooperation**. Establishing this positive rapport requires the teacher to work and communicate frequently with students' families. Doing so creates an inviting learning atmosphere in which family members feel welcomed and included as **equal contributors** to the educational program. This sentiment empowers and encourages family members to take an active role in their children's education, thus strengthening students' support system and enhancing the overall learning experience. In addition, family members that feel a strong connection to their children's school are more likely to model positive attitudes toward education and reinforce learning at home. When teachers and family members communicate frequently, they develop a mutual sense of trust for one another. This allows for **productive collaboration** and the exchange of valuable insight regarding how to best support students' learning needs both within and outside of the classroom.

APPROPRIATE COLLABORATION AND COMMUNICATION WITH FAMILIES

To effectively collaborate and communicate with students' families, the teacher must carefully consider appropriate methods for doing so. Communication and collaboration must always be **positive**, **respectful**, and **inclusive** to all families to ensure they feel welcomed as equal participants in their children's education. As such, the teacher must be mindful and responsive to the fact that students come from a variety of backgrounds, family dynamics and living situations. This includes demonstrating **cultural competency** when interacting with families from different backgrounds, providing multiple and varied opportunities for family involvement, and communicating through a variety of means. Doing so ensures that families of varying situations have access to pertinent information and feel equally included in the educational program. The teacher must also be mindful of the nature and purpose of communication in order to ensure that sensitive details about individual students are shared only with appropriate family members. General classroom information, such as important dates, events, or assignments, may be shared publicly among the classroom community, whereas such matters as individual student progress or behavior records must be reserved for private communication with the appropriate family members.

INVOLVEMENT OF FAMILIES, PARENTS, GUARDIANS, AND LEGAL CAREGIVERS
STRATEGIES TO ENCOURAGE ENGAGEMENT

As students' family dynamics are diverse, it is important that the teacher implement a variety of methods to engage parents, guardians, and legal caregivers into the educational program. Doing so creates an inviting atmosphere in which family members of all situations feel encouraged to participate in their children's education. Efforts to engage families must always be **positive, inclusive**, and **accommodating** to a variety of needs, schedules, and situations. This includes ensuring that all opportunities for involvement are culturally sensitive, meaningful, and accepting of all families. Utilizing a variety of **communication methods**, such as weekly newsletters, calendars, phone calls, and electronic communication, ensures that opportunities to engage in the educational program are accessible to all families. Providing **multiple** and **varied** opportunities for involvement, such as family nights, field trips, award ceremonies, or inviting families to participate in classroom activities, further encourages family engagement in the educational program. This enables families in various situations to become involved in their children's education in the way that best suits their needs and abilities.

FORMS OF ACTIVE INVOLVEMENT

Active involvement in the educational program can take a variety of forms both within and outside of the classroom to accommodate differences in families' schedules, dynamics, and abilities. Providing multiple avenues for involvement engages families of various situations to actively participate in their children's education. Within the classroom, family members can **volunteer** their time to assist as teacher's aides, tutors, or chaperones. In addition, if a family member is skilled in an area related to instruction, the teacher can ask them to come in to speak or teach a lesson. Inviting family members to **visit the classroom** or participate in special class activities allows them to actively engage in the learning process and gain insight into the educational program. Outside of daily classroom activities, family members can be encouraged to participate by attending **family nights, school social events, fundraisers**, or **parent-teacher association meetings**. Active involvement in the educational program can also occur at home. By frequently communicating with teachers, assisting with projects or homework, and emphasizing the importance of learning at home, family members can be informed and actively involved in their children's education.

IMPORTANCE IN CHILDREN'S EDUCATION

As students spend a great deal of time between school and home, the degree to which their family is involved in the educational program significantly influences the quality of the learning experience. When teachers take measures to engage families in their children's education, they establish a welcoming tone that facilitates relationships founded on mutual respect, understanding, and acceptance. These positive relationships are necessary for encouraging and empowering families to actively participate in the learning process. Such involvement contributes to establishing a **positive learning community** in which teachers and families can collaborate productively to enhance students' learning. When students' families are actively involved in their education, it strengthens the **support system** in both influential areas of their lives, thus establishing a sense of security that allows them to confidently engage in learning. Families that participate in the educational program are more likely to emphasize its value at home by extending and reinforcing learning outside of the classroom. This is highly beneficial in promoting positive attitudes toward learning, academic achievement, and social and emotional development.

INFLUENCE ON STUDENT LEARNING AND DEVELOPMENT

The degree of family involvement in the educational program significantly influences the quality of students' learning and development. Learning is more effective when parents, guardians, or legal caregivers are actively engaged in their child's education, as this promotes positive relationships between students' school and home lives that strengthen their **support system** and encourage the extension of learning beyond the classroom. Families that participate in the educational program are likely to emphasize and model its importance at home, thus influencing students to adopt the same positive attitudes toward learning. This facilitates **academic achievement, decreased absences** from school, and **positive learning habits**. In addition, when families are actively involved in the educational process, they are more effectively able to support students with resources at home that reinforce concepts learned in the classroom to strengthen connections and understanding. Students develop healthy **social and emotional skills** as well when their families are actively involved in the educational program. This facilitates positive self-esteem and interpersonal skills that contribute to academic success and fewer behavioral issues in the classroom.

BENEFITS FOR PARENTS, FAMILIES, GUARDIANS, AND LEGAL CAREGIVERS

Families, parents, guardians, and legal caregivers that are actively involved in the educational program gain greater **insight**, **understanding**, and **resources** that enable them to support their children's learning more effectively both within and outside of the classroom. Active engagement in the educational program fosters a positive rapport founded on mutual respect and support among family members, teachers, and school. This provides family members with a sense of **confidence** in the merits of the educational program while contributing to the sense that they are **equal participants** in the learning process. These family members are more informed regarding what is being taught in the classroom, as well as beneficial resources to reinforce learning at home. This leaves family members feeling more **empowered** and willing to reinforce their students' learning. In addition, participating in the learning process provides family members with a greater understanding of the characteristics and capabilities of their children's developmental level, thus equipping them with the knowledge to effectively support learning and growth.

BENEFITS FOR EFFECTIVE TEACHING

The involvement of families, parents, guardians, and legal caregivers in the educational program is highly beneficial for effective teaching. Family members that actively participate in the learning process are likely to develop a greater sense of **understanding** and **appreciation** of the teacher's role within it. Such involvement also facilitates positive and frequent communication with families that fosters relationships founded on mutual respect and increases the teacher's **morale**, and therefore effectiveness, in the classroom. Active engagement from family members also allows the teacher to gain a better understanding of how to support individual students' needs. Family members provide valuable insight regarding students' cultures, values, beliefs, educational goals, and learning needs to allow for more effective teaching. In addition, family members that are involved in their children's education are more likely to reinforce and extend learning at home, thus allowing for more effective teaching in the classroom.

POSITIVE RAPPORT

A positive rapport between teachers and families enhances the quality of the learning experience. Establishing these positive relationships requires that teachers frequently take measures to engage families in the educational program in ways that are **meaningful**, **relevant**, and **responsive** to varying situations, backgrounds, and needs. In doing so, teachers communicate the sentiment that all families are welcomed, valued, and considered equal participants in the learning process. This serves to create an open, inviting learning atmosphere in which family involvement is encouraged, thus fostering the **participation** and **communication** necessary for developing a mutual positive rapport. Working to build positive relationships strengthens the connection between schools and families that facilitates productive **collaboration** to best support and enhance students' learning.

INTERACTING WITH FAMILIES OF VARIOUS BACKGROUNDS
DIVERSITIES THAT MAY BE ENCOUNTERED

Appropriate interaction when working and communicating with students' families requires the teacher to recognize the wide range of diversities in characteristics, backgrounds, and needs that they will inevitably encounter. With **culturally diverse** families, the teacher will likely experience variances in language, values, traditions, and customs, including differences in beliefs regarding best practices for raising and educating children. **Socioeconomic** differences may influence the degree to which families have the ability and access to resources to support their children in learning. In some instances, socioeconomic differences may also impact the level of education that family members have attained and potentially the value they place on the importance of education. The teacher must also be mindful of the diversities that exist among **family dynamics**. Some families may have a single caregiver, whereas others may have many. Students may be only children, have several siblings, or come from a blended family. Differences in dynamics also include varying work schedules, lifestyle demands, and living situations that the teacher must consider when working and communicating with families. By acknowledging the diverse characteristics, backgrounds, and needs of students' families, the teacher can take measures to ensure appropriate and inclusive interactions that enhance the learning experience.

APPROPRIATE AND PRODUCTIVE INTERACTIONS

Recognizing the diverse nature of students' cultures, backgrounds, and experiences provides teachers with insight regarding how to interact with their families appropriately and productively. By self-educating to become **culturally competent** and building relationships with students, teachers develop an understanding of the unique characteristics, values, beliefs, and needs of each family. This enables teachers to tailor their communication with individual families in a way that is respectful, **culturally sensitive**, and responsive to their concerns and needs. Doing so ensures that all families feel welcomed and supported in the school environment, thus establishing positive relationships that encourage families to actively engage in the educational program and collaborate productively with teachers to enhance students' learning.

POSSIBLE OBSTACLES

As teachers work and interact with families of diverse backgrounds and experiences, they likely will encounter obstacles that must be addressed to facilitate effective communication. **Cultural differences** in values, beliefs, language, and nonverbal communication may cause misinterpretations between teachers and families that make it difficult to understand one another. It is, therefore, important that the teacher educate themselves regarding students' backgrounds to learn how to communicate in a culturally sensitive manner. When language barriers are present, learning common words and phrases in the language or utilizing an interpreter is beneficial in facilitating communication. Family members may have experienced **negative interactions** with teachers in the past that affect their willingness to engage in communication. Taking measures to establish an inviting, accepting atmosphere that promotes open communication is beneficial in encouraging these families to become involved. **Lifestyle differences**, including varying work schedules, living situations, and family dynamics, may make it difficult to establish effective communication. In addition, **accessibility issues**, including lack of access to transportation, technology devices, or the internet, may hinder family members' abilities to maintain frequent communication. To address these issues, teachers must utilize several communication methods that accommodate families' varying needs and situations.

CONSIDERATIONS TO ENSURE BENEFICIAL INTERACTIONS

The ultimate goal when working and communicating with families is to benefit students' learning and development. When teachers and families develop a positive rapport between one another, it fosters productive collaboration to support the students' educational and developmental goals. Doing so requires that teachers ensure all interactions with students' families are appropriate, respectful, and considerate. This includes demonstrating awareness of varying **backgrounds, characteristics**, and **needs** of each family and interacting in a way that is responsive and accepting of differences. Teachers must practice **cultural competency** when communicating with families, including recognizing differences in perspectives, values, beliefs, and nonverbal communication. Teachers must also consider families' unique situations, including differing **work schedules, living**

arrangements, and **family dynamics** to ensure that all interactions are considerate of their time, accommodating to their needs, and supportive of their role in the educational program. When interacting with families, it is important that teachers practice active listening and respond appropriately, meaningfully, and constructively. This communicates to families that their opinions, goals, and concerns related to the educational program are respected, thus encouraging them to actively participate in supporting their children's progress and development.

REGULAR COMMUNICATION WITH FAMILIES

STUDENTS' PROGRESS AND IMPORTANT CLASSROOM INFORMATION

Frequent communication regarding individual student progress and important classroom information is essential to actively engaging family members as equal contributors to the educational program. Doing so creates an inviting atmosphere focused on open and productive dialogue to enhance students' learning and development. Regular communication with families through a variety of methods establishes a strong connection between students' school and home lives that supports their achievement. When families are consistently updated and informed regarding their children's progress in the educational program, they can more effectively collaborate with the teacher to **proactively** address concerns and **implement necessary supports** for successful learning. Frequently communicating important classroom information, including curriculum, assignments, events, and opportunities for involvement, ensures that families are always informed regarding their children's educational program and ways in which they can actively participate. This equips family members with the knowledge and resources necessary to effectively support and reinforce learning both in the classroom and at home.

> **Review Video: Collaborating with Families**
> Visit mometrix.com/academy and enter code: 679996

POSITIVE RAPPORT THAT ENHANCES TEACHING AND LEARNING

Regularly interacting and working with students' families facilitates the **continuous** and **open** line of communication necessary to establishing and sustaining a positive rapport. Building such positive relationships is integral to quality teaching and learning, as frequent communication allows families and teachers to develop a sense of mutual respect, trust, and understanding over time. By frequently communicating with families, teachers create a welcoming, inclusive learning environment in which family members feel encouraged and empowered to contribute as **equal participants** in their child's educational program. This facilitates productive collaboration between teachers and families that supports and enhances students' learning. Developing a positive rapport with family members is also valuable in providing teachers with insight regarding strategies to best support and accommodate students' learning styles, needs, and individual differences. When teachers and families have a positive relationship with one another, students feel more supported in their learning both within and outside of the classroom, thus promoting positive attitudes toward learning and academic achievement.

LISTENING AND RESPONDING TO FAMILIES' CONCERNS

Actively **listening** and **responding** to students' families when interacting with them is an important part of building positive relationships that enhance teaching and learning. By listening attentively to families' concerns, ideas, and information regarding their child and the educational program, teachers gain a greater awareness of their unique backgrounds, characteristics, and experiences. With this understanding in mind, teachers can ensure that they respond to family members in a **sensitive**, **accepting**, and **empathetic** manner to promote the development of a mutual positive rapport. Doing so conveys the sentiment that family members are valued and respected as equal participants in the educational program, thus encouraging them to engage in positive communication to support their children's learning. Families can provide valuable insight regarding their children's learning styles, needs, and behaviors. When teachers listen and respond constructively to this information, they foster positive relationships with families by validating and including them in the learning process. In addition, listening and responding appropriately to students' families indicates acknowledgement and appreciation for their participation in the educational program that contributes to building positive relationships and encourages continued communication.

CONFERENCES

BUILDING POSITIVE RELATIONSHIPS BETWEEN SCHOOLS AND FAMILIES

Frequently conducting conferences with parents, guardians, and legal caregivers facilitates the consistent **in-person communication** necessary for building positive relationships founded on mutual understanding and respect. The conference setting provides a space in which teachers, school staff, and families can discuss the educational program and the student's individual progress, as well as address concerns and collaborate in developing goals. By conducting conferences regularly, teachers, school staff, and families can maintain a continuous, **open dialogue** that provides insight regarding one another's perspectives, intentions, and roles in the educational program. This allows for increased understanding and appreciation for one another that contributes to building positive relationships. Families that attend conferences regularly feel more included in the educational program as equal contributors to their children's learning, thus encouraging them to establish positive strong connections with the school.

SUPPORT OF STUDENTS' SUCCESS IN LEARNING

Effective conferences between teachers and families are focused on open communication, productive collaboration, and strengthening the connection between students' home and school lives. When families and teachers work together in conferences to benefit the student, it strengthens their **support system** in both influential areas of their lives. This is beneficial in enhancing students' **academic achievement**, promoting **healthy development**, and encouraging **positive attitudes toward learning**. Conducting conferences frequently ensures that family members are consistently **informed** and **involved** as equal participants in their child's progress and the educational program. This equips families with the information, understanding, and resources to more effectively support their child's learning both within and outside of the classroom. In addition, effective conferences provide teachers with insight from families regarding students' learning needs, behaviors, and individual situations. With this knowledge in mind, teachers can work with families to develop a plan and implement strategies that best support students' learning and development.

GUIDELINES FOR EFFECTIVENESS

Family conferences are a valuable opportunity to discuss students' individual progress, collaborate to develop educational goals, and address concerns. To ensure conferences are productive, teachers must take measures to make families feel welcomed, respected, and included in the process. Conferences must be scheduled at a **convenient time** for all attending family members in order to accommodate varying needs and situations. It is also important that conferences take place in a comfortable, **inviting atmosphere**, as this establishes a positive tone and facilitates discussion. Teachers must arrive **on time** and **prepared** with specific information to discuss regarding the student, including positive remarks that highlight their strengths. This demonstrates that teachers know the student well and want them to succeed, thus making family members feel comfortable in discussing their child. Asking **open-ended questions**, encouraging families to talk, and practicing active listening is important in facilitating productive discussion, as well as ensuring families feel heard and respected in their concerns. **Direct criticism** of the student must always be avoided;

166

rather, teachers should focus on discussing ways that student can apply their strengths to improve in other areas.

FAMILY SUPPORT RESOURCES THAT ENHANCE FAMILY INVOLVEMENT

Families that are supported through school, community, and interagency resources are equipped to effectively support their child's learning and development. Often, families may be hesitant to become actively involved in their children's education because they lack the skills and understanding of how to do so. These support systems are beneficial in providing family members with the **tools, knowledge**, and **resources** that prepare them to effectively participate in the educational program and extend learning outside of the classroom. Such resources are valuable in educating families on the characteristics, needs, and abilities of their children's developmental level, as well as strategies for developing and engaging in age-appropriate activities that support learning at home. This instills a sense of confidence within families regarding their ability to successfully support their children's learning that empowers and encourages them to become actively involved.

When families are supported through **school**, **community**, and **interagency** resources, they are able to more effectively become involved in the educational program. Numerous resources dedicated to educating families on ways they can support their children's learning are available to accommodate varying situations, needs, and abilities. Within the school, **teachers**, **guidance counselors**, and other **staff members** can provide valuable information regarding students' developmental characteristics, needs, and abilities, as well as ways families can become involved to enhance learning within and outside of the classroom. **Support groups** hosted by the school enable families to share experiences and discuss ways to become involved in the learning process. Community support resources are often tailored to address the specific needs of families within the community. These resources offer **family education services** such as classes, meetings, or programs designed to provide families with the training, strategies, and knowledge necessary to become actively involved in their children's education. Several **national family support agencies** are also available to educate families on ways to become involved in their children's learning. Such agencies often have multiple locations, as well as an array of digitally printed information, discussion forums, and training opportunities to enhance family involvement in learning.

Chapter Quiz

Ready to see how well you retained what you just read? Scan the QR code to go directly to the chapter quiz interface for this study guide. If you're using a computer, simply visit the bonus page at **mometrix.com/bonus948/oaeapkma** and click the Chapter Quizzes link.

OAE Practice Test #1

1. Prior to the start of his first year of teaching, a language arts teacher asks other teachers for advice on how to best organize his class for group work. Which of the following is the best advice for this teacher to take to organize his classroom?

   a. Make sure all supplies are in a central location for groups to easily access
   b. Display posters around the classroom about how to properly work and behave in groups
   c. Organize students into rows and assign them to groups early in the school year
   d. Arrange desks in groups of four to five and create spaces for students to collect materials and turn in assignments

2. The alphabetic principle would be best introduced at which of Piaget's cognitive stages of development?

   a. Sensorimotor stage
   b. Preoperational stage
   c. Concrete operational stage
   d. Formal operational stage

3. Which of the following is a common symptom of spina bifida?

   a. Motor dyspraxia/apraxia
   b. Lower-body paresis
   c. Athetosis
   d. Spasticity

4. Which of the following is *not* part of the process of closing a lesson?

   a. Extended practice.
   b. Review of key points.
   c. Preview of future lessons.
   d. Demonstration of student work.

5. When presenting information, effective teacher communication is best achieved when the teacher uses which of the following types of phrases?

   a. because, for example
   b. not many, not very
   c. somewhere, somehow
   d. generally, usually

6. All of the following statements are true about the evaluation component of a lesson except:

    a. Evaluation may be group-wide instead of individual

    b. Evaluation must occur in some form with every lesson

    c. Evaluation may occur on an on-going basis

    d. Evaluation may occur again; for example, during a unit test

7. How can teachers establish positive, productive learning environments for students whose developmental levels vary within the same classroom?

    a. Observe levels/types of children's play and provide only activities matching these.

    b. Give older elementary and middle school students high school-type collaboration.

    c. Do not expect new preschoolers sharing, but do model, encourage, and reward it.

    d. Confine productive learning environments in high school classes to the classrooms.

8. What is the most productive order to structure a class period?

    a. Seatwork, class discussion, content development

    b. Class discussion, seatwork, content development

    c. Seatwork, content development, class discussion

    d. Content development, class discussion, seatwork

9. Which example best demonstrates a student making an accommodation to existing schema, as suggested by Piaget?

    a. A child knows that periods are used at the ends of sentences. When given a question to punctuate for the first time, she uses a period.

    b. After using the writing process to write a narrative text, a child applies the process to write an expository text.

    c. A child does not like bees until learning about the role they play in pollination. She then believes that bees are helpful.

    d. A toddler learns about lions from a picture book and practices saying, "Roar!" She hears a tiger making a similar sound at the zoo and calls it a lion.

10. According to the Family Educational Rights and Privacy Act (FERPA), which of the following is true?

    a. Students of any age can refuse to disclose educational records to their parents

    b. Parents of children under 18 can inspect and request amendments to their children's educational records on demand

    c. Teachers need written authorization from parents in order to disclose a student's educational record to a school official with a legitimate educational interest

    d. Written authorization from parents is required before a school releases a student's educational records to a school to which that student is transferring

11. Which of the following is true of students whose parents are highly aware of and involved in their academic progress?

    a. They are always from high-income families

    b. They typically perform better in school than students whose families are less involved

    c. They are always near the top of their classes

    d. They are typically lower-performing students, because parents are only interested in their children's academic progress if they are not doing well

12. As an approach for managing student behavior, what is a characteristic of the "simple authority statement" from the teacher?

    a. It causes emotional distress but stops misbehavior authoritatively.
    b. It models reasonable, respectful use of authority with little upset.
    c. It expresses teacher disapproval of student behavior subjectively.
    d. It expresses teacher disapproval authoritatively, but it takes time.

13. What is the most accurate predictor of a student's achievement in school?

    a. Socio-economic background of a student's peers
    b. Family involvement in student's life
    c. Education level of parents
    d. Marital status of parents

14. What is the best way to ensure overall good behavior from your students?

    a. Establish a set of rules for your classroom, give the students a written copy, and go over the rules at the beginning of the year or semester
    b. A good teacher is a strict teacher. From the very beginning be gruff with the students, and show them that you have no tolerance for "nonsense."
    c. Wait a few days before setting ground rules. Students will respect you more if you give them more leeway in the beginning as they are settling in.
    d. Change your rules frequently to keep the students on their toes.

15. Which of the following is the best step to address the concerns of parents who feel their child is being assigned too much homework in a class?

    a. Explain the merits of completing homework on time, and have data ready to present to the parents
    b. Listen to the parents' worries, explain the study skills that are taught, and establish a plan to assist the student
    c. Ask the parents how much time it takes the student to complete their homework every day
    d. Ask a counselor to work with the student to help them learn how to better do their homework

16. Mike, a student in your 10th grade geometry class, is rapidly falling behind in class because he is having a harder time grasping concepts than are most of the other students. You have set up a meeting with Mike's parents and want to discuss options such as encouraging them to hire a private tutor, or possibly even transferring him to a remedial math class. What might be the best way to begin the discussion?

    a. "Mike is working very hard in my class, but he is having a very tough time. I wanted to discuss a few ideas with you, and also to hear your input about what we can do to help him."
    b. "Mike currently has one of the lowest averages in my class. I want to be frank with you. If something does not change, I'm afraid he will fail the class."
    c. "Have you been working much with Mike at home to help him with his geometry? He just does not seem to be cutting it."
    d. "Mike is having a little trouble with his geometry. I'm sure he will do fine, but I just wanted to let you know."

17. During in-class assignments and small group activities, how can a teacher best ensure that all of the students are on-task and not getting behind?

a. Watch the class quietly from the teacher's desk
b. Respond to students promptly when they raise their hands
c. Collect all student work several times during the class, check it, and then hand it back so that they can continue working
d. Circulate among the students regularly to observe the students' work up close

18. A second-grade teacher is participating in a regionwide professional development course focused on creating culturally responsive classrooms. For an upcoming assignment, the teacher plans to discuss his experiences working with ethnically diverse groups of students. Which of the following does this teacher have the legal and professional responsibility to do prior to submitting the assignment?

a. Take measures to protect the confidentiality of students' identities.
b. Ensure the assignment includes only factual accounts of his experiences.
c. Request permission from the school administration to disclose students' educational records.
d. Inform students' families of his intention to include them in the assignment.

19. Which one of the following statements about objectives is *not* true?

a. Objectives are a communications tool aimed specifically at the students, not other audiences.
b. Objectives provide a way to evaluate student learning.
c. Objectives help focus and motivate students.
d. Objectives provide a way for teachers to measure their own effectiveness.

20. Which example best demonstrates a student learning in his zone of proximal development?

a. Being taught to apply a decoding strategy while reading a book at the instructional level
b. Practicing fluency using a familiar reading passage
c. Listening to an audio version of a story that is too difficult to read independently
d. Pairing up with a struggling reader to model use of a comprehension strategy

21. Strategies for establishing a verbal-linguistic learning environment include all except which one of the following?

a. Classroom discussions
b. Stories told by the teacher
c. Task Cards
d. Word walls

22. In a unit about the Vietnam War, a high school history teacher wants to use the song "Fortunate Son," by Creedence Clearwater Revival to help teach students about the cultural reaction of the war in the United States. Can this teacher play this song for their class?

a. No, because the teacher has not obtained copyright permission to play the song
b. No, because the song is inappropriate to use in an educational setting
c. Yes, because an educator can play a song for instructional purposes under fair use
d. Yes, because fair use allows teachers full rights to use all media over 20 years old for educational purposes

23. What is the relationship between project-based learning and technology?

   a. Technology is a fundamental characteristic of project-based learning
   b. Technology should only be used in project-based learning after students are in middle school
   c. Technology should generally not be used in project-based learning
   d. Technology can strengthen project-based learning

24. Mrs. Sanchez is a new teacher of 9th grade literature. She truly loves her subject, and the highlight of each class period is when she holds a 20-minute class discussion of the previous day's reading assignment. She is very enthusiastic about these discussions and encourages the students to form and express their own opinions. She often asks provocative questions and pushes the students to consider the motives of characters from different points of view. Many of the students enjoy this, but an observer notices some problems. Misbehavior by a few students is getting out of hand. And a couple of students seem to just zone out. What common mistake is Mrs. Sanchez making?

   a. She is not being strict enough.
   b. She is devoting too much time to discussions.
   c. She is concentrating all her attention on the discussions and not noticing everything that is going on in the classroom.
   d. Her enthusiasm makes her look weak to the students.

25. Which of the following is *not* a benefit of flexible grouping practices?

   a. Allows students to work at individual interest levels.
   b. Allows students to pick their own groups for better cooperation.
   c. Allows students to work according to readiness levels.
   d. Allows students to work on specific skills identified as deficient through assessments.

26. Which of the following activities would be most developmentally appropriate to include in a prekindergarten reading center?

   a. A consonant blend word sort
   b. Word cards that students can sequence to form sentences
   c. Letter outlines for students to fill in with beans
   d. Compound word puzzles

27. In addition to engaging parents by inviting them to observe and help in classrooms, what is true about other common teacher outreach efforts to parents?

   a. Parents mostly view teachers' home visits as unwanted intrusions.
   b. Parents only want phone calls about problems, not for good news.
   c. Parents will not read a newsletter that a teacher sends every week.
   d. Parents support students far better if periodically given information.

28. What is the primary reason teachers should strive to read educational articles and publications related to their own subjects?

   a. It allows teachers to take ownership of their learning so they can model independent study
   b. It enables teachers to identify the professional goals that they need to work on improving
   c. It allows the educator to learn from other professionals in their field to ensure they are teaching current content
   d. It allows educators the opportunity to find new research and studies that they can bring to meetings at their school

29. A teacher wants to help her students develop critical thinking skills. Which assignment would best help students develop this skill while in her social studies class?

    a. Ask students to create a law they feel should exist and defend their reasoning

    b. Have students interview an adult who works in government

    c. Have students write a report on the history of their state government

    d. Give an assignment to create a list of laws passed in the last year

30. As a cognitive element of the learning process, what is a characteristic of planning?

    a. Planning requires concrete thinking, not abstract thinking.

    b. Planning requires both abstract thinking and imagination.

    c. Planning requires organizational, not imaginative abilities.

    d. Planning is on a lower level of higher-order thinking skills.

31. Which of the following would be the most effective in helping students take better ownership of their own individual learning processes?

    a. Allow students to choose which of their assignments should be graded

    b. Have students self-grade each assignment to say what grade they think they should receive

    c. Provide checklists and rubrics to students to let them know what is expected on assignments

    d. Have a designated place in each student's binder to record each grade and track their progress

32. During her annual review, Mr. Ainsley is told by the school principal that his teaching is good overall, but that his portfolio shows that he does not assess his students as often or as effectively as he should. What actions should Mr. Ainsley take first to correct this problem?

    a. Write a letter to the principal stating that he thinks this assessment of his teaching is unfair, and explaining his reasons for his failure to assess his students adequately

    b. Use available professional development resources on assessment to develop a plan to improve his use of assessment in the classroom and present it to the principal for review

    c. Confer with other teachers to find out if the principal made similar suggestions to them about improving their assessment techniques

    d. Sign up for an assessment workshop that will occur in a few months and let the principal know that he will need to take a few days off work to attend the workshop

33. A history teacher has assigned his final research project of the semester. For this project, he sets the requirement of four online sources and three print sources. Over the next few days, several students express their concern over being unable to find the necessary sources to complete their project due to their lack of computer access at home. What can the teacher do to make sure all students have fair access to complete this project?

    a. Make and arrangement media center specialists for students to stay after school to gather the necessary research materials for the project

    b. Schedule time in your class period for students to go to the media center and computer lab to gather the necessary research

    c. Provide clear instructions for the project so that students know what is expected of them

    d. Pair students together so that students with access to resources work with students without access to resources

34. Which of the following is an example of extrinsic motivation?

a. A student works hard in all classes because his parents give him $20 for every "A" grade he receives

b. A student volunteers to walk dogs at an animal shelter after school because he wants to help animals in tough situations

c. A student wants to audition for the school play because they want to learn how to perform in front of an audience

d. A student works on developing their conversational skills because they want to make friends at their new school

35. Which of the following is a valid technique to use with non-native English speakers in your class if they are having trouble and your school has very limited ESL resources?

a. Ask the student's parents to hire a translator to sit with the child in class

b. Use more visual aids and illustrative hand gestures while teaching

c. Speak as rapidly as possible so that the student will get used to hearing English faster

d. Repeat everything you say twice

36. Which equipment should be arranged first when deciding upon a classroom floor plan?

a. The teacher's desk

b. Computer workstations

c. Filing cabinets

d. Overhead projector

37. A class is about to receive a new student in the middle of the school year. This student has cerebral palsy and uses a device for communicating. What could the teacher do prior to the student's arrival to help the student feel more welcome when they arrive in class?

a. Instruct students to not use their voices for one class day to empathize with the new student's situation

b. Demonstrate how the device works and how the student will use it to communicate

c. Assign each student a day of the month where they are assigned to assist the new student

d. Allow students to play with and investigate a similar device

38. Whose responsibility is it to ensure that a teacher remains current with new teaching techniques?

a. The county school system is required to set the standards and provide opportunities for teachers to learn new skills.

b. The principal is responsible for ensuring that the teachers in his or her school do not fall behind.

c. The senior teachers for each grade are responsible for taking the less experienced teachers under their wing.

d. Every teacher is responsible to taking the initiative for learning and applying new teaching methods as appropriate for the classes they teach.

39. "Language load" refers to:

a. The basic vocabulary words a first grader has committed to memory.

b. The number of unrecognizable words an English language learner encounters when reading a passage or listening to a teacher.

c. The damage that carrying a pile of heavy books could cause to a child's physique.

d. The number of different languages a person has mastered

40. Suppose the students in your computer science class vary greatly in the amount of experience and knowledge they have about computers. What can you do as a teacher to make student evaluations fair to everyone?

    a. Evaluate how much each student learns in addition to whether or not the student gets the correct answers on tests

    b. Grade class tests on a curve

    c. Put more weight on class research projects than on tests

    d. Grade students only according to test results

41. What common misconception often makes it difficult to keep parents closely involved with their children's school life at the middle and high school levels?

    a. Many parents mistakenly believe that by high school, that their child's scholastic abilities have already been established, and so there is little point in parent involvement.

    b. Many parents mistakenly believe that their input is not welcomed by the school and teachers.

    c. Many parents mistakenly believe that being more involved at school will humiliate their child.

    d. Many parents mistakenly believe that becoming less involved in a child's school life will encourage the child to mature and become more responsible.

42. The day before a unit test over the Civil War, a teacher builds in a day to allow her students to review. She wants her students to work together to review the material. Which of the following would be the best way to have her students prepare for the test?

    a. Allow students to decide how they should review for tomorrow's test

    b. Students work in groups of two or three to complete a study guide for the test

    c. Have students watch a video reviewing key battles and moments of the Civil War

    d. Assign students to work in groups to create a concept map over the Civil War unit

43. Which of the following is the best example of giving ESL students appropriate feedback in response to their developing English-language skills?

    a. Correcting every single mistake every time a student makes one

    b. Pointing out serious errors after the class has finished an activity

    c. Disregarding student errors in planning additional class practicing

    d. Accepting good work via silence while highlighting only mistakes

44. When a student considers whether an information source is reputable, has been proven objectively, and is accepted by experts in its discipline, which element of critical thinking does the student demonstrate?

    a. Evaluating supporting evidence

    b. Judging the quality of material

    c. Distinguishing fact from opinion

    d. Finding evidence/no evidence

45. Mr. Krick recently read an article about a new interactive computer game that is very effective at getting children interested in history. Although he has never seen the game himself, he is interested in the possibility of using it with his class. What is the best course of action for Mr. Krick?

    a. Go the local computer store, buy the game, and try it out with his class the next day

    b. He should forget about it. Computer games are bad for children.

    c. Make a copy of the article, note the website of the game, and consult with the school's technology coordinator to see if the coordinator knows anything about the product

    d. Ask the class if they have heard of the game and if they think the game would be helpful to them in class.

46. According to research findings, which of these predict(s) parents' involvement in their children's education the most?

    a. Racial or ethnic status of parents

    b. The marital status of the parents

    c. The educational levels of parents

    d. School policies, teacher practices

47. Mrs. Hanson gives a brief lecture and asks students to discuss a list of questions in pairs before the class as a whole discusses them. This technique is effective for facilitating class discussion primarily because:

    a. It gives students the opportunity to try out their answers in a "safe" environment before stating them in front of the class

    b. It encourages students to compare their answers to those of their classmates and revise them if they are not socially acceptable

    c. It develops students' higher-order thinking skills by demonstrating that there are differing perspectives

    d. It provides Mrs. Hanson with the opportunity to see which questions are most interesting to the students before the classroom-wide discussion commences

48. Which of the following scenarios is the most probable indicator that a 4-year-old might have a developmental disability?

    a. The student is having trouble reading at the same level as his peers

    b. Student cannot tell their left from their right

    c. Their play is largely imagination-based

    d. Student is very anxious when away from their parents.

49. What is the best starting point for deciding on the floor plan of your classroom?

    a. Make sure that all student desks are oriented with their backs to the windows, so as to ensure that no students will become distracted by events going on outside

    b. Consider the size and shape of the room and decide where the optimal position would be for you to carry out most of your instruction

    c. Arrange student desks so that they all face the chalkboard

    d. Use whatever arrangement is already there. School administrators spend a lot of time before the beginning of the school year optimizing the floor plans of every classroom in the building.

50. **Which of the following strategies would foster students' intrinsic motivation to learn?**
    a. Helping students to develop a personal connection to and interest in the material they're learning
    b. Emphasizing the rewards associated with academic success (recognition, a good job) and consequences associated with academic failure (shame, punishment by parents)
    c. Both A and B
    d. Neither A nor B

51. **Getting the classroom ready for the first day of school can be overwhelming for a new teacher. As the big day comes, one often must make some hard choices and leave a few things to be done later. Which of the following could wait a few more days if necessary?**
    a. Optimize arrangement of student desks
    b. Decorate all bulletin boards and set them up for display
    c. Make sure that you have enough textbooks and that they are all in satisfactory condition
    d. Verify that equipment such as overhead projectors and computer workstations are functional and ready to use

52. **At one high school, a large proportion of ESL students are very recent immigrants to America. To help these students and their families understand the protocols and culture of the school better before the school year starts, the ESL teachers will host an orientation event. What should the teachers do first to enable understanding and present helpful information most effectively during this event?**
    a. They should provide families with a detailed analysis of the district ESL program.
    b. They should ask the ESL students to function as interpreters with their families.
    c. They should provide families with pertinent materials in their native languages.
    d. They should arrange discussion groups for all families on their native languages.

53. **In preparation for the upcoming school year, the test results shared with the teachers who will be working with the students the following year. How will this information be most useful to the students' new teachers?**
    a. It will determine which students should be placed in remedial classes
    b. It will help the teachers plan their instruction based on the strengths and needs of the incoming students
    c. It will help determine which students should repeat a grade
    d. It will help the teachers decide whether or not they should use team teaching

54. **How are teachers required to ensure educational equity?**
    a. By delivering uniform instruction to all students
    b. By offering different opportunities to students
    c. By treating students less fairly if they deserve it
    d. By using materials reflecting multicultural views

55. What is the best way that a teacher can utilize the data from standardized tests from the previous year?

a. Seat students with similar deficiencies together in class to make it easier to facilitate learning
b. Identify the highest and the lowest achievers and enact a plan for the highest achievers to assist the lowest achievers
c. Identify the achievement gaps of each student and create a plan that addresses the largest gaps
d. Compare data with other teachers in the grade level to evaluate the best methods for instruction

56. In today's public schools, who are most often responsible for instructing special education students?

a. Educational specialists
b. Special education teachers
c. The most applicable therapists
d. The regular classroom teachers

57. How should a teacher initially plan to manage a highly diverse classroom?

a. On the first day of class, the teacher should ask each student to complete a survey to determine the students' cultural, ethnic, and racial background.
b. A good teacher should be intimately familiar with the major cultures within the local school district.
c. A teacher should plan lessons so that new material is introduced using a variety of different approaches.
d. Guest teachers from different ethnic backgrounds should occasionally be invited to teach, so that all students will feel more comfortable.

58. Which of the following categories of cognitive disabilities most consistently includes the characteristic of a marked gap between intellectual ability and school performance?

a. Autism spectrum disorders (ASDs)
b. Intellectual disabilities (ID)
c. None of these includes such a gap
d. Specific learning disabilities (SLDs)

59. After a month of class, Mr. Gupta notices that his 12th grade physics class has fallen well behind his planned curriculum. In-class experiments and other activities have taken significantly longer to complete than the teacher expected. What should he do?

a. Cease holding in-class experiments and stick rigidly with following the units in the textbook
b. Ignore the planned curriculum; the students will learn more from doing the experiments than from lectures and written assignments.
c. Increase the amount of homework in order to catch up
d. Evaluate way students are carrying out experiments and develop more organized procedures to keep the students on track

60. Which of the following is least likely to cause a sudden academic decline:

 a. Parental divorce
 b. Drug abuse
 c. Eating disorders
 d. Participation in a school sports team

61. Of the following, which is a principle wherein Albert Bandura's theory *agrees with* behaviorist learning theory?

 a. Consequences reinforce or punish behaviors.
 b. Learning always results in a change in behavior.
 c. Internal cognitive processes must be examined.
 d. Social interactions are very important in learning.

62. When teaching Shakespeare's *Romeo and Juliet*, which technique might help students maintain interest despite the difficult language?

 a. Give the students a glossary of archaic English words commonly found in the play
 b. Include a discussion of some modern interpretations of the story (movies such as *Romeo+Juliet*, or even *West Side Story*) and have students identify differences between the modern versions and the original
 c. Have the students read the parts out loud
 d. Hold a detailed discussion of English syntax and grammar of the period

63. In the middle of the school year, a high school teacher learns that a new student with moderate vision loss will be joining her classroom. What can the teacher do to help the student feel comfortable and safe in her classroom?

 a. Set aside a time during the student's first week in class for other students to ask questions about his disability and limitations
 b. Arrange a time to discuss any concerns or requests the student may have in private
 c. Hold a class discussion on how to make students with disabilities feel welcome in the classroom
 d. Allow the student's parents to observe the class any time they desire

64. ESL teacher Mr. Rogers is working with a diverse high school student body. He invites his students to articulate their widely varied perspectives, gives them debating and role-playing exercises to practice seeing others' viewpoints, and assists them in expressing their emotions as well as teaching them English language use and academic subject content. For which goal are his practices most relevant?

 a. Recognizing, understanding, analyzing, and alleviating cultural identity crises
 b. Decreasing conflicts among students from lack of intercultural understanding
 c. Working with multicultural students to improve their academic achievements
 d. Acknowledging the linguistic diversity among his students and addressing this

65. A special education classroom has several students with differences in their physical characteristics and physical development. What is the best way that the teacher can make sure not to exclude any student in activities that they may plan for classroom instruction?

    a. Allow students of differing physical abilities to pair up so those with more coordination can help those with less coordination

    b. Interchange activities between those that account for their physical differences and those that do not

    c. Take care to not plan any activities that require students to leave their desks

    d. Take care to not exclude students when planning activities that require specific levels of coordination

66. A student has begun struggling in several content areas where previously they did not demonstrate any deficiencies. Which of the following would be the most appropriate in terms of delivering this information to the parents of the child at a meeting?

    a. Create a chart comparing the student's progress to the progress of a typical student in their grade

    b. Ask the parents what they think the teacher should do for their child

    c. Bring multiple samples of the student's work to the parents that demonstrate the areas of concern

    d. Compare the student's work to the work of their classmates to show how the child is struggling

67. Of the following, which represents a descriptor for English Language Learners at the intermediate proficiency level in speaking?

    a. Speaking in simple sentences without need for hesitation

    b. Speaking in detailed sentences with sufficient vocabulary

    c. Speaking in simple sentences with mostly present tenses

    d. Speaking in sentences people unused to ELLs understand

68. In a lower-income school district, which strategy at an elementary school is likely to work best for promoting literacy in students' homes?

    a. Use school funds to create a well-stocked library and encourage parents and students to spend time reading together at home

    b. Assign creative projects about books for students to complete with their parents at home

    c. Send home a weekly update of what literacy skills are being taught so that parents can reinforce those skills at home

    d. Ask parents to come in weekly to read their favorite stories to the students

69. Among school personnel, who is most likely to help classroom teachers by informing them about activities for developing fine motor and daily living skills?

    a. Physical therapist

    b. Occupational therapist

    c. Special education staff

    d. Any IEP team member

70. Objectives should be designed to teach something that is worth learning. Practicing skills is a good learning objective if the practice is embedded within application opportunities. Which of the following, however, may be a pointless practice?

   a. Reading to practice word attack skills.
   b. Solving problems to practice number facts and computations.
   c. Writing a composition to practice spelling and penmanship.
   d. Copying definitions of words to improve vocabulary.

71. Which of the following assessment methods would be most useful for fostering middle school students' ownership of their learning?

   a. Providing students with charts showing their improvement over the course of a year
   b. Giving the students pre- and post-tests for each instructional unit so that they can see their learning progress
   c. Giving students detailed feedback on their performance and providing opportunities to incorporate the feedback and demonstrate improvement
   d. Creating an environment wherein students openly compete to achieve the best grades, but are also rewarded for improvement

72. A new law is passed by the state that changes what will be taught in certain science classrooms. Who is accountable for ensuring that this is carried out in classrooms?

   a. The Department of Education
   b. The state government
   c. The local government
   d. Each individual school

73. Ms. Mattingly has received her fourth grade class' standardized test results, and they show that her students are significantly behind the other fourth grade classes in the district in both reading and math. She didn't realize her students were so far behind, because they had been doing well on in-class assessments. How should Ms. Mattingly respond to this situation?

   a. Since standardized tests are an imperfect measure of achievement, she should ignore the results as long as her students are doing well in her class
   b. She should confer with her principal and other fourth grade teachers to determine whether her grade level expectations for academic achievement align with those of the district as a whole
   c. She should change her instructional methods to "teach to the test" and include more practice taking multiple choice tests for her students
   d. She should send a letter to her students' parents informing them that their children need tutoring in reading and math

74. Ms. Frank conducts an assessment and discovers that most students in her fourth grade class are auditory learners, while a few are visual or kinesthetic learners. When teaching students a new concept, which of the following strategies would be most effective for the largest number of her students?

   a. Having her students write an explanation of the new concept in their own words
   b. Teaching the students a song that explains the new concept
   c. Writing an explanation of the new concept on the chalkboard
   d. Teaching the students to describe the concept using sign language

75. At the start of a unit on the life cycle of plants, a fourth-grade teacher instructs her students to write an open-ended response on what they already know in their daily journals. How can the teacher best use this data to guide her instruction?

    a. Use the student responses to create her assessment on the unit
    b. Gauge how interested her students are in the topic
    c. Evaluate which students are the most advanced
    d. Assess each student's background knowledge

76. Mr. Bennet's fourth-grade students are practicing digital literacy skills as part of a math unit on financial literacy. They will be completing two digital assignments during this unit. One assignment is to write a blog post on budgeting that will be published on the school website. Another assignment is to write an email to a friend describing something they are saving up to buy. Which topic would be most beneficial for Mr. Bennet to teach to assist students with successfully completing both of these assignments?

    a. Verifying online sources
    b. Selecting relevant search keywords
    c. Navigating nonlinear writing and hyperlinks in digital texts
    d. Adjusting formality of language based on audience

77. Which of the following would be an unethical use of school property?

    a. Mr. Jackson takes home a school-owned laptop because there is publishing software installed on it that will help him prepare handouts for class.
    b. Mrs. Wallenstein goes to the school supply room and takes a box of colored chalk to use for drawing pie charts on the board for his math class.
    c. Mr. Calhoun uses his classroom after school to sell Girl Scout cookies for his daughter.
    d. Mr. Martinov asks the school secretary to requisition a laser pointer for his lectures.

78. What is the best method for improving students' memorization skills?

    a. Repetition
    b. Break the item to be memorized into small sections and then learn the sections one at a time
    c. Students should read the item once as rapidly as possible and then immediately try to repeat as much as they can recall
    d. Play a distinctive piece of music in the background

79. A math teacher spends a week teaching her advanced students a new concept. After giving a quiz, she notices that four students in her class are still having difficulty mastering the subject. What should this teacher's next step be in helping these students learn the material?

    a. Assign the other students an enrichment activity while using targeted instruction with the group of four
    b. Allow the struggling students the opportunity to retake assessments to see if they improve
    c. Assign each of the four students a peer tutor in the classroom to assist them with their work
    d. Assign the students extra homework to see if their work improves in class

80. Mr. Stratton has assigned his fifth grade social studies class to write a research report about a historical period that they have learned about in class during the year. To ensure that students understand what is expected of them and are able to complete the project on schedule, the best approach for Mr. Stratton to take would be to:
    a. Take time to explain how to do the research and set several 'checkpoints' before projects are due
    b. Pair students who have never completed a research project before with students who have
    c. Hold after-school tutoring sessions to help students brainstorm ideas and conduct research
    d. Send a note home to parents telling them about the project and the due date

81. In an inclusion classroom, a student with profound hearing loss is regularly mocked by students when she speaks. How should the classroom teacher and resource teacher work to solve this issue?
    a. Correct inappropriate behavior immediately when it occurs in class
    b. Create and put in place a strict no-bully policy for all students in the classroom
    c. Move the child back to a self-contained environment for her protection
    d. Contact the parents and guardians of all students to explain what is occurring

82. Ms. Schneider, a fifth grade teacher, has been assigned a paraprofessional who comes to her class three times a week to work with the mainstreamed special education students. For the past week, the paraprofessional has arrived late to the classroom and appeared distracted and disinterested in his duties. What should be the first step that Ms. Schneider takes to resolve the problem?
    a. Ask the school principal to assign a different paraprofessional to her class
    b. Send a note to the special education teacher explaining the problem
    c. Take the paraprofessional aside and explain her concerns
    d. Help the special education students write a letter to the paraprofessional explaining how his behavior is affecting their learning

83. Which of the following assessment methods is most likely to be used in a learner-centered classroom?
    a. A method that provides different alternatives for students to demonstrate their knowledge
    b. A method that allows students to complete the assessment in groups
    c. A structured method that allows students' mastery to be compared with that of other students
    d. A multiple-choice test which students help to construct and grade

84. Which learning theory is based on the idea that students are actively involved in constructing their own meaning, and that teachers should guide students through scaffolding rather than using instructor-led teaching techniques?
    a. Behaviorism
    b. Cognitivism
    c. Constructivism
    d. Social learning theory

85. What is true about how teachers can support student development of intrinsic motivation?

    a. Teachers can interest students in content without being interested in it themselves.
    b. Teachers strongly interested in content need not show it to develop this motivation.
    c. Teachers can develop intrinsic student motivation without knowing student interests.
    d. Teachers can develop intrinsic motivation by connecting content to student interests.

86. A teacher wanting to show items from various cultures to the children in her classroom asks a child of Chinese heritage to bring a coolie hat to school. The family is insulted by the teacher's assumption that all Chinese are/were coolies. What is the best response for the teacher once she has realized her mistake?

    a. Apologize and let the issue drop.
    b. Rescind the request to other families for cultural items to avoid more problems.
    c. Ask the family to send whatever it feels appropriate.
    d. Have the child make a coolie hat in class since one was not available at home.

87. Ellen, a student, has been diagnosed with a serious illness and will be out of school for several months. Ellen's parents have asked her teachers to send her worksheets home to her in electronic form. All but which of the following could be used to send electronic copies of paper worksheets?

    a. Copy machine
    b. Scanner
    c. Flash drive or disc
    d. Email

88. Which of the following is an advantage of using anecdotal notes to assess student work?

    a. Teachers can use these to collect information both during assessment and outside of it.
    b. Unless a teacher adds norms or criteria for comparison, these notes lack standardization.
    c. Teachers cannot record observations of individual student behaviors as with most tools.
    d. Writing anecdotal notes can yield valuable insights but often lack any supporting context.

89. A special education teacher is working to create an IEP for one of her students. To complete her IEP, she needs to record when the student reached certain developmental and academic milestones. Who is the best person to reach out to in order to get this information?

    a. The student's pediatrician
    b. The student's previous teachers
    c. The school counselor
    d. The student's parent or guardian

90. There are differences among planned activities that are necessary classroom routines, activities that are fun and provide a break, and activities that are directly related to the curriculum. Of the following, which is an activity for taking a break?

    a. Singing a song.
    b. Packing up to go home.
    c. Playing math games.
    d. Taking a field trip.

91. A fifth grade science teacher has used a new textbook this year, and she wants to evaluate its effectiveness compared with that of the textbook she used in previous years. Which of the following strategies would be most appropriate?

   a. Comparing this year's students' performance on standardized tests to the standardized test scores of the students she taught in previous years using the old book
   b. Comparing this year's students' performance on norm-referenced in-class tests to the test scores of the students she taught in previous years using the old book
   c. Comparing current students' improvement on a criterion-referenced test administered at the beginning and the end of the year to previous students' improvement on that same test throughout the year
   d. Surveying current students' interest in science and comparing it to previous students' interest in science

92. How should teachers distribute the cognitive levels of the questions they ask relative to student grade levels?

   a. All elementary and secondary grades should be asked half higher- and half lower-level questions.
   b. More than half the questions should be at higher cognitive levels for all student grades.
   c. More than half at higher levels for secondary grades, below half in elementary grades.
   d. More than half the questions should be at lower cognitive levels for all student grades.

93. How can including cooperative learning strategies in the classroom teach practical life skills to students?

   a. Students learn to work independently, even when others are around.
   b. Students learn interpersonal problem-solving skills that they will need later in life.
   c. Students learn ways to score better on standardized tests.
   d. Students learn the importance of physical exercise in their daily lives.

94. A large school has divided its departments into multiple professional learning communities (PLCs) within the school. What should be the main goal of PLCs regarding teacher participation?

   a. Each should be led by the teacher or teachers with the most experience
   b. They should strictly follow the curriculum and guidelines sent from the district's main office
   c. They should strive to listen to and incorporate everyone's opinions and thoughts
   d. They should remain the same throughout the school year for consistency

95. Which of the following teacher behaviors impedes rather than promotes school-home communication?

   a. Listening to the parents and/or families of students
   b. Mutually exchanging teacher and family expertise
   c. Instructing parents and/or families in what to do
   d. Brainstorming supportive strategies together

96. During a class discussion, a teacher has posed a question to her class, but no student has responded. What should she do?

   a. Continue to wait until a student answers
   b. Repeat the question
   c. Rephrase the question
   d. Tell the students the answer

97. How can project-based learning help foster student learning?

a. By encouraging students to explore content in a variety of ways
b. By teaching students new content in a methodical approach
c. Allowing students to take ownership of their own learning
d. By introducing students to new knowledge and learning materials

98. An English Language Development (ELD) teacher notices that one of his English learners is refusing to use his home language in school. He has started to hang out with native English speakers and dressing similarly to them. What is this phenomenon known as?

a. Accommodation
b. Biculturalism
c. Culture shock
d. Assimilation

99. Teachers can positively communicate expectations in such a way as to make students eager to learn. Of the following statements, which one would be the least effective?

a. "We're going to think like scientists in this class."
b. "You might not like this practice, but it will help you to get a good grade."
c. "I know you are all curious about how to make a puppet."
d. "This project is one of my hobbies, so I wanted to share it with you."

100. A new teacher wants to make her students feel like their contributions during class discussions are important and vital to the flow of the classroom. What can this teacher do to ensure that students understand this while they are in her classroom?

a. Always be sure to ask follow-up questions when students contribute to the discussion
b. Offer extra credit when students participate in class
c. When students speak, allow other students a chance to respond to what the student said
d. Provide appropriate wait time and necessary cues when students are participating in class

Answer Key and Explanations

1. D: Arranging desks in groups of four to five is a good start for a first-year teacher who wants his students to work in groups. Additionally, creating designated spaces in the classroom where students know they can find material and turn in their work is extremely helpful for both teachers and students alike. These locations do not necessarily need to be centralized in the classroom, as it is more important that the locations remain consistent throughout the year and that students simply know where they are. Posters could be an added tool for this teacher to consider, but it is not the best advice for having the students work in groups successfully. Groups of desks are generally better than rows of desks for group work because it allows students to more easily communicate with each other.

2. B: When children reach the preoperational stage, they begin to think symbolically. At this point, they are able to begin understanding the relationship between letters (symbols) and sounds, also known as the alphabetic principle. Children are typically in the sensorimotor stage until about age 2, and they are not yet able to think symbolically in this stage. The concrete operational stage lasts from ages 7 to 12, and the formal operational stage lasts from age 12 until adulthood.

3. B: Spina bifida is the condition of incomplete closure of the neural tube in the spinal column. As such, it affects the spinal nerves and commonly causes paresis (paralysis) or weakness in the lower body. Motor dyspraxia or apraxia (A) is caused by damage to the parts of the brain's cerebrum that control and coordinate muscular movements. Athetosis (C) involves involuntary, uncontrolled body movements, while spasticity (D) is caused from excessive muscular rigidity and tension, which is a common symptom in cerebral palsy patients.

4. A: Extended practice should be part of the lesson when the teacher's evaluation shows that extended practice is needed to solidify the lesson or ensure that all students have learned the objective. The closing of the lesson is too late to try to back up and insert extended practice. When closing a lesson, it is natural to review key points, perhaps as demonstrated by work done by the students during the lesson, and giving the students a preview of the next or other related lessons builds student anticipation and desire to learn.

5. A: Words like "because" and "for example" have to be followed by a reasonably precise explanation that gives clarity to the communication. Clarity is critical to good communication. Vague or confusing language can reduce the effectiveness of presentations. Answer B gives examples of negated intensifiers; that is, the use of words such as "many" and "very" that indicate something big, but that are qualified by a "not", which communicates a nebulous state. Answer C indicates an ambiguous designation or destination – how is the student supposed to figure out needed specific information, even how to find supplies in the closet, if the directions are so vague? Answer D has words with the problem of vague probability; the student doesn't know exactly how often or what percentage.

6. A: The teacher needs to know how well each student is doing and must teach each child. The teacher is striving for a quality learning experience for every child rather than averages or high percentages measured by a group-wide evaluation. It is true that evaluation must be part of every lesson, in some form or another, or else the teacher will not know if the objective was reached, and if some or all students need a re-teach. This evaluation can continue with retention checks in other lessons; that is, on an on-going basis, and may be repeated in overall unit tests.

7. C: Preschool is a time in life in which students are highly likely to be at different developmental levels in the same classroom. Instead of expecting students to share, as might be above their current developmental skill level, teachers should promote sharing with modeling, encouraging, and rewarding sharing. Considering developmental levels for positive classroom environments, teachers can observe children's levels/types of play (unoccupied, independent, onlooker, parallel, associative, cooperative) and offer them not only matching activities (a), but also experiences at the next higher levels/types. Teachers must remember that older elementary and middle school students have not developed the social interaction skills of high school students, and accordingly guide them in peer collaboration (b). They should not expect new preschoolers to share, but instead should model, encourage, and reward sharing (c). For high school students, teachers can extend learning environments beyond classrooms (d) to surrounding communities, including service projects.

8. D: The teacher should first instruct the class on the subject matter, then the class should discuss it, and then the students should engage in independent activity. This order insures that the students have the most opportunity to absorb the new material before attempting to complete a related assignment on their own.

9. C: Accommodation occurs when something challenges a person's existing schema and causes it to be altered. In choice C, the child has a negative opinion of bees until she learns the role that they play in pollination. Her schema is altered, and she now views them as helpful. The other options demonstrate examples of assimilation, which occurs when someone takes in new information and adds it to existing schema rather than changing it. In choice A, the student applies the information she knows about sentences to punctuate the question. In choice B, the student applies information about the writing process to a new type of text. In choice D, the child assumes that the tiger is a lion because it makes the same sound.

10. B: The FERPA stipulates that parents of children under 18 can inspect and request amendments to their children's educational records on demand (B). However, once students reach the age of majority, they become "eligible students." This means that this right is transferred to them and their permission is required to disclose their educational records to anyone, including their parents. Written permission from parents or the eligible student is not required in order to disclose records to a school official with a legitimate educational interest (C) or to a school to which the student is transferring (D).

11. B: While parental involvement does not guarantee academic success, students whose parents are involved in their schooling typically perform better than students whose families are less involved. While many factors contribute to this outcome, one important factor is that by being involved, parents convey to their children their belief that education is valuable.

12. B: The approach of the teacher's "simple authority statement" authoritatively stops student misbehavior with a minimum of emotional distress (a); models reasonable, respectful use of authority for students (b); and expresses teacher disapproval of student behavior as objectively as possible (c), and does so immediately (d).

13. B: Studies have shown that no other factor affects a student's performance in school as much as the degree to which the student's family is involved in his or her life. All of the other factors listed also have their influence too, but if a student's family takes an active interest in the student's performance in school, the other factors are more likely to be overcome, and the student's grades, attitude, and likelihood of graduation are all likely to be higher. Whatever a teacher can to encourage this is to the student's advantage.

14. A: Establishing a clear set of rules for your classroom from the very beginning is the best way to let your students know what is expected of them. Giving the students the rules in writing ensures that they have no excuse to not know what the rules are. Answer B works for some teachers, but not for all. Moreover, it is not necessarily to your advantage to establish yourself in a negative light before your students. Answer C is a very bad idea. Waiting to establish the rules will likely result in chaos, and students will get the idea that they can get away with anything. Answer D is also unhelpful. Your rules should be consistent. Changing them often will confuse your students, and might cause them to take your rules less seriously.

15. B: Parents need opportunities to express their concerns when something is not working for their child in a classroom. Teachers should strive to be empathetic to parental concerns and attempt to work out resolutions to problems that can work for all involved. Explaining why homework is important and providing data to the parents likely will not make a difference in the stresses they are experiencing at home with their child. Asking their parent how long it takes their student to complete homework will likely come up in the conversation, but the question itself does not work to address the problem that the family is experiencing. A counselor could be a useful tool to help the student next if the strategies the parents and teacher discuss prove to be ineffective.

16. A: This approach clearly communicates the problem, while at the same time showing respect for the student. Additionally, it invites input from the parents. This is a very good way to lay the groundwork for a cooperative discussion. Answer B needlessly compares Mike's performance to the other students in the class, and worse yet, it offers no solution. Answer C would likely put the parents on the defensive since it questions whether they are helping Mike. Answer D does not effectively communicate the seriousness of the problem. The parents will leave the meeting thinking that it's no big deal.

17. D: Circulating around the class allows the teacher to observe firsthand how things are going without interrupting the students' work. Answer A does not permit the teacher to see how the students are doing. Answer B is much too passive, and does not allow the teacher a chance to solve problems before they happen. Answer C is not practical, since it requires too much time.

18. A: The Family Educational Rights and Privacy Act (FERPA) prohibits teachers from disclosing any information related to students' educational records without consent from the parents, authorized persons, or the individual student upon reaching the age of eighteen. This includes academic or behavioral records, medical history, and personally identifiable information, such as names, birthdates, or student identification numbers. As such, this teacher has the legal and professional responsibility to take measures for ensuring that information included in his assignment does not infringe upon his students' right to confidentiality prior to submitting it. While he may refer to his experiences working with ethnically diverse students in a general sense, he may not disclose any personal information that may reveal the students' identities.

19. A: The objective is like a public declaration for all to see – not only the students, but also other teachers, administrative staff, and parents who want to know what is going on that day and whether the objective has been clearly communicated to the students. One of the benefits of a clearly written, focused objective is that the teacher knows exactly what to evaluate – did the students learn the objective for the day? Another benefit is that the evaluation works in reverse also – providing a measure for the teacher to judge his/her own effectiveness. It is the primary purpose of an objective to focus the students on what they are to learn that day; in addition, a well-written objective might also motivate students to want to learn the day's lesson.

20. A: According to Vygotsky, activities in the zone of proximal development are ones that students are almost able to complete independently, but they require some scaffolding. The activities are not too easy or too difficult, but just challenging enough to allow some growth to occur. Reading books at the instructional level with teacher guidance is an example of an activity in the zone of proximal development. Choices B and D represent activities that are easy for the student. Choice C demonstrates a way to make a text accessible for a student when it is too difficult for the student to read independently.

21. C: Task cards are a strategy best used as a manipulative for tactile-kinesthetic learners. While a task card may have writing on it, the value to tactile learners is that a card is something that the students can touch, which makes the writing more real to them. Students who are dominantly verbal-linguistic learners will learn best when listening, speaking, reading, and writing. Consequently, activities such as classroom discussions, listening to a story read by the teacher, or reading the words listed on the classroom word wall are good strategies for reaching the verbal-linguistic learners in the class.

22. C: Under the fair use doctrine, educators can use certain copyrighted works in the classroom for educational purposes. Playing a song in class is one of the allowed items under the fair use doctrine. Teachers need to ensure that materials they are using in the classroom are not infringing on copyright laws, and the fair use doctrine provides guidance as to what teachers can use. Media specialists, curriculum chairs, and other leaders in the school should also be able to provide guidance on what resources can be used by teachers without violating copyright laws.

23. D: Technology is a tool that, when used properly, can strengthen project-based learning in the classroom. When teachers incorporate good technological tools into class, it can greatly strengthen the learning that occurs, and make students more independent. While not all project-based learning projects will use technology, a great number of them are likely to use it at least some for students to gather the necessary materials. With proper supervision and education, elementary school students should be able to use technology in project-based learning just as well as middle and high school students.

24. C: Many new teachers make the mistake of getting so caught up in their lesson that they fail to notice problem behavior in the classroom before it gets out of hand. Teachers must learn to divide their attention between all aspects of the class environment, and to periodically scan the room and take account of what is going on. Like juggling, this is a skill that takes time and practice to develop. All new teachers must work hard to become competent at it.

25. B: Allowing students to pick their own groups defeats the purposes outlined above and will most likely result in groups that were chosen by the students so that they could be with friends rather than good working partners. Flexible grouping is designed to put students together in groups that work well for various purposes. One type of group would be one in which the students can work according to similar interests. Others would group students according to readiness levels or specific skill levels. In other words, the grouping would be teacher-selected according to assessments that indicate the needed diversity or similarities to make the group efficient.

26. C: Prekindergarten students are likely in the emergent stage of reading development, where they are developing an understanding of the concepts of print. In this stage, they are in the beginning stages of learning to recognize letters and letter/sound relationships. Therefore, an activity that focuses on letter identification is most developmentally appropriate. The other activities require more complex phonics skills and would be more appropriate for students in the early stage of reading development.

27. D: Some common teacher outreach efforts include home visits, which more parents welcome than find intrusive (A); phone calls from teachers with good news about their children instead of only hearing from them about problems (B); weekly newsletters, not only explaining class activities but also offering parents ideas for working with students at home, which many parents read and appreciate (C); and periodically sending information to parents (e.g., papers explaining the stages of reading and writing development, informing milestone anticipation and progress monitoring). This enhances parental support, which in turn dramatically accelerates student mastery (D).

28. C: Teachers should continually strive to improve their professional knowledge of the subjects that they teach. It allows them to stay abreast of current topics in the field, as well as any educational studies or changes in the field that may change their day-to-day instruction. It also helps teachers remain leaders in their subjects so that they are up to date on current events related to their field. Continual professional knowledge and development is a characteristic that top-level teachers strive to always be working on because it helps them to remain leaders in the school by knowing what is currently occurring in their field.

29. A: Option A is correct because critical thinking involves analyzing and synthesizing information to reach a solution. By having the student create a law and defend their reasoning, they are actively participating in critical thinking. Option B is incorrect because, while interviewing someone in government will teach the student about how government works, it will not help students develop critical thinking skills. Option C is incorrect because simply writing a report does not work on expanding students' critical thinking skills. Option D is incorrect because creating a list requires a low level of thinking and engagement and does not help advance skills related to critical thinking.

30. B: Planning requires abstract thinking (A), as it involves mentally representing actions before actually performing them, and imagination (B) to envision doing things not done yet. Planning both requires and promotes organization as well as imagination (C). Planning is identified as being on a higher level among higher-order thinking skills, not lower (D).

31. C: Providing checklists and rubrics to students is a valuable way to teach students to take ownership of their learning. It helps the students know what is expected so that they can self-check their own work and progress along the way. Students generally should not choose which of their assignments should be graded, nor should they be required to self-grade each assessment prior to turning it in. Having students keep an established place in their binder to track their grades is a helpful way to allow students to monitor their progress, but is not the most effective way to teach students to take ownership.

32. B: Mr. Ainsley should respond to the principal's suggestion by using available professional development resources on assessment to develop a plan to improve his use of assessment in the classroom and present it to the principal for review. This approach will provide the most immediate and effective way to resolve the flaw in his instructional approach, and it will also allow him to get feedback from the principal so that he knows that he has correctly understood and responded to the principal's suggestion.

33. B: When teachers assign projects that require the use of technology and independent research, they should ensure that all students have reasonable access to the materials they need to complete the project. In this case, if the teacher can schedule time for students to go to the media center and computer lab during class, this would help students gather the materials they need and ensure that all students have a fair chance to complete the project. Asking students to stay after school may be difficult for students who rely on the school bus for transportation or who have other responsibilities after school. Clear instructions should always be given on assignments, but clear instructions will not help students who do not have the means to complete the assignment. Pairing students together for the assignment is likely not what the teacher wants to do for a final research project that he was anticipating students complete alone. It would be best for him to make sure all students have access to the resources they need.

34. A: Extrinsic motivation is behavior that is motivated by external rewards like money or grades. Offering a child money based on good grades is a prime example of extrinsic motivation. Extrinsic motivation can also include praise, rewards, and other motivators unrelated to the target activity. The other answer choices in this scenario are all related to intrinsic motivation. Intrinsic motivation is the motivation to complete an action, assignment, or project because of inherent benefit related to the activity, such as feeling accomplished after a successful performance, as in answer C.

35. B: Using additional visual aids and hand gestures will help get your points across more clearly. Answer A is inappropriate. The parents should not have to pay for a translator, and such a strategy would also not encourage the student to increase her English skills. Answer C would make it even harder for the student to understand. Answer D would be unfair to the other students, since it would greatly slow down you class and make it impossible to you to cover your material on schedule.

36. B: The placement of computer workstations is dictated by the location of electrical outlets and Internet connections. Therefore it is highly desirable to arrange their location before bringing in other equipment. Answer A, the teacher's desk, is less critical, but should be positioned so that it affords the teacher a good view of the classroom when the teacher is working. Answer C, filing cabinets, are the least critical item, and may usually be left until last, since the only issues concerning their placement are that they should be out of the way of student traffic and should be easily accessible from the teacher's desk. Answer D, the overhead projector, needs to be position within a direct line of sight to the projection screen, but since these projectors are often on wheeled carts, they can be easily moved out of the way when not in use.

37. B: Demonstrating how the device works and explaining how the student will use the device to communicate will help potentially ease the child's entrance into the classroom. Students should have fewer questions and be more willing to engage with the student if they know more about what to expect. Instructing students to refrain from using their voices for a day trivializes the struggle the student deals with for his life and is not the best activity to have in class to help this student feel welcome. While it may be helpful to assign a helper to the student, the student might not want his peers helping him in class and it would be better to ask the student privately if that is something he might like. Allowing students to play with a similar device may help them learn how it works, but they may need more explanation and instruction to understand and empathize with the student who uses the device.

38. D: The individual teacher is ultimately responsible for keeping up with the latest ideas. The school system, the principal, and other teachers can often be excellent resources, and may even set up programs or continuing education requirements to help teachers stay current, but this does not always occur, and in any case, it remains a teacher's responsibility to ensure that his or her skills are constantly improving.

39. B: Language load is the number of unrecognizable words an English language learner encounters when reading a passage or listening to a teacher. Language load is one of the barriers English language learners face. To lighten this load, a teacher can rephrase, eliminate unnecessary words, divide complex sentences into smaller units, and teach essential vocabulary before the student begins the lesson.

40. A: Evaluating individual student progress will make evaluation much fairer in such a situation. Answer B is more about making the teacher look good than about fairness to the students. Answer C, shifting the grading priority to research projects, will not necessarily make the evaluations fairer if student progress is not considered. Answer D is the opposite of what a teacher should do in this situation.

41. D: Many parents assume that as their children approach adulthood, the parents should step back and let them make the children make own mistakes. While children at this age do need to have a little more freedom and responsibility, this age range is actually a particularly critical time in students' development and they need the involvement and guidance of their families more than ever. A teacher does have the power to help change this by reaching out to the parents and creating more opportunities for them to be involved in class activities. It also helps to try and get your school more involved with parents in general.

42. D: The best way to have her students prepare for the test is to assign students to work in groups to complete a concept map over the Civil War. Students working together to gather data and make connections should activate prior learning to help them focus on both what they have already learned and the connections they have made in the unit. While the other options are all somewhat acceptable methods to review for a test, instructing students to complete a concept map should activate a deeper understanding of the unit to help students retain more information long-term about the Civil War.

43. B: If a teacher corrects ESL students every single time they make any kind of mistake (A), many of them would feel so inhibited they would be afraid to say anything. Many grammatical errors do not significantly interfere with communication. While serious errors should be corrected, teachers do better to make notes of these and then point them out after a class activity is over rather than interrupting the activity's/discussion's flow. Teachers should also make use of student errors to inform themselves of further student learning needs when they plan additional practice for the class (C). Rather than only highlighting errors, teachers should equally acknowledge good work at expressing ideas in English with encouraging words (D) during oral activities, and with check marks or similar written feedback on written assignments.

44. A: Each of the answer choices describes an element of critical thinking. The student's described actions correspond to evaluating evidence used to support arguments or statements (a), since the student should consider whether a source is reputable, proven, and accepted by authorities in the field before using evidence from that source. Judging the quality of material (b) or information can be done by comparing it to other material/information, consulting one's own previous experience, and listening to one's own intuition. Distinguishing fact from opinion (c) in text or speech is done by looking for objectivity, facts, and proof vs. subjectivity, non-factual information, and absence of proof. Identifying whether a source contains evidence or no evidence (d) to support the writer's or speaker's arguments can be done by examining the ideas and information in the text or speech. The quality of a source, the source's use of fact and opinion, and whether the source contains evidence that supports an argument are all factors that should be considered when evaluating evidence. Since the student's described actions are also used to evaluate supporting evidence, Choice A is the correct answer.

45. C: It might be a good idea, but it is best to do a little research first and talk to the technology coordinator. It is important to make sure that the game is truly educational, is practical for class use, and also that it is appropriate for use with the age group of the students in his class. Answer A is risky. At the very least the teacher should spend some time with the game and verify that it looks promising. Answer B is closed minded. After all, there are indeed some useful educational games that can successfully be used in class. Answer D is unreliable, since most students would be happy to play a game instead of listening to a lecture.

46. D: Research finds that teacher practices and school policies are more predictive of how involved parents will be in their children's educations than the parents' race or ethnicity (a), the marital status of the parents (b), or the parents' own levels of education (c) are.

47. A: Allowing students to discuss the questions in pairs gives students the opportunity to try out their answers in a "safe" environment before stating them in front of the class. This will make students more comfortable participating in the discussion, thus making it more effective.

48. D: Option D is correct because a child should be able to be away from their parents for periods of time by the age of 4. Option A is incorrect because reading is too advanced for many 4-year-olds and is not a skill that students are expected to have mastered by this age. It is not a developmental concern if students cannot read by this age. Option B is incorrect because this is too advanced for a typical 4-year-old and is the developmental milestone of a 6-year-old. Option C is incorrect because imagination and fantasy are typical at this stage of development.

49. B: Classrooms come in a variety of shapes and sizes. Moreover, the arrangement that works for one class will not necessarily work for another. Answer C, with the desks facing the chalkboard, seems logical and might work in many cases, but you need to consider the needs of your class first. For example, some teachers prefer to use an overhead projector instead of a chalkboard. Also, some classrooms have more than one chalkboard. Answer A is not a good idea unless there really is a major source of distraction outside the window. Answer D is absurd. School administrators do not spend any time optimizing the floor plans of classrooms. The previous teacher's arrangement will not necessarily work for you.

50. A: intrinsic motivation can be fostered by helping students to develop a personal connection to and interest in the material they're learning. Intrinsic motivation refers to a person's desire to do something (like a hobby) without any apparent material motivation and without any threat of punishment should the activity not be done. In contrast, answer B refers to extrinsic motivation. This type of motivation propels a person to do something not because they enjoy the activity for its own sake, but because they fear punishment or desire rewards produced by that activity.

51. B: Bulletin boards are a great way to make your classroom more appealing to students and can also be a useful way to communicate rules, schedules, and other information. However, it is not absolutely essential that the bulletin boards be perfect on the first day of school. Answer A is much more important since students must have a good view of the main teaching area and if you have to move them around, it will make it harder for you to learn their names. Answer C is essential so that all students have access to the materials necessary for the class. Of course, this is not as critical with materials that will not be used until later in the term. Answer D is equally important if you intend to rely on these items in your teaching.

52. C: By providing recent immigrant families with materials pertinent to the orientation in their native languages, the teachers will ensure that the families understand the content of the materials. Providing the families with a detailed analysis of the district ESL program (A) will not give them an understanding of all of the school's protocols and culture, but of only one component. Asking the ESL students to interpret for their families (B) does not acknowledge that many of these recent immigrant students may not have the English-language proficiency to interpret, and doing so could activate the students' affective filters. Arranging discussion groups about the families' native languages (D) can promote communication among these families, but it will not help students' parents understand the information the teachers are presenting to them during the orientation event.

53. B: This information will help the teachers plan their instruction based on the strengths and needs of the incoming students. Standardized test information should not be the sole basis on which students are given remedial instruction (A); their class performance should be strongly considered as well. D is incorrect because team teaching can be effective regardless of how well or poorly students perform on standardized tests, and C is incorrect because the decision to repeat a grade typically does not involve a student's future teachers, and should not be based solely on standardized test results.

54. D: Because of diverse student needs, teachers are required to ensure educational equity by differentiating their instruction accordingly with student abilities (a), offering equal opportunities to all students (b), treating all students fairly (c), and choosing and/or adapting instructional materials to reflect multicultural perspectives (d) to which multicultural students can relate.

55. C: The best way that a teacher could use standardized test data in her classroom is to use it to analyze gaps in learning that their students may have. They could potentially identify common gaps among the students and identify which students struggled more on specific standards than other students. It allows for the teacher to have an opportunity to plan out what she wants her students to improve upon in the upcoming year and enact a plan to see them achieve.

56. D: Because inclusive education is a federal legal mandate and mainstreaming is the commonest means of compliance today, regular classroom teachers most often have the responsibility for the instruction of special-needs students—even if these students are also assigned educational specialists (a), special education teachers (b), and whichever therapists are most applicable (c) to an individual student's needs. Classroom teachers collaborate with these personnel, but still usually have the main responsibility for instruction.

57. C: Introducing new material using several different strategies will help make it more accessible to a larger group of students, regardless of their specific backgrounds. All three of the other answers represent a shallow approach to diversity that presumes that different cultures adhere to stereotypes. The truth is that different students think differently, and using a wider variety of teaching methods will cast a wider net.

58. D: Students with specific learning disabilities (SLDs) do not have intellectual impairments; they have impairments in processing information. Therefore it is most typical of students with SLDs to show a marked gap between intellectual ability and school performance. Students with ASDs (a) can have any degree of intellectual impairment or none. Those with high IQs may excel academically but have difficulty with social interactions, transitions, and sensory input, and/or demonstrate rigid routines and schedules, restricted interests, and repetitive behaviors. Students with ID (b) typically learn the same ways as others, but more slowly. Generally their intellectual ability and school performance are less disparate than those of students with SLDs. Hence (c) is incorrect.

59. D: If Mr. Gupta knows that it the experiments are where the time is being lost, then he needs to closely evaluate why they are taking so long. Are the students spending more time talking that working? Are they getting stuck and waiting a long time for Mr. Gupta to get around to them? Are some of the experiments simply too ambitious for this class? In any case, he must determine where the problem is, and then reorganize the way experiments are conducted to make the process more efficient. Answer A is too drastic, and deprives students of an important opportunity to gain a hands-on understanding of the principles being covered. Answer B is also not the way to go. This will eventually result in a class that fails to cover a lot of important material. Answer C is unfair to the students. Mr. Gupta should not overburden the students because he failed to properly organize the class in the first place.

60. D: A sudden decline in academic performance could be caused by any of the factors listed. Certain eating disorders can cause declines in academic performance because of physical symptoms like lethargy and the students' attendant lack of motivation. Drug use can also cause lethargy, inattentiveness, and/or hyperactivity that can affect schoolwork. Parental divorce can cause depression and inability to focus, which can also contribute to a decline in academic achievement. However, it is important to remember that these problems do not always cause declines in academic achievement. Joining a sports team may cause sudden change in a student's life, causing them to need to adjust to perform well in both sporting and academic pursuits. Once the student is adjusted, participation in a school sports team should not cause problems with academics and, in fact, may reinforce study habits if the team requires the student to achieve a certain grade point average.

61. A: Whereas behaviorist learning theorists believe that learning always results in some change in behavior, Bandura disagrees, finding children could learn something new without necessarily producing new or different behaviors. Bandura agrees with the behaviorist concept that consequences (events immediately following behaviors) either reward them, reinforcing and increasing their probable recurrence, or punish them, decreasing their probable recurrence. Unlike behaviorists who insist only externally observable, measurable behaviors can be changed, Bandura emphasizes the importance of internal cognitive processes in learning and thus of examining their roles (C), as well as social interactions in learning (D).

62. B: This will bring the story into a modern context, making it easier to understand. Having them search for differences will ensure that they actually read the original as well. Answer A would certainly be helpful, but by itself is not likely to prevent students from losing interest. Answer C is also a useful practice, but without a real understanding of the context, much of the drama will be lost upon the students. Answer D will almost certainly put most of the students to sleep, and is unnecessary for studying a single play.

63. B: Arranging a time in private to discuss concerns or requests with the visually impaired student is an essential first step in helping the student feel welcome in the classroom. It is likely the teacher has already received a list of accommodations for this student from the teenager's case manager. However, setting aside a time for a conversation with the student can help the teacher learn more about their needs and if there are any extra steps that can be taken to make the student more comfortable and successful. Setting aside time in the class for the student to be asked questions by their peers might be something the student could suggest to the teacher, but it should not be done without the student's approval. The same can be said for a class discussion because it may make the student feel like an outcast. Inviting the parents to observe any time they want is a lot to ask for the teacher, and while the parents should be allowed to observe class if both they and their child feel it would be helpful, it should only be expected on a mutually agreed upon date, and not at any time they wish.

64. B: Mr. Rogers' practices are most relevant to promoting understanding and empathy among students from diverse cultures and preventing student conflicts by helping them express their diverse viewpoints, relate to each other's perspectives, and discuss their emotions in the school context. The question does not identify any students as experiencing cultural identity crises (A). While it does describe Mr. Rogers as teaching English language use and academic subject content, it does not describe any practices for specifically improving academic achievements (C). It does not describe any practices for specifically acknowledging and addressing student linguistic diversity (D).

65. D: When classrooms include students at different levels of physical abilities, it is important for the teacher to make sure not to accidentally exclude students from activities because of their ability level. Their ability level could include both physical and mental limitations that should be accounted for when planning instruction. This does not mean that teachers should not plan any activities that require coordination, but rather that they should account for any accommodations the students may need, which may include pairing some students with paraprofessionals for certain activities. While occasionally a teacher might choose to pair up students of differing physical ability levels, they should not solely rely on that as a means of accommodation. Additionally, interchanging activities is a good plan, but it is not a way to ensure that student needs are always addressed, nor is never planning any activities that allow students to move around the classroom.

66. C: Parents need to be kept up to date with their child's progress in school. When areas of concern arise, teachers should be ready with concrete examples of specific struggles that their child is experiencing. Concrete examples include projects, tests, and written work samples. Charts and grade printouts do not effectively demonstrate what the specific areas of concern are for the student. While parents should be consulted for ideas on how to help their child, it is not the best way to convey that a child is struggling. By comparing the child's work to the work of his classmates, parents may become defensive and upset about the progress of their children. It is generally best practice to not compare the work of specific children, particularly when holding conversations with parents and guardians.

67. C: One of the descriptors for ELL students at the Intermediate level of Speaking proficiency is speaking in simple sentences, using mostly present tenses. Another is that they may often need to hesitate for long times (A) to figure out how to express themselves. Another descriptor is that they seldom have sufficient vocabulary to speak in more detail (B). People used to interacting with ELLs usually understand their pronunciation, but people unused to ELLs often will not (D).

68. A: Using school funds to make sure there is a large variety of books for families to choose from is the best way to promote literacy at home in a lower-income school. Having access to books that the students can borrow for free and enjoy at home gives lower-income students the opportunity to enjoy books that they may have never had the opportunity to read. The more students read at home, the better they will become at reading in school, which will help increase their confidence in other subjects. Assigning creative projects about books for students to complete at home will likely cause added stress on families with limited resources in lower-income schools and should be avoided when possible. Sending home a weekly brochure that covers what skills students are learning can be a helpful tool for parents to follow what their students are learning about, but it should not be expected that parents spend their time at home to reinforce those skills with their children. Requesting that lower-income parents come into school weekly to read to their students would likely be a struggle for many of the parents and should not be expected of lower-income families.

69. B: The occupational therapist is most qualified to inform classroom teachers of activities that develop student fine motor skills and skills for completing activities of daily living (ADL). The physical therapist (A) is more qualified to inform teachers of exercises and activities that develop gross motor skills, and to make and adapt assistive devices. The special education teacher (C) is more qualified to help classroom teachers adapt/modify curriculum and instruction for special student needs and provide strategies for inclusive and differentiated instruction. The OT's specific expertise is not equally available from any other IEP team members (D).

70. D: Although copying definitions might help to cement the meaning of a word, if the word is not one that is relevant to the lesson, it will be quickly forgotten. Answer D violates the guideline that practicing skills should be embedded within application opportunities and is busy-work practice with no point to the effort. Reading does help students to improve word attack skills, as well as many other skills, so Answer A is a worthwhile objective. If the objective is to improve number facts and computations, solving problems is a good practice, so Answer B is also a worthwhile objective. In the process of writing an essay, the student has to practice spelling and penmanship skills, so this assignment achieves a good objective, as stated in Answer C.

71. C: By giving students detailed feedback on their performance and providing opportunities to incorporate the feedback and demonstrate improvement, a teacher can give students a sense of control over their learning. For example, a teacher might provide students with detailed feedback on an essay, and then give them a chance to rewrite and improve it to achieve a higher grade.

72. C: The local government is responsible for making sure that the new changes will be carried out in schools. This is generally carried out by each individual school district, who passes the changes on to each school in their district. While the state government is responsible for mandating what should be taught in schools, local governments are responsible for ensuring that they are implemented.

73. B: In order to begin resolving the problem, Ms. Mattingly should first confer with her principal and other fourth grade teachers to determine whether her grade level expectations for academic achievement align with those of the district as a whole. Since she was previously unaware of the fact that her students were falling behind, the most logical explanation for this situation is that her academic expectations for her students are not as high as those used by school administrators in constructing the test. She should definitely not ignore the standardized test results (A) or ask the students' parents to resolve the problem themselves (D). She may not need to change her instructional methods either (C), if the problem is simply that her expectations are too low.

74. B: Since most of the students in Ms. Frank's class are auditory learners, she would reach the majority of her students by teaching them a song about the new concept that they're learning. Auditory learners remember and comprehend concepts best using their sense of hearing.

75. D: Option D is correct because asking the students to write an open-ended response will give the teacher a valuable opportunity to investigate what students already know about the life cycle of plants. Option A is incorrect because the teacher should be creating her assessment on what she wants her students to know by the end of the unit. Option B is incorrect because an open-ended response does not indicate how much interest her students would have in the topic. Some students might not know anything yet but will become interested as they learn more. Option C is incorrect because prior knowledge on a topic is not correlated with how advanced a student might be.

76. D: Although all of the skills listed are part of digital literacy, the main focus of this assignment is to create writing on the same topic for two very different audiences. Students will therefore need to know how to adjust the formality of their writing so that it is appropriate for each audience. A post on the school website, which will be seen by numerous community members, should use a more formal tone than an email to a friend. Therefore, choice D is the most relevant skill for this particular assignment.

77. C: Though many people would look the other way, Mr. Calhoun would be committing an ethical violation by selling products such as Girl Scout cookies on school property. It may not seem like much of an offense, but it does not benefit the school in any way, and some parents might complain about a teacher who is selling sweets to their children. Moreover, Mr. Calhoun's students might even get the idea that if they do not buy Mr. Calhoun's cookies, that they will not get good grades.

78. B: Breaking the item in to smaller sections makes memorization much easier. Answer A is an important part of memorization, but without breaking a topic up into smaller sections, many students will have a hard time. Answer C is ineffective unless the student has a photographic memory. Playing music in the background is helpful to some, but later the student may have difficulty if the same music is not playing when the student tries to recall the subject matter.

79. A: When a small group of students have trouble understanding a new concept, a teacher should attempt to help remediate those students. One of the best ways to handle this during class time is to provide an enrichment activity to the students who have mastered the concept while providing additional instruction to the students still working on mastery. Retaking assessments can also be utilized, but material should be retaught before having students retake assessments. Taking the time to try to help students understand concepts is particularly important in math classrooms because concepts tend to build upon each other, and teachers should try to incorporate this into their lesson plans when students are struggling.

80. A: If Mr. Stratton's goal is to ensure that students understand what is expected of them and that they are able to complete the project on schedule, the best approach for him to take would be to explain how to do the research and set several 'checkpoints' before the final product is due. By explaining the research process, Mr. Stratton ensures that all students understand what they're expected to do. Setting checkpoints, (for example, asking students to submit a brief description of their project one month before it is due and asking them to submit a rough draft one week before it is due), Mr. Stratton can make sure that all of his students are on track to complete the project as scheduled.

81. B: Creating and enacting a no-bullying policy should be one of the first steps that the classroom teacher and the resource teacher should work together to help improve the classroom environment. This should not only educate the students on why it is inappropriate to tease the child with hearing loss, but should prevent other children from being bullied in the class as well. No-bully policies can be implemented by setting guidelines for appropriate behavior and administering consequences when bullying occurs. Correcting inappropriate behavior is a good step to take, but it is not always appropriate to correct behavior immediately because it may single out students who do not understand what they are saying and how it is inappropriate. Moving the child to a self-contained environment does not allow for the least restrictive environment for the student and is not an acceptable solution. Contacting all parents and guardians to explain what is occurring in class is not a feasible solution without first trying other solutions.

82. C: Ms. Schneider should take the paraprofessional aside and explain her concerns. She should attempt to find out what is causing the behavior, and help the paraprofessional find a way to improve his performance. She should only begin approaching others regarding the problem after she has discussed the problem directly with the paraprofessional and given him a chance to improve his performance.

83. A: Learner-centered assessment provides alternatives that allow different students to be assessed differently. Although student participation in assessment creation (D) is also an important part of learner-centered assessment, a multiple choice test does not reflect the goals of learner-centered assessment because it does not provide an authentic assessment experience.

84. C: Constructivism is a learning theory based on the idea that people are actively involved in the learning process, rather than being passive receivers of knowledge. Constructivism suggests that children learn best by solving real-world problems, gathering information, testing ideas, and other active processes, with teachers guiding and scaffolding them along the way.

85. D: To encourage student development of intrinsic motivation, teachers can interest students in learning content by having a strong interest in it themselves (a); demonstrating their own interest in the content to students (b); getting to know students and their individual interests (c); and moreover, connecting learning content to those student interests (d).

86. C: The offended family will be given the opportunity to educate the teacher and the class about their culture. The activity should continue so that the other students aren't denied an opportunity to share because of the teacher's mistake. Most definitely, the teacher should not compound the error by persisting in asking for something that s/he has been told is offensive. Teachers who make assumptions based on cultural stereotypes could offend students with inappropriate statements or requests. It is good practice to have the students share about their cultures in a "Show and Tell" activity, for example. However, should the teacher make a mistake about cultural practices, s/he should apologize to anyone offended and not let the matter drop but follow up with another option and continue the activity for everyone. The teacher should give careful thought to the mistake and correct any misconceptions.

87. A: In order to send Ellen electronic copies of paper worksheets, a scanner and email, a disc or flash drive would probably be needed, but a copy machine would not be necessary. The teachers could scan the documents using a scanner and send them as an email attachment or save them to a disc. The disc could then be sent home and Ellen could download the documents and print them out, or Ellen could open and print the email attachment.

88. A: One advantage of writing anecdotal notes as an assessment tool is that teachers can collect information about student skills and behaviors outside of assessment activities as well as during them; this can help teachers realize valuable insights into student learning and behavior. The fact that such notes are not standardized unless the teacher incorporates norms or criteria for comparison (b) is a disadvantage. An advantage of anecdotal notes is that teachers *can* record observations of individual student behaviors, which standard test instruments, checklists, and most other tools do *not* allow (c). The fact that anecdotal notes often lack any supporting context (d) is a disadvantage.

89. D: The parent/guardian is the best person to consult for this information. Parents and guardians have been with their children for their entire lives and would have much more information than any other source. They should have access to the student's medical records and will have information from before their children started attending school. Previous teachers and school counselors likely would not have access to most developmental milestones and would likely be missing other pertinent information.

90. A: Singing a song is the answer because this is a pleasant activity that the children enjoy and that helps them to relax. Singing a song is good for a break, especially a break that transitions into a new lesson or activity. Although some songs may also enhance a lesson, the students perceive singing a fun song as just that: fun. Packing up to go home is a routine activity that is part of the classroom management structure. Playing math games is an activity that is directly related to the math curriculum and reinforces a lesson. Taking a field trip is also related to the curriculum and is supposed to be designed to illustrate or enhance a lesson.

91. C: The most effective way to evaluate the effectiveness of the new textbook would be to compare current students' improvement on a criterion-referenced test over the course of a year to previous students' improvement on that same test. This method would help to eliminate intervening variables (standardized test difficulty and changing focus, as well as variations in students' initial level of academic achievement) that would make the other measures suggested problematic.

92. C: Teachers should ask more than half of their questions at higher cognitive levels (i.e., requiring students to apply, analyze, evaluate, and synthesize or create information) for students in secondary grades, and include smaller proportions at this level for students in elementary grades, rather than by dividing question types equally for all grades (A), giving more high-level questions to all grades (B), or giving more low-level questions (i.e., requiring students only to remember and understand information) to all grades (D).

93. B: Cooperative learning exercises (working in small groups) teach students how to solve problems in groups. These skills are essential to success in many jobs. Answer A is the opposite of cooperative learning. Answers C and D are unrelated to the topic of the question.

94. C: Professional learning communities (PLCs) should strive to listen to and incorporate all members' opinions and thoughts while in the community. The purpose of PLCs is to collaborate, share skills and knowledge, and work to improve both the skills of the teachers in the community and the teachers in the school, as well as improve student performance. PLCs do not necessarily have to be led by the teachers with the most experience, nor do they have to generally follow guidance from the district office. They also do not have to remain consistent throughout the year and can change as the school year progresses.

95. C: Teacher behaviors that promote school-home communication include devoting equal time to listening to parents/families (a), mutually exchanging teacher and family expertise (b) with each other, and brainstorming with families to find strategies supporting individual students (d). However, when teachers limit their behaviors with families to telling them what to do (c), this impedes school-home communication.

96. C: The teacher should try rephrasing the question before telling students the answer. Often, students fail to answer because they simply don't understand what information the teacher is looking for, rather than because they actually don't know the information. The teacher might try asking the question from a different angle, providing a hint, or using different terminology.

97. A: Project-based learning is a meaningful tool that allows students to investigate topics in depth and apply what they know to investigate new material. Students examine content in depth and generally have a choice for how they choose to approach their learning. It is not a methodical approach to learning, but rather is a way for students to learn how to formulate a plan, research, and apply knowledge to real-world topics. While students may have a choice in how they approach the topic, they are not in charge of their own learning because the teacher should act as the facilitator and give guidance. It also is not necessarily introducing students to new knowledge, but instead may be allowing enrichment on topics students are already familiar with.

98. D: Assimilation is the process in which an individual tries to adopt the culture of the dominant culture and rejects his or her culture. Accommodation is a process in which members of the mainstream culture and the minority culture both learn to adapt to one another. Biculturalism is when an individual is able to function in two different cultures. Culture shock occurs once the initial excitement of being in a new culture wears off and the individual feels frustrated by the confusion and differences between the two cultures.

99. B: The answer uses a negative and is just like saying, "Eat your spinach because it is good for you." Kids want to do what they like, not necessarily what's good for them. Answer A is a positive communication that creates anticipation for learning because the teacher is setting expectations and giving students a goal for achieving a skill that might be interesting. Answer C sets up an expectation of curiosity that encourages students to want to find out more. Answer D is another way that a teacher can interest students who have a curiosity about the teacher's personal life, and is very inviting because it offers to share something with the students.

100. D: Allowing appropriate wait times for student responses in class is an important way to show students that their opinions are important to the classroom. Additionally, providing cues to students who need help answering a question will let them know that their contributions are appreciated in the classroom. This helps students feel safe and valued, which can improve their self-esteem and motivation in school.

OAE Practice Tests #2 and #3

To take these additional OAE practice tests, visit our bonus page:
mometrix.com/bonus948/oaeapkma

How to Overcome Test Anxiety

Just the thought of taking a test is enough to make most people a little nervous. A test is an important event that can have a long-term impact on your future, so it's important to take it seriously and it's natural to feel anxious about performing well. But just because anxiety is normal, that doesn't mean that it's helpful in test taking, or that you should simply accept it as part of your life. Anxiety can have a variety of effects. These effects can be mild, like making you feel slightly nervous, or severe, like blocking your ability to focus or remember even a simple detail.

If you experience test anxiety—whether severe or mild—it's important to know how to beat it. To discover this, first you need to understand what causes test anxiety.

Causes of Test Anxiety

While we often think of anxiety as an uncontrollable emotional state, it can actually be caused by simple, practical things. One of the most common causes of test anxiety is that a person does not feel adequately prepared for their test. This feeling can be the result of many different issues such as poor study habits or lack of organization, but the most common culprit is time management. Starting to study too late, failing to organize your study time to cover all of the material, or being distracted while you study will mean that you're not well prepared for the test. This may lead to cramming the night before, which will cause you to be physically and mentally exhausted for the test. Poor time management also contributes to feelings of stress, fear, and hopelessness as you realize you are not well prepared but don't know what to do about it.

Other times, test anxiety is not related to your preparation for the test but comes from unresolved fear. This may be a past failure on a test, or poor performance on tests in general. It may come from comparing yourself to others who seem to be performing better or from the stress of living up to expectations. Anxiety may be driven by fears of the future—how failure on this test would affect your educational and career goals. These fears are often completely irrational, but they can still negatively impact your test performance.

Elements of Test Anxiety

As mentioned earlier, test anxiety is considered to be an emotional state, but it has physical and mental components as well. Sometimes you may not even realize that you are suffering from test anxiety until you notice the physical symptoms. These can include trembling hands, rapid heartbeat, sweating, nausea, and tense muscles. Extreme anxiety may lead to fainting or vomiting. Obviously, any of these symptoms can have a negative impact on testing. It is important to recognize them as soon as they begin to occur so that you can address the problem before it damages your performance.

The mental components of test anxiety include trouble focusing and inability to remember learned information. During a test, your mind is on high alert, which can help you recall information and stay focused for an extended period of time. However, anxiety interferes with your mind's natural processes, causing you to blank out, even on the questions you know well. The strain of testing during anxiety makes it difficult to stay focused, especially on a test that may take several hours. Extreme anxiety can take a huge mental toll, making it difficult not only to recall test information but even to understand the test questions or pull your thoughts together.

Effects of Test Anxiety

Test anxiety is like a disease—if left untreated, it will get progressively worse. Anxiety leads to poor performance, and this reinforces the feelings of fear and failure, which in turn lead to poor performances on subsequent tests. It can grow from a mild nervousness to a crippling condition. If allowed to progress, test anxiety can have a big impact on your schooling, and consequently on your future.

Test anxiety can spread to other parts of your life. Anxiety on tests can become anxiety in any stressful situation, and blanking on a test can turn into panicking in a job situation. But fortunately, you don't have to let anxiety rule your testing and determine your grades. There are a number of relatively simple steps you can take to move past anxiety and function normally on a test and in the rest of life.

Physical Steps for Beating Test Anxiety

While test anxiety is a serious problem, the good news is that it can be overcome. It doesn't have to control your ability to think and remember information. While it may take time, you can begin taking steps today to beat anxiety.

Just as your first hint that you may be struggling with anxiety comes from the physical symptoms, the first step to treating it is also physical. Rest is crucial for having a clear, strong mind. If you are tired, it is much easier to give in to anxiety. But if you establish good sleep habits, your body and mind will be ready to perform optimally, without the strain of exhaustion. Additionally, sleeping well helps you to retain information better, so you're more likely to recall the answers when you see the test questions.

Getting good sleep means more than going to bed on time. It's important to allow your brain time to relax. Take study breaks from time to time so it doesn't get overworked, and don't study right before bed. Take time to rest your mind before trying to rest your body, or you may find it difficult to fall asleep.

Along with sleep, other aspects of physical health are important in preparing for a test. Good nutrition is vital for good brain function. Sugary foods and drinks may give a burst of energy but this burst is followed by a crash, both physically and emotionally. Instead, fuel your body with protein and vitamin-rich foods.

Also, drink plenty of water. Dehydration can lead to headaches and exhaustion, especially if your brain is already under stress from the rigors of the test. Particularly if your test is a long one, drink water during the breaks. And if possible, take an energy-boosting snack to eat between sections.

Along with sleep and diet, a third important part of physical health is exercise. Maintaining a steady workout schedule is helpful, but even taking 5-minute study breaks to walk can help get your blood pumping faster and clear your head. Exercise also releases endorphins, which contribute to a positive feeling and can help combat test anxiety.

When you nurture your physical health, you are also contributing to your mental health. If your body is healthy, your mind is much more likely to be healthy as well. So take time to rest, nourish your body with healthy food and water, and get moving as much as possible. Taking these physical steps will make you stronger and more able to take the mental steps necessary to overcome test anxiety.

Mental Steps for Beating Test Anxiety

Working on the mental side of test anxiety can be more challenging, but as with the physical side, there are clear steps you can take to overcome it. As mentioned earlier, test anxiety often stems from lack of preparation, so the obvious solution is to prepare for the test. Effective studying may be the most important weapon you have for beating test anxiety, but you can and should employ several other mental tools to combat fear.

First, boost your confidence by reminding yourself of past success—tests or projects that you aced. If you're putting as much effort into preparing for this test as you did for those, there's no reason you should expect to fail here. Work hard to prepare; then trust your preparation.

Second, surround yourself with encouraging people. It can be helpful to find a study group, but be sure that the people you're around will encourage a positive attitude. If you spend time with others who are anxious or cynical, this will only contribute to your own anxiety. Look for others who are motivated to study hard from a desire to succeed, not from a fear of failure.

Third, reward yourself. A test is physically and mentally tiring, even without anxiety, and it can be helpful to have something to look forward to. Plan an activity following the test, regardless of the outcome, such as going to a movie or getting ice cream.

When you are taking the test, if you find yourself beginning to feel anxious, remind yourself that you know the material. Visualize successfully completing the test. Then take a few deep, relaxing breaths and return to it. Work through the questions carefully but with confidence, knowing that you are capable of succeeding.

Developing a healthy mental approach to test taking will also aid in other areas of life. Test anxiety affects more than just the actual test—it can be damaging to your mental health and even contribute to depression. It's important to beat test anxiety before it becomes a problem for more than testing.

Study Strategy

Being prepared for the test is necessary to combat anxiety, but what does being prepared look like? You may study for hours on end and still not feel prepared. What you need is a strategy for test prep. The next few pages outline our recommended steps to help you plan out and conquer the challenge of preparation.

STEP 1: SCOPE OUT THE TEST

Learn everything you can about the format (multiple choice, essay, etc.) and what will be on the test. Gather any study materials, course outlines, or sample exams that may be available. Not only will this help you to prepare, but knowing what to expect can help to alleviate test anxiety.

STEP 2: MAP OUT THE MATERIAL

Look through the textbook or study guide and make note of how many chapters or sections it has. Then divide these over the time you have. For example, if a book has 15 chapters and you have five days to study, you need to cover three chapters each day. Even better, if you have the time, leave an extra day at the end for overall review after you have gone through the material in depth.

If time is limited, you may need to prioritize the material. Look through it and make note of which sections you think you already have a good grasp on, and which need review. While you are studying, skim quickly through the familiar sections and take more time on the challenging parts.

Write out your plan so you don't get lost as you go. Having a written plan also helps you feel more in control of the study, so anxiety is less likely to arise from feeling overwhelmed at the amount to cover.

STEP 3: GATHER YOUR TOOLS

Decide what study method works best for you. Do you prefer to highlight in the book as you study and then go back over the highlighted portions? Or do you type out notes of the important information? Or is it helpful to make flashcards that you can carry with you? Assemble the pens, index cards, highlighters, post-it notes, and any other materials you may need so you won't be distracted by getting up to find things while you study.

If you're having a hard time retaining the information or organizing your notes, experiment with different methods. For example, try color-coding by subject with colored pens, highlighters, or post-it notes. If you learn better by hearing, try recording yourself reading your notes so you can listen while in the car, working out, or simply sitting at your desk. Ask a friend to quiz you from your flashcards, or try teaching someone the material to solidify it in your mind.

STEP 4: CREATE YOUR ENVIRONMENT

It's important to avoid distractions while you study. This includes both the obvious distractions like visitors and the subtle distractions like an uncomfortable chair (or a too-comfortable couch that makes you want to fall asleep). Set up the best study environment possible: good lighting and a comfortable work area. If background music helps you focus, you may want to turn it on, but otherwise keep the room quiet. If you are using a computer to take notes, be sure you don't have any other windows open, especially applications like social media, games, or anything else that could distract you. Silence your phone and turn off notifications. Be sure to keep water close by so you stay hydrated while you study (but avoid unhealthy drinks and snacks).

Also, take into account the best time of day to study. Are you freshest first thing in the morning? Try to set aside some time then to work through the material. Is your mind clearer in the afternoon or evening? Schedule your study session then. Another method is to study at the same time of day that you will take the test, so that your brain gets used to working on the material at that time and will be ready to focus at test time.

STEP 5: STUDY!

Once you have done all the study preparation, it's time to settle into the actual studying. Sit down, take a few moments to settle your mind so you can focus, and begin to follow your study plan. Don't give in to distractions or let yourself procrastinate. This is your time to prepare so you'll be ready to fearlessly approach the test. Make the most of the time and stay focused.

Of course, you don't want to burn out. If you study too long you may find that you're not retaining the information very well. Take regular study breaks. For example, taking five minutes out of every hour to walk briskly, breathing deeply and swinging your arms, can help your mind stay fresh.

As you get to the end of each chapter or section, it's a good idea to do a quick review. Remind yourself of what you learned and work on any difficult parts. When you feel that you've mastered the material, move on to the next part. At the end of your study session, briefly skim through your notes again.

But while review is helpful, cramming last minute is NOT. If at all possible, work ahead so that you won't need to fit all your study into the last day. Cramming overloads your brain with more information than it can process and retain, and your tired mind may struggle to recall even previously learned information when it is overwhelmed with last-minute study. Also, the urgent nature of cramming and the stress placed on your brain contribute to anxiety. You'll be more likely to go to the test feeling unprepared and having trouble thinking clearly.

So don't cram, and don't stay up late before the test, even just to review your notes at a leisurely pace. Your brain needs rest more than it needs to go over the information again. In fact, plan to finish your studies by noon or early afternoon the day before the test. Give your brain the rest of the day to relax or focus on other things, and get a good night's sleep. Then you will be fresh for the test and better able to recall what you've studied.

STEP 6: TAKE A PRACTICE TEST

Many courses offer sample tests, either online or in the study materials. This is an excellent resource to check whether you have mastered the material, as well as to prepare for the test format and environment.

Check the test format ahead of time: the number of questions, the type (multiple choice, free response, etc.), and the time limit. Then create a plan for working through them. For example, if you have 30 minutes to take a 60-question test, your limit is 30 seconds per question. Spend less time on the questions you know well so that you can take more time on the difficult ones.

If you have time to take several practice tests, take the first one open book, with no time limit. Work through the questions at your own pace and make sure you fully understand them. Gradually work up to taking a test under test conditions: sit at a desk with all study materials put away and set a timer. Pace yourself to make sure you finish the test with time to spare and go back to check your answers if you have time.

After each test, check your answers. On the questions you missed, be sure you understand why you missed them. Did you misread the question (tests can use tricky wording)? Did you forget the information? Or was it something you hadn't learned? Go back and study any shaky areas that the practice tests reveal.

Taking these tests not only helps with your grade, but also aids in combating test anxiety. If you're already used to the test conditions, you're less likely to worry about it, and working through tests until you're scoring well gives you a confidence boost. Go through the practice tests until you feel comfortable, and then you can go into the test knowing that you're ready for it.

Test Tips

On test day, you should be confident, knowing that you've prepared well and are ready to answer the questions. But aside from preparation, there are several test day strategies you can employ to maximize your performance.

First, as stated before, get a good night's sleep the night before the test (and for several nights before that, if possible). Go into the test with a fresh, alert mind rather than staying up late to study.

Try not to change too much about your normal routine on the day of the test. It's important to eat a nutritious breakfast, but if you normally don't eat breakfast at all, consider eating just a protein bar. If you're a coffee drinker, go ahead and have your normal coffee. Just make sure you time it so that the caffeine doesn't wear off right in the middle of your test. Avoid sugary beverages, and drink enough water to stay hydrated but not so much that you need a restroom break 10 minutes into the